9199

Science and Technology Breakthroughs

Science and Technology Breakthroughs

From the Wheel to the World Wide Web

Volume **2**

Leonard C. Bruno

U·X·L ®

AN IMPRINT OF GALE

Detroit New York Toronto London

Science and Technology Breakthroughs

From the Wheel to the World Wide Web

by Leonard C. Bruno

Staff

Sonia Benson, *U•X•L Senior Editor*
Carol DeKane Nagel, *U•X•L Managing Editor*
Thomas L. Romig, *U•X•L Publisher*

Mary Beth Trimper, *Production Director*
Evi Seoud, *Assistant Production Manager*
Shanna Heilveil, *Production Associate*

Cynthia Baldwin, *Product Design Manager*
Barbara J. Yarrow, *Graphic Services Supervisor*
Mary Claire Krzewinski, *Art Director*

Marco Di Vita, Graphix Group, *Typesetter*

Library of Congress Cataloging-in-Publication Data
Science and technology breakthroughs : from the wheel to the world wide web / Leonard C. Bruno
      p. cm.
      Includes bibliographical references and indexes.
      Summary: Emphasizes current technology in providing information on the invention, manufacturing, and future uses of thirty common high-interest products.
      ISBN 0-7876-1927-2 (alk. paper). — ISBN 0-7876-1928-0 (alk. paper). — ISBN 0-7876-1929-9 (alk. paper)
      1. Science—Miscellanea—Juvenile literature. 2. Technology—Miscellanea—Juvenile literature. #. Inventions—Miscellanea—Juvenile literature. M[1. Discoveries in science. 2. Science—History. #. Technology—History.] I. Title
      Q173.B896 1997
      502'.02—dc21
                                            97-34-39
                                              CIP

∞™ This book is printed on acid-free paper that meets the minimum requirements of American National Standard for Information Sciences—Permanence Paper for Printed Library Materials, ANSI Z39.48-1984.

Printed in the United States of America

10 9 8 7 6 5 4 3 2

Table of Contents

Table of Contents

Reader's Guide

For a comprehensive account of the milestones in the history of science and technology, there's no better place to turn than *Science and Technology Breakthroughs: From the Wheel to the World Wide Web*. Written in clear, accessible language, this two-volume reference provides approximately 1,300 paragraph-length entries that unravel the mysteries of the universe as they unfolded to the pioneers in science, as well as chronicling the origins of everyday things we generally take for granted.

This resource is arranged chronologically, from ancient times to the present, by twelve fields of study, making it easy to locate subjects of interest quickly. Readers will be fascinated by breakthroughs related to:

- Agriculture and Everyday Life
- Astronomy
- Biology
- Chemistry
- Communications
- Earth Sciences
- Energy, Power Systems, and Weaponry
- Medicine
- Mathematics
- Physics
- Transportation

The chronological format of *Science and Technology Breakthroughs* encourages browsing as well as helping students to complete homework assignments and general readers to track down elusive facts. From identifying the tiniest subatomic particles to mapping the farthest galaxies, or from the first submarine voyage to walking on the moon, each break-through in science and technology is an exciting story in itself.

Science and Technology Breakthroughs includes additional features, such as:

- "Words to Know" section that defines scientific and technology terms
- Sidebars that highlight fascinating facts
- Cross references that direct readers to related entries
- 150 photos and technical drawings
- "Further Reading" section including sources of general interest and by field

About the Author

Leonard C. Bruno is a science manuscript historian in the Manuscript Division of the Library of Congress. He has written two major works for the Library, *The Tradition of Science* (1987) and *The Tradition of Technology* (1995). Both books discuss the landmark works in each field that are found in the vast collections of the Library of Congress. As curator of two Library exhibitions, he has written *Creativity: Its Many Faces* (1981) and *"We Have a Sporting Chance": The Decision to Go to the Moon* (1979). Among his other publications are *On The Move: A Chronology of Advances in Transportation* (1993) and *Science & Technology Firsts* (1997), both published by Gale Research.

Suggestions

We welcome any comments and suggestions on *Science and Technology Breakthroughs: From the Wheel to the World Wide Web.* Please write: Editors, *Science and Technology Breakthroughs*, U•X•L, Gale Research, 835 Penobscot Bldg., Detroit, Michigan 48226-4094; call toll-free: 800-877-4253; or fax to: 313-961-6348.

Words to Know

A

Aberration of light: The apparent displacement or movement in the observed position of a star from its true place in the sky.

Absorption: The taking up of one substance by another (like a sponge soaking up water).

Acoustics: The science concerned with the production, properties, and propagation of sound waves.

Acupuncture: The Chinese practice of treating disease or pain by inserting very thin needles into specific sites in the body.

Adsorption: The taking up of one substance by another, but only on the surface of the first (such as a filter).

Aerodynamic drag: The retarding force exerted on a moving body by a fluid medium (like the air).

Aerodynamics: The study of the motion of gases (particularly air) and the motion and control of objects in the air.

Affinity: A measure of the ability of one element or compound to react with another. The greater the affinity, the stronger the reaction.

Algae: A group of simple, plant-like organisms that make their own food by photosynthesis.

Algebra: The use of letters or symbols to represent quantities in calculations.

Allotrope: The different physical form of the same element.

Alternator: An electric generator that produces an alternating current (as opposed to direct current).

Amniocentesis: The drawing of amniotic fluid (that surrounds the fetus during pregnancy) by a needle through the abdominal wall to aid in diagnosing fetal abnormalities.

Anaerobic respiration: A type of respiration that does not involve oxygen.

Analgesic: A pain-relieving substance.

Analog: A way of showing the quantity of something in terms of another quantity.

Analytic geometry: The geometry that deals with the relation between algebra and geometry, using graphs and equations of lines, curves, and surfaces to prove relationships.

Anatomy: The study of the structure of living things.

Anesthesia: The absence of sensation, especially pain, following the injection or inhalation of anesthetic drugs.

Antibody: A protein in the blood that locks on to a specific foreign substance and renders it harmless.

Antihistamine: A drug that treats allergies by reducing the effects of histamine in the body.

Antiseptic: A substance that checks the growth and multiplication of microorganisms in or on living tissue.

Aqueous rock: Rock that is formed by the influence of water.

Artificial intelligence: The ability of a computer to think, learn, and work like a human being.

Assay: To make chemical tests to determine the relative amount of metal in an ore.

Asteroid: A small, rocky object in the solar system, also called a minor planet.

Astrophysics: The branch of modern astronomy that is described as the physics and chemistry of the stars.

Atomic number: The number of protons in the nucleus of each atom of an element (which if changed, transforms it into a different element).

Atomic weight: A quantity indicating atomic mass that tells how much matter there is in something or how dense it is, rather than its weight.

Atomism: The theory that everything is composed of ultimately small, indivisible particles.

Atmospheric pressure: The pressure exerted by the atmosphere at the Earth's surface due to the weight of the air.

Aurora borealis: The luminous, colored pattern in the Earth's upper atmosphere caused by charged particles put out by the Sun. This glowing phenomenon in the night sky is also called the Northern Lights.

Autonomic nervous system: The part of the nervous system that controls involuntary actions.

Autopsy: An examination, usually by dissection, of a body after death to determine the cause of death, extent of injuries, or other factors.

B

Bacteria: Any of a large group of one-celled microorganisms found in soil, water, and air, some of which can cause disease. (Bacterium, singular).

Barbiturate: A drug that depresses brain activity and was used to treat convulsions and to tranquilize.

Basalt: A fine-grained, dark-colored igneous (volcanic) rock.

Binary number: A number made up only of the digits 0 and 1, with each digit having twice the value of the digit to its right.

Biogeography: The study of the distribution and dispersal of plants and animals throughout the world.

Bioluminescence: The chemical phenomenon in which an organism can produce its own light.

Bit: A single numeral in a binary number used by a computer. It is short for "binary digit."

Black hole: A region of space where the gravitational force is so strong that not even light can escape. It is formed when matter collapses in on itself and concentrates into a super-dense collapsed star.

Blood pressure: The pressure exerted by the blood upon the walls of the blood vessels.

Boolean algebra: A system that applies algebra to logic. Also called symbolic logic, it converts logic into mathematical symbols.

Buoyancy: The tendency of a fluid to exert a lifting effect on a body immersed in it.

Byte: A binary code signal with eight bits, which is also the amount of computer memory needed to store a single character.

C

Calculus: The branch of mathematics that uses algebra to calculate changing quantities and motion.

Capillary: An extremely fine blood vessel that supplies individual cells with blood.

Caravel: A small sailing vessel with a broad bow, high poop (upper deck in the rear), and lateen sails.

Cardiac arrest: The sudden stoppage of heart output and blood circulation that results in death if untreated.

Cardiovascular system: An animal's closed circulatory system composed of the heart, blood, and blood vessels.

Carrack: A sailing ship with high castles (structures raised above the main deck) fore and aft (front and back) for combat and work purposes.

CAT Scan: Computerized axial tomography is a method for examining the body's soft tissues with x rays. It is now called Computed Tomography (CT).

Catalyst: A substance that speeds up a chemical reaction but that does not change itself.

Causality: The principle that every effect is a consequence of a preceding cause or causes.

Celestial mechanics: The study of the motions of celestial bodies such as planets, moons, and stars, moving in gravitational fields of force.

Cellular pathology: The study of the nature and causes of cell disease.

Cellulose: An insoluble carbohydrate that plants use as building material to make their cell walls.

Cerebellum: The part of the brain that coordinates movement. It is located at the bottom rear of the brain.

Cerebral localization: The phenomenon in which a specific part of the brain controls a specific area of the body.

Cerebrum: The folded mass of nerve cells that sits over the rest of the brain and coordinates voluntary movements. It is also essential for memory, learning, and sensing things.

Chaos: The mathematical study of pattern or order in turbulence and disorder.

Chemical thermodynamics: That part of chemistry dealing with heat changes accompanying chemical reactions.

Chlorination: Adding the element chlorine to water for the purpose of purifying it.

Chlorofluorocarbons: Synthetic gases that build up in the atmosphere and react with ozone, making that protective layer thinner.

Chlorophyll: The main pigment necessary for photosynthesis in green plant cells.

Chromatic aberration: A defect in the lens of refracting telescopes that results in a false color or blurring around the image. The problem arises because light of different wavelengths is focused at different distances from the lens.

Chromosome: A structure in the cell's nucleus that carries part or all of a cell's hereditary material (DNA).

Circadian rhythm: The behavior of animals when influenced by the 24-hour day/night cycle.

Circumference: The distance around a circle.

Clinker: A method of building a ship's hull in which the planks overlap.

Cloning: A technique of genetic engineering in which an offspring is produced asexually (without joining egg and sperm) that has the exact same genes as its donor organism.

Clutch: The connecting mechanism between the power source and the shaft it is turning.

Coherer: A device used to detect radio waves.

Coke: A fuel made by baking bituminous coal in a closed oven to drive off gases and other elements. It is about 88 percent carbon.

Combustion: Any chemical reaction in which heat, and usually light, is produced. It is commonly the burning of organic substances during which oxygen from the air is used to form carbon dioxide and water vapor.

Comet: An icy body orbiting in the solar system, which partially vaporizes when it nears the Sun, and develops a diffuse envelope of dust and gas as well as one or more tails.

Comparative anatomy: The study of the similarities and differences of the structure of living things.

Comparative zoology: The study of the similarities and differences of animals.

Compound microscope: A multiple-lens microscope (two or more lenses housed in a long tube).

Computer virus: A program or set of instructions that attacks and destroys information stored in a computer.

Conduction: The flow of heat through a solid (also called thermal conduction).

Conservation of energy: The law that states that the total amount of energy in a system always stays constant. It is also stated by saying that energy cannot be created or destroyed.

Contraceptive: A mechanical or biochemical means of preventing fertilization (the union of the male and female sex cells) and thus of preventing pregnancy.

Convection: The flow of heat through a fluid (being a liquid or a gas).

Cornea: The outer, transparent part of the eye through which light passes to the retina.

Corona: The outermost layers of the Sun.

Coronary artery: One of a pair of arteries that branch from the aorta and supply the heart with blood.

Cosmic radiation: High-speed, extremely energetic elementary particles that travel through the universe near the speed of light and reach Earth.

Cosmology: The study of the universe as a whole, its nature, and the relations between its various parts.

CPR: Cardiopulmonary resuscitation is an emergency procedure consisting of external heart massage and artificial respiration.

Crop rotation: The growing of different crops in a specified order, on the same field, for the purpose of protecting the soil and increasing production.

Cross-pollination: The pollination of one plant by another plant of the same species.

Crust: The hard, outer shell of the which floats upon the softer, denser mantle.

Cryosurgery: The use of extreme cold to destroy unwanted tissue.

Crystal: A solid mineral with surfaces that are smooth, angular, and regularly arranged.

Crystallography: The study of crystals.

Cuneiform writing: A pictographic type of ancient writing in which objects were represented by pictures, and numbers by the use of strokes and circles.

Cutaneious: Pertaining to the skin.

Cybernetics: The study of communications and feedback control in machines and humans.

Cytogenics: The study of physical changes in the cell's hereditary material.

D

Dark matter: Matter thought to exist in the universe but not yet detected.

Decimal fraction: The expression of a fractional number in decimal form.

Density: The mass of a substance compared to its volume.

Dialysis: A medical procedure that filters waste products from the blood of kidney-disease patients.

Diffraction: The way in which light rays bend outward as they pass the edges of an object.

Diffusion: The natural mingling of two or more substances to form a mixture or solution.

Digital: The opposite of analog, it is a way of showing the quantity of something directly as digits or numbers.

Dirigible: A large, cigar-shaped balloon with a rigid metal interior frame attached to a passenger cabin and engines. It is also called an airship.

Displacement: The moving out of place of an equal volume of fluid by a body completely or partially immersed in it.

Dissection: Cutting and separating the body along its natural cleavage lines to allow scientific examination.

Dissociation: Also called ionization or electrolytic dissociation, it occurs when compounds dissolve or melt (and sometimes join up again in new combinations).

Distillation: The process of changing a liquid into a vapor by heating and then condensing the vapor back to a liquid. This separates two liquids with different boiling points and also purifies liquids.

DNA: Deoxyribonucleic acid is made up of two twisted strands held together by chemical bases. The exact sequence of these bases forms genetic information that determines the total, unique make-up of an individual living organism.

Doppler effect: The apparent change in pitch produced when the source of a sound is moving relative to the listener.

E

Echolocation: A method of detecting objects by using sound waves.

Eclipse: A phenomenon in which the light from a celestial body is temporarily cut off by the presence of another. Lunar eclipses occur when the Moon passes into the shadow of the Earth.

Ecologist: A scientist who studies the relationships between living things and their environments.

Ectoderm: The outer layer of cells in an animal that gives rise to the skin and nerves.

EEG: An electroencephalogram (EEG) is a graphic recording that shows and measures the changing strength of the brain's electric field.

EKG: An electrocardiogram is a graphic recording of the electrical activity of the heart. It is also called an ECG.

Electrolysis: The use of an electric current to split up a substance.

Electromagnetic induction: The use of magnetism to produce electricity.

Electromagnetic radiation: Waves of energy with a wide range of frequencies and lengths that travel through space and come from the Sun, stars, and galaxies. It can also be produced artificially.

Electromagnetic spectrum: The complete range of frequencies of electromagnetic radiation (radio waves, visible light, and very short radiations such as X rays).

Electromagnetism: The study of the magnetism produced by an electric charge in motion.

Electron: A negatively-charged subatomic particle that moves in a path around the nucleus of an atom.

Electrophysiology: The study of the electrical properties of living tissue.

Element: A substance that cannot be decomposed by normal chemical action into simpler substances.

Elliptical orbit: An orbital path which is egg-shaped or resembles an elongated circle.

Embryology: The study of early development in living things.

Endoderm: The inner layer of cells in an animal that gives rise to the digestive system, lungs, and other organs.

Energy: The ability to cause an action or for work to be done.

Entropy: In a closed system, a quantity of thermal energy that is not available to do work.

Enzyme: A protein catalyst that speeds up chemical reactions in living things.

Erythrocytes: Red blood cells that carry oxygen.

Ether: The medium that was once believed to fill space and to be responsible for carrying light and other electromagnetic waves.

Etiology: The study of the causes of disease.

Eugenics: The study of human improvement by genetic means.

Evolution: The process by which groups of living things undergo gradual genetic change as one generation succeeds another.

F

Fauna: The animal life of an area.

Feedback: A process that allows an automatic machine to operate under its own control and to adjust its performance.

Fermentation: A biochemical process that consists of the breakdown of sugars by bacteria.

Fiber optics: The use of glass threads or fibers to carry light rays.

Fission: The splitting of nuclei to release energy. Also called nuclear fission, it takes place in nuclear reactors and nuclear weapons.

Flora: The plant life of an area.

Fractals: Visual representations of great complexity that are made from disorderly growth patterns.

Fusion: The combining of nuclei to release energy. Also called nuclear fusion, it takes place in the Sun and in thermonuclear weapons and reactors.

G

Galaxy: A family of stars or a star system that is held together by mutual gravitational attraction.

Game theory: The study of games of strategy, which is concerned primarily with probability.

Gear: A pair of toothed wheels or system of wheels that are connected so that one wheel turns another.

Gene: The basic unit of heredity that carries the instructions needed to make a particular protein.

Generator: A machine that converts mechanical energy (movement) into electrical energy. It is also called a dynamo.

Genetic recombination: The mixing of genes or genetic material to produce new combinations.

Genetics: The study of how inherited characteristics are passed on.

Genotype: The genetic information that a living thing inherits from its parents that affects its makeup, appearance, and function.

Genus: A classification group (plural, genera) that contains one or more closely related species.

Geocentric: A geocentric model of the solar system places a stationary Earth at the center of the solar system, with the Sun and planets orbiting the Earth.

Geochemistry: The study of the Earth's chemical composition and the distribution of its elements.

Geometry: The branch of mathematics that deals with points, lines, and shapes.

Geophysics: The study of the Earth's history, structure, and composition.

Glacier: A large mass of ice formed from snow that has packed together and which moves slowly down a slope under its own weight.

Globular cluster: A roughly spherical, densely packed cluster of hundreds of thousands or even millions of stars.

Governor: A feedback device that controls the speed of a machine.

Gravity: The force of mutual attraction between all bodies.

H

Half-life: The time it takes for a radioactive substance to decay or lose half of its radioactivity.

Hardware: The physical machinery or basic parts of a computer.

Heimlich maneuver: An emergency procedure to help someone choking on an object or food by abruptly pushing upward, from behind, just below the sternum (breastbone).

Heliocentric: A heliocentric model of the solar system places the Sun at the center with the planets and the Earth orbiting around it.

Hemisphere: Either of two parts of the brain's cerebrum.

Hemoglobin: An iron-containing protein in red blood cells that carries oxygen.

Hemorrhage: To undergo heavy or uncontrollable bleeding.

Heredity: The genetic link between successive generations of living things.

Hieroglyphic writing: A stylized form of Egyptian picture-writing.

Histamine: A compound in cells that is released in allergic and inflammatory responses and causes small blood vessels to widen, decreases blood pressure, increases gastric secretions, and constricts smooth muscles.

Histology: The study of tissues and organs.

Hologram: A three-dimensional image made with a laser light.

Homeostasis: The maintenance (by controlled response to change) of stable conditions or a constant internal environment in a cell or a living thing.

Homologous: A structure found in different species that has the same evolutionary origin.

Hormone: A chemical messenger released by the body that carries instructions from one set of cells to another.

Horsepower: A measurement of power (or the rate of doing work) equal to 745.7 watts.

Hybrid: The offspring of parents from two different species.

Hydra: A group of species of cnidarian (an invertebrate with a digestive cavity that has only one opening) that lives in fresh water.

Hydraulic: A system operated by the pressure or movement of a liquid.

Hydrocephalus: An abnormal condition in which cerebrospinal fluid builds up in the brain's spaces and can result in enlargement of the head, brain damage, and death.

Hydrofoil: A wing-like projection that lifts the hull of a moving vessel out of the water and generates thrust to propel the vessel.

Hydrostatics: The study of fluids at rest and objects immersed in fluids.

Hydrothermal vents: Underground jets of mineral-rich hot water.

I

Igneous rock: Rock that forms as molten magma or lava solidifies.

Immunization: The process by which resistance to an infectious disease is increased.

Immunology: The study of the body's response to foreign invasion.

Incandescence: Glowing due to heat.

Inert gases: The elements argon, helium, krypton, neon, radon, and xenon are unreactive gases and form few compounds with other elements. They are also called rare or noble gases.

Infusoria: A group of minute organisms found in decomposing matter and stagnant water.

Insulin: A hormone secreted by the pancreas that is essential to the metabolism of carbohydrates and is used to control and treat diabetes mellitus.

Integrated circuit: A complete set of electronic components in one unit.

Internal combustion engine: An engine that develops power through the expansive force of a fuel that is burned inside a closed chamber or cylinder.

Intravenous injection: The insertion of a hypodermic needle into a vein to instill a fluid, withdraw or transfuse blood, or start an intravenous feeding.

Invertebrate zoology: That part of zoology that studies animals without a backbone.

In vitro: Pertaining to an artificial condition, as in a test tube or laboratory. It is the opposite of in vivo, meaning in a living organism.

Irradiation: A method of preservation that treats food with low doses of radiation to deactivate enzymes and to kill microorganisms and insects.

Isochronism: The maintenance of same period of vibration or having a regular periodicity.

Isomer: A compound that has the same number and type of atoms in its molecules as another compound.

Isostacy: The balancing between the above-ground heights of a mountain and the depth of its below-ground "roots" or foundation — both of which float on the Earth's mantle.

Isotope: A form of an element with a different number of neutrons in the nuclei of its atoms than other forms of the same element. It is basically a different version of the same element.

K

Kinetic energy: A form of energy possessed by a body because of its motion.

L

Laryngology: A branch of medicine dealing with diseases of the larynx (voice box).

Lateen: A triangular sail hung on a long yard (horizontal spar) that is attached at an angle to a short mast (vertical spar).

Latitude: The angular distance north or south of the Earth's equator measured in degrees.

Leukocytes: White blood cells that are an important part of the body's defense mechanism.

Light year: The distance travelled through a vacuum by light in one year.

Liquefaction: The change-in-state from a vapor to a liquid caused by an increase in pressure.

Lithography: The process of writing or putting designs on stone with a greasy material and of making printed impressions from it.

Lock: A section of a waterway or canal that is closed off with gates in which vessels are raised or lowered by raising the water level in the enclosed section.

Logarithms: An alternative way of expressing numbers by means of exponents or powers used with a base number.

Longitude: The angular distance east or west of some arbitrary point measured in degrees.

M

Mach number: The ratio of the (supersonic) speed of an object to the speed of sound in the surrounding medium.

Magnetosphere: The region of the Earth's magnetic field that resembles a teardrop in shape, with its tail pointing away from the Sun.

Mantle: The soft interior of the Earth that lies above the core and below the crust.

Mass: The amount of matter in an object (different from its weight).

Mechanics: The study of the effects of forces upon objects.

Medulla: The part of the brain that controls involuntary processes like breathing and heartbeat. It is an extension of the spinal cord.

Mesoderm: The middle layer of cells in an animal that gives rise to bone, muscle, blood, and sex cells.

Metabolism: All the chemical processes that take place in a living thing.

Metallurgy: The science of the extraction of metals from their ores, and of refining metals and forming alloys.

Metamorphic rock: Rock formed by the alteration of other rocks (by heat or pressure).

Microwaves: Electromagnetic waves with a short wavelength (similar to radio waves but with a higher frequency).

Milky Way: A band of hazy light circling the night sky that is made up of large numbers of faint.

Mineral: A naturally occurring substance with a definite chemical composition. Most have a crystal form.

Mineralogy: The branch of geology that studies the minerals from which rocks are made.

Mitosis: The division of a cell nucleus to produce two identical cells.

Modem: A device that connects a computer to the telephone system and converts a computer signal into a telephone signal and back again.

Momentum: The mass of a moving object multiplied by its velocity.

Mouse: A hand-held device that controls the movements of a cursor or pointer on a computer screen.

MRI: Magnetic resonance imaging is a noninvasive diagnostic technique that produces detailed computerized images of internal body tissues.

N

Neolithic: A time period in early mankind's history characterized by the use of stone tools shaped by polishing or grinding. It precedes the appearance of metal tools in the Bronze Age and follows the age of stone-chipped tools (Paleolithic Period).

Neuron: An individual nerve cell that transmits electrical signals or impulses.

Neurotransmitter: A chemical substance that transmits nerve impulses within the nervous system.

Neutron: A subatomic particle with no electric charge found in the nucleus of an atom.

Neutron star: The remnant of a massive star that has collapsed and is extremely dense and tiny.

Non-Euclidean geometry: Any geometry not based on Euclid's assumptions.

Nucleic acid: A complex organic compound stored in the cell nucleus that carries genetic information.

Nucleus: The center of a cell that directs its activities and contains its chemical instructions.

Nutation: The small, slow variation or "nodding" of the Earth's axis due to the influence of the Moon.

O

Obstetrics: The branch of medicine concerned with the care of women during pregnancy, childbirth, and immediately afterward.

Oceanography: The study of the chemistry of the oceans, as well as their currents, marine life, and the ocean bed.

Operating system: The programs or instructions that a computer needs in order to perform its basic tasks.

Ophthalmology: The study of the eye and its development, structure, function, defects, diseases, and treatment.

Optics: The study of the nature of light and its properties.

Organic chemistry: The study of the compounds of carbon, natural or synthesized.

Ornithology: The branch of zoology that deals with the study of birds.

Orthodontics: The branch of dentistry concerned with irregularities of the teeth and their correction.

Oscillation: A repeated back-and-forth movement.

Osmosis: The flow of water through a permeable membrane from a weak to a strong solution. It continues until the two solutions are of equal strength.

P

Paleontology: The study of the geologic past that involves analysis of plant and animal fossils.

Papyrus: A tall, aquatic plant used in ancient Egypt as both a material on which to write and as building material for reed boats.

Parabolic: A plane curve formed by the intersection of a right circular cone and a plane parallel to an element of the cone.

Parallax: The difference in direction or change of position of an object in the sky when it is viewed from two different points on Earth.

Parchment: The processed skins of certain animals, like goats and sheep, on which writing is inscribed.

Pasteurization: The process of slow heating that kills bacteria and other microorganisms.

Pathogenic: Something causing or capable of causing disease.

Percussion: An examination technique of tapping parts of the body to learn the condition of internal organs by listening to the sound produced.

Petri dish: A shallow, circular dish with a loose-fitting cover that is used to culture or grow bacteria or other microorganisms.

Petrography: A branch of petrology that describes rocks and their grouping into classes.

Petrology: The study of the origin, composition, and occurrence of rocks.

pH: A measure of the acidity or alkalinity of a substance.

Phagocytosis: The process by which certain cells engulf and digest microorganisms and consume debris and foreign bodies in the blood.

Pharmacopoeia: A book listing the properties and uses of all known drugs.

Phenotype: The visible characteristics or physical shape produced by a living thing's genotype.

Phlogiston theory: The incorrect idea that the material substance phlogiston was what gave something the ability to burn.

Photoconductivity: The increase in the ability of a material to allow an electric current to flow in it when struck by light.

Photoelectric effect: The phenomenon in which light falling upon certain metals stimulates the emission of electrons and changes light into electricity.

Photon: A particle of electromagnetic radiation.

Photosphere: The bright, visible surface of the Sun.

Photosynthesis: A plant process that uses the energy in sunlight to carry out a chain of chemical reactions to make food.

Photovoltaic cell: A device that changes sunlight into electricity using the photoelectric effect.

Phylum: A classification group (plural, phyla) that contains one or more classes of living things.

Physiology: The study of the processes, activities, and phenomena of living things.

Piezoelectricity: Electricity produced when a crystal is squeezed or made to vibrate.

Planetoid: An asteroid or a minor planet.

Plasma: Matter in the form of electrically charged atomic particles that form when a gas becomes so hot that electrons break away from the atoms.

Plate tectonics: The theory that the Earth's surface is covered by a number of relatively thin plates which move over the material below.

Platelet: A disk-shaped cell in the blood that is essential for blood clotting.

Pollen: Dust-like grains or particles produced by a plant that contain male sex cells.

Pollination: The transfer of pollen from the male parts of flowers to the female parts.

Polymerization: A chemical process in which molecules of the same compound combine to form a long chain of large molecules called a polymer (like a plastic).

Positional notation: A number system in which the position of a symbol or digit in a numeral determines its value. It is also called the place value system.

Preformation: The incorrect idea that the egg contains the organism already fully formed, and that development consists merely in an increase in size.

Prenatal: Prior to birth.

Prism: A triangular or wedge-shaped block of glass that breaks up light into its constituent colors.

Probability: The degree of chance that something might happen.

Projective geometry: The geometry that studies properties and spatial relationships of figures as they are projected.

Prominences: Masses of glowing gas, mainly hydrogen, that rise from the Sun's surface like flames.

Prothrombin: A protein essential to blood being able to clot.

Proton: A positively charged subatomic particle in the nucleus of an atom.

Protozoa: A group of single-celled organisms (singular protozoon) that live by taking in food rather than making it by photosynthesis.

Psychiatry: The branch of medicine dealing with the study of the mind and the diagnosis, treatment, and prevention of emotional and behavioral disorders.

Psychology: The study of the mind especially as it relates to behavior.

Psychosurgery: Surgery of the brain, usually involving the interruption of certain nerve pathways to relieve severely abnormal psychological symptoms.

Pulsar: A rotating neutron star characterized by rapidly varying bursts of radio waves.

Q

Quasar: A very remote, small, extragalactic object that is incredibly bright.

R

Radio astronomy: The exploration of the universe through the detection of radio emissions from celestial objects.

Radioactivity: The emission of high-energy rays or particles by certain elements.

Radiometric dating: Finding the age of rocks by measuring radioactive decay.

Radius: The distance from the center of a circle to an edge.

Random-access memory: The part of a computer's memory whose contents can be changed.

Reaction engine: An engine that develops thrust by the forced expulsion of ignited fuel gases.

Redshift: The lengthening of the wavelength of light from a body that is moving away from the observer. The farther light must travel the more its waves are stretched, and long waves are associated with the red end of the light spectrum.

Reflecting telescope: A telescope whose main light-collecting element is a concave mirror.

Reflex action: A rapid, automatic response to a stimulus. It is built into the nervous system and does not have to be learned.

Refracting telescope: A telescope whose lens bends (refracts) light rays from a straight path to a focus near the eye where a second lens magnifies the image.

Rejection: An immunological response of the body against an invading microorganism or a transplanted organ.

Respiration: The physical process that supplies oxygen to an animal's body. It also describes a series of chemical reactions that take place inside cells.

Retina: The light-sensitive part of the eyeball that receives images and transmits visual impulses through the optic nerve to the brain.

Richter scale: A scale that measures the magnitude of an earthquake. Its readings are taken on a seismograph.

RNA: Ribonucleic acid (RNA) is a group of nucleic acids that carry out several important tasks in the synthesis of proteins. Unlike DNA, it has only a single strand.

Rock: A large mass of mineral matter that makes up the solid mass of the Earth's crust.

S

Seafloor spreading: The formation of new oceanic crust and the gradual widening of the oceans.

Sedimentation: The process of forming sediments (material deposited in water which settle on the bottom and form layers over time).

Seismology: The study of earthquakes.

Semiconductor: A material that varies in electrical conductivity and can therefore produce and process electrical signals.

Serum: The clear, thin, sticky fluid of the blood that contains no cells or platelets.

Servomechanism: A device for increasing the power used to operate a machine.

Smelt: To separate a metal from its ore by heating the ore with a suitable reducing agent.

Software: The instructions or programs that control the functioning of a computer's hardware.

Solar spectrum: The range of colors in the Sun's light.

Solar wind: A flow of atomic particles, mostly protons and electrons, that streams out from the Sun in all directions.

Solstice: The time when the midday Sun is directly overhead at one of the tropics. This happens twice a year (winter solstice and summer solstice).

Solution: A liquid with a substance dissolved in it.

Solvent: A substance in which something is dissolved.

Sounding: Determining the depth of water, often by acoustic means.

Species: A group of living things that can breed together in the wild.

Spectroscope: An instrument used to split up the light of a star or other shiny object.

Spermatozoon: A sperm (plural, spermatozoa) is a male sex cell produced by the testis.

Spontaneous generation: The incorrect theory that living things can be generated from nonliving things. It is also called abiogenesis.

Spore: A small, usually one-celled reproductive body that is capable of growing into a new organism.

Static electricity: A form of electricity produced by friction in which the electric charge does not flow in a current but stays in one place.

Statics: The study of the forces acting on bodies that do not move.

Stratigraphy: The study of the distribution and order of rock layers.

Sublimation: The process of changing a solid to a vapor by heating, and then cooling the vapor and changing it directly back to a solid.

Sunspot: A region of the Sun where the temperature is lower than that of the surrounding surface region and consequently appears darker. The presence of a strong, concentrated magnetic field produces the cooling effect.

Superconductivity: The ability of a substance to conduct electricity without resistance.

Supernova: A star that explodes, sending much of its material into space. For a short time, it sends out a tremendous amount of energy and can be seen over vast distances.

Symbiosis: A relationship between two different species from which both benefit.

Symbolic logic: The use of symbols to express logic or reasoning.

Synapse: A junction or space between two neurons that allows one neuron to pass signals to another.

T

Taxonomy: The laws and principles of classifying living things.

Thalamus: The large, oval-shaped mass of gray matter in the cerebrum that relays sensory impulses.

Thermodynamics: The branch of physics that deals with the relationships between heat and other forms of energy.

Therapeutics: The branch of medicine concerned with treatment.

Time sharing: A technique of organizing a computer so that several users can interact with it simultaneously.

Tissue: A group of similar cells that work together.

Torque: A measure of the turning effect or force. It is the amount of force multiplied by its distance from the pivot.

Tracheotomy: The surgical operation of cutting into the trachea (windpipe) through the neck to allow the passage of air.

Tranquilizer: A drug that produces a calming effect and lessens anxiety and tension.

Transduction: A process in which a virus transfers genetic information from its host organism to another.

Transformer: A device that changes the voltage and type of current of a supply of electricity.

Transit: The passage of a smaller celestial body across the visible disc of a larger one.

Transplant: The transfer of an organ or tissue from one person to another to replace a diseased organ.

Triboelectrification: The production of an electrical charge by rubbing together two dissimilar substances. It is also called frictional electricity.

Trigonometry: The branch of mathematics that deals with the sides and angles of triangles and their measurements and relations.

Turbine: A motor in which a set of blades rotates when struck by a moving stream of gas or liquid.

Typography: The process of printing with movable type.

U

Ultrasound: The reflection of sound waves at very high frequencies that produce an image of an internal body structure to aid in a diagnosis .

Universal gravitation: The notion of the constancy of the force of gravity between two bodies.

V

Vaccination: The introduction of weakened or dead viruses or microorganisms into the body to create immunity by the production of specific antibodies.

Vacuum: A physical state completely empty of matter or particles.

Vacuum tube: A sealed glass tube in which the conduction of electricity takes place through a vacuum or gas.

Valency: The power or ability of an element to form bonds.

Variable star: Any star whose light output varies in any way (brightening or fading).

Vellum: An especially fine type of parchment made from the more delicate skins of kids or calves.

Virus: A package of chemicals that are far smaller than living cells they infect. Viruses are not classified as living organisms, since they cannot grow and reproduce on their own, but rely on a host cell to make copies of themselves.

Volume: The amount of space occupied by a three-dimensional object.

Vulcanization: The process of producing rubber that is strong and not sticky by combining it with sulfur in the presence of heat and pressure.

W

Woodcut: A block of wood out of which a design has been cut and from which a print can be made.

Word processor: A computer program that enables a person to write letters and documents in an efficient manner.

Work: The transfer of energy (when a force moves the position of a body against an opposing force).

Further Reading

General Science and Technology

Asimov, Isaac, *Asimov's Chronology of Science and Discovery*. New York: Harper & Row, 1989.

Bunch, Bryan H., and Alexander Hellemans, *The Timetables of Technology*. New York: Simon and Schuster, 1993.

Calder, Ritche, *The Evolution of the Machine*. Toronto: McClelland and Stewart Ltd., 1968.

Cipolla, Carlo M., and Derek Birdsall, *The Technology of Man*. New York: Holt, Rinehart and Winston, 1979.

De Bono, Edward, ed., *Eureka! How and When Great Inventions Were Made*. London: Thames and Hudson, 1974.

Dummer, G. W. A., *Electronic Inventions: 1745-1976*. New York: Pergamon Press, 1977.

Finniston, Monty, Trevor Williams, and Christopher Bissell, eds., *Oxford Illustrated Encyclopedia of Invention and Technology*. Oxford: Oxford University Press, 1985.

Gascoigne, Robert Mortimer, *A Chronology of the History of Science: 1450-1900*. New York: Garland Publishing, Inc., 1987.

Giscard d'Estaing, Valerie-Ann, *The Second World Almanac Book of Inventions*. New York: World Almanac, 1986.

Great Scientific Achievements: The Twentieth Century. Pasadena: Salem Press, 1990.

Hellemans, Alexander, and Bryan H. Bunch, *The Timetables of Science*. New York: Simon & Schuster, 1988.

Further Reading

Magill, Frank N., *Great Events from History II: Science and Technology Series.* Pasadena: Salem Press, 1991.

Marcorini, Edgardo, ed., *The History of Science and Technology: A Narrative Chronology.* New York: Facts on File, 1988.

Mount, Ellis, and List, Barbara A., *Milestones in Science and Technology.* Phoenix: Oryx Press, 1994.

Newton, David E., Rob Nagel, and Bridget Travers, *U•X•L Encyclopedia of Science.* Detroit: U•X•L, 1998.

Ochoa, George, and Melinda Corey, *The Timeline Book of Science.* New York: The Stonesong Press, 1995.

Presence, Peter, ed., *Purnell's Encyclopedia of Inventions.* Bristol: Purnell & Sons Ltd., 1976.

Ronan, Colin A., *Science: Its History and Development Among the World's Cultures.* New York: Facts on File, 1982.

Schmittroth, Linda, Mary Reilly McCall, and Bridget Travers, *Eureka! Scientific Discoveries and Inventions That Shaped the World.* Detroit: U•X•L, 1995.

Scientists: Their Lives and Works, four volumes. Detroit: U•X•L, 1996-97.

Travers, Bridget, *World of Invention.* Detroit: Gale, 1994.

Travers, Bridget, *World of Scientific Discovery.* Detroit: Gale, 1994.

Williams, Brian, *Inventions and Discoveries.* New York: Warwick Press, 1979.

Williams, Trevor I., *The Triumph of Invention: A History of Man's Technological Genius.* London: Macdonald Orbis, 1987.

Williams, Trevor I., *Science: A History of Discovery in the Twentieth Century.* Oxford: Oxford University Press, 1990.

Wolf, Abraham, *A History of Science, Technology, and Philosophy in the Eighteenth Century.* New York: Macmillan Co., 1939.

Wolf, Abraham, *A History of Science, Technology, and Philosophy in the 16th & 17th Centuries.* London: George Allen & Unwin Ltd., 1950.

Agriculture and Everyday Life

Du Vall, Nell, *Domestic Technology: A Chronology of Developments.* Boston: G. K. Hall, 1988.

Schapsmeier, Edward L., *Encyclopedia of American Agricultural History.* Westport, CT: Greenwood Press, 1975.

Smith, Maryanna S., *Chronological Landmarks in American Agriculture.* Washington: Department of Agriculture, 1980.

Trow-Smith, Robert, *Man the Farmer.* London: Priory Press Ltd., 1973.

Astronomy

Engelbert, Phillis, *Astronomy and Space: From the Big Bang to the Big Crunch*, three volumes. Detroit: U•X•L, 1997

Herrmann, Dieter B., *The History of Astronomy from Herschel to Hertzsprung.* Cambridge: Cambridge University Press, 1984.

McGraw-Hill Encyclopedia of Astronomy. New York: McGraw-Hill, 1993.

Moore, Patrick, *History of Astronomy.* London: Macdonald & Co., 1983.

Motz, Lloyd, *The Story of Astronomy.* New York: Plenum Press, 1995.

Pannekoek, Anton, *A History of Astronomy.* New York: Dover Publications, 1989.

Biology

Gardner, Eldon J., *History of Biology.* Minneapolis: Burgess Publishing Co., 1972.

Green, Joseph Reynolds, *A History of Botany, 1860-1900. Being a Continuation of Sach's History of Botany.* New York: Russell & Russell, 1967.

Hooper, Tony, *Genetics.* Austin: Raintree Steck-Vaughn Publishers, Inc., 1978.

Magner, Lois N., *A History of Life Sciences.* New York: M. Dekker, 1994.

Mayr, Ernst, *The Growth of Biological Thought.* Cambridge, MA: Belknap Press, 1982.

Morton, Alan G., *History of Botanical Science: An Account of Botany from Ancient Times to the Present Day.* New York: Academic Press, 1995.

Nordenskiold, Erik, *The History of Biology.* St. Clair Shores, MI: Scholarly Press, 1976.

Sachs, Julius, *History of Botany, 1530-1860.* New York: Russell & Russell, 1967.

Chemistry

Brock, William Hodson, *The Norton History of Chemistry.* New York: W. W. Norton, 1993.

Kaufman, Morris, *The First Century of Plastics*. London: Plastics Institute, 1963.

Partington, James R., *A History of Chemistry*. London: Macmillan, 1961-1970.

Communications

Clair, Colin, *A Chronology of Printing*. New York: Frederick A. Praeger, 1969.

Dunlap, Orrin E., *Radio & Television Almanac*. New York: Harper & Brothers, 1951.

Gassan, Arnold, *A Chronology of Photography*. Athens, OH: Handbook Co., 1972.

A History of Paper. New York: Fraser Paper, 1964.

Hunter, Dard, *Papermaking: The History and Technique of an Ancient Craft*. New York: Dover Publications, Inc., 1978.

Lemagny, Jean-Claude, and Andre Rouille, eds., *A History of Photography*. Cambridge: Cambridge University Press, 1987.

Computers

Augarten, Stan, *Bit by Bit: An Illustrated History of Computers*. New York: Ticknor & Field, 1984.

Ralston, Anthony, and Edwin D. Reilly, eds., *Encyclopedia of Computer Science*. New York: Van Nostrand Reinhold, 1993.

Veit, Stan, *Stan Veit's History of the Personal Computer*. Asheville, NC: WorldComm, 1993.

Williams, Michael R., *A History of Computing Technology*. Englewood Cliffs, NJ: Prentice-Hall, Inc., 1985.

Earth Sciences

Engelbert, Phillis, *The Complete Weather Resource*, three volumes. Detroit: U•X•L, 1997.

Faul, Henry, *It Began with a Stone: A History of Geology from the Stone Age to the Age of Plate Tectonics*. New York: J. Wiley, 1983.

Gohau, George, *A History of Geology*. New Brunswick, NJ: Rutgers University Press, 1990.

Thompson, Susan J., *A Chronology of Geological Thinking from Antiquity to 1899*. Metuchen, NJ: Scarecrow Press, 1988.

Energy, Power Systems, and Weaponry

Bloom, Alan, *250 Years of Steam*. Tadworth, Surrey: World's Work Ltd., 1988.

History of Energy. Washington: Department of Energy, 1980.

Muller, Heinrich, *Guns, Pistols, Revolvers*. New York: St. Martin's Press, 1980.

Mathematics

Boyer, Carl B., and Uta C. Merzbach, *A History of Mathematics*. New York: John Wiley & Sons, 1989.

Eves, Howard W., *An Introduction to the History of Mathematics*. Philadelphia: The Saunders Series, 1990.

Swetz, Frank J., *From Five Fingers to Infinity: A Journey Through the History of Mathematics*. Chicago: Open Court, 1994.

Medicine

Bendiner, Jessica, and Elmer Bendiner, *Biographical Dictionary of Medicine*. New York: Facts on File, 1990.

Bordley, James III, and A. McGehee Harvey, *Two Centuries of American Medicine: 1776-1976*. Philadelphia: W. B. Saunders Co., 1976.

Castiglioni, Arturo, *A History of Medicine*. New York: J. Aronson, 1975.

Garrison, Fielding H., *An Introduction to the History of Medicine*. Philadelphia: W. B. Saunders Co., 1929.

Magner, Lois N., *A History of Medicine*. New York: M. Dekker, 1992.

McGrew, Roderick E., *Encyclopedia of Medical History*. New York: McGraw-Hill, 1985.

Mez-Mangold, Lydia, *A History of Drugs*. Basel, Switzerland: F. Hoffmann-La Roche & Co., 1971.

Mould, Richard F., *A Century of X Rays and Radioactivity in Medicine*. Bristol: Institute of Physics Publishing, 1993.

Physics

Sambursky, Samuel, ed., *Physical Thought from the Presocratics to the Quantum Physicists*. London: Hutchinson, 1974.

Weaver, Jefferson Hane, ed., *The World of Physics*. New York: Simon & Schuster, 1987.

Westcott, Gerald F., *Mechanical and Electrical Engineering*. London: Her Majesty's Stationery Office, 1955.

Transportation

Braun, Werner von, and Frederick J. Orway III, *History of Rocketry and Space Travel*. New York: Thomas Y. Crowell Co., 1966.

Bruno, Leonard C., *On the Move: A Chronology of Advances in Transportation*. Detroit: Gale, 1993.

Lay, M. G., *Ways of the World: A History of the World's Roads and of the Vehicles That Used Them*. New Brunswick, NJ: Rutgers University Press, 1992.

Picture Credits

The photographs and illustrations appearing in *Science and Technology Breakthroughs: From the Wheel to the World Wide Web* were received from the following sources:

On the cover (from top to bottom): scientist performing gene therapy (**photograph by Philippe Plailly. National Audubon Society Collection/Photo Researchers, Inc. Reproduced by permission.**); Nicolaus Copernicus (**The Library of Congress**); motorcycle racer (**photograph by Patrick Ward. Corbis. Reproduced by permission.**).

JLM Visuals. Reproduced by permission: pp. 3, 8, 450; **National Audubon Society Collection/Photo Researchers, Inc. Reproduced by permission:** p. 5; **Courtesy of the Library of Congress:** pp. 10, 13, 16, 19, 21, 32, 33, 38, 40, 71, 73, 75, 81, 88, 115, 117, 123, 124, 131, 132, 135, 138, 139 (right and left), 157, 158, 163, 165, 166, 168, 174, 175, 176, 185, 197, 199, 201, 204, 206, 209, 213, 262, 315, 321, 331, 333, 336, 337, 348, 349, 350, 353, 356, 359, 362, 377, 394, 395, 405, 411, 416, 424, 428, 430, 431, 452; **NASA:** 28, 45, 61, 65, 149, 188, 218, 477, 478, 481; **Illustration by Hans & Cassady. Gale Research:** pp. 42, 86, 89, 92, 143, 194, 283, 308, 339, 412, 454, 460, 463, 468; **Photograph by Francois Gohier. Photo Researchers, Inc. Reproduced by permission:** p. 49; **Photograph by Julian Baum. Science Photo Library, National Audubon Society Collection/Photo Researchers, Inc. Reproduced by permission:** p. 51; **Photograph by Tony Ward. Photo Researchers, Inc. Reproduced by permission:** p. 55; **Photograph by Ludek Pesek. National Audubon Society Collection/Photo Researchers, Inc. Reproduced by permission:** p. 58; **NASA/Mark Marten. National Audubon Society Collection/Photo Reserachers, Inc. Reproduced by permission:** p. 66; **Photograph by**

Robert J. Huffman. Field Mark Publications. Reproduced by permission: pp. 78, 342; **Illustration by Robert L. Wolke. Reproduced by permission: pp. 103, 280, 431; Photograph by Scott Camazine. National Audubon Society Collection/Photo Researchers, Inc. Reproduced by permission: pp. 108, 433; Photograph by Philippe Plailly. National Audubon Society Collection/Photo Researchers, Inc. Reproduced by permission: pp. 110, 390; Photograph by Martin Dohrn. National Audubon Society/Photo Researchers, Inc. Reproduced by permission: pp. 121, 379; Photograph by Charles D. Winters. National Audubon Society Collection/Photo Researchers, Inc. Reproduced by permission: p. 145; Photograph by J. Berhnholz et al, North Carolina State University/Science Photo Library, National Audubon Society Collection/Photo Researchers, Inc. Reproduced by permission: p. 151; Photograph by Spencer Grant. National Audubon Society Collection/Photo Researchers, Inc. Reproduced by permission: p. 215; Photograph by Doug Handel. Stock Market. Reproduced by permission: p. 221; Reuters/Bettmann. Reproduced by permission: p. 224; Photograph by Tom Van Sant. Stock Market. Reproduced by permission: pp. 254; U.S. Geological Survey Photographic Library: pp. 258, 268; Photograph by John Buitenkant. National Audubon Society Collection/Photo Research, Inc. Reproduced by permission: p. 265; Photograph by Mark Newman. Phototake NYC. Reproduced by permission: p. 270; Photograph by C. D. Miller. U.S. Geological Survey Photographic Library: p. 275; Photograph by Francis Leroy. Biocosmos/Science Photo Library, National Audubon Society Collection/Photo Researchers, Inc. Reproduced by permission: p. 288; Photograph by Chris Hamilton. Stock Market. Reproduced by permission: p. 296; Photograph by Mark Gamba. Stock Market. Reproduced by permission: p. 301; Photograph by Phil Jude. National Audubon Society Collection/Photo Researchers Inc. Reproduced by permission: p. 305; U.S. Department of Energy, Washington DC: pp. 311, 313; Photograph by Yoav Levy. Phototake NYC. Reproduced by permission: p. 317; Photograph by Robert Visser. Greenpeace. Reproduced by permission: p. 323; Photograph by Mug Shots. Stock Market. Reproduced by permission: p. 370; Photograph by T. McCarthy. Custom Medical Stock Photo, Inc. Reproduced by permission: p. 372; Photograph by A. Glauberman. National Audubon Society Collection/Photo Researchers, Inc. Reproduced by permission: p. 374; Photograph by Will & Deni McIntyre. National Audubon Society Collection/Photo Researchers, Inc. Reproduced by permission: p. 384; Photograph by James Steveson. National Audubon Soci-**

Science and Technology Breakthroughs

Earth Sciences

c. 5000 B.C. · Age of quarrying and mining dawns. Primitive quarrying and mining begins with the Neolithic Revolution. A quarry is an open cavity dug from the Earth's surface, whereas a mine implies some degree of underground operations. This time period is characterized by the use of stone tools that are shaped by polishing or grinding, and it follows the Paleolithic Age or age of chipped-stone tools. It in turn is followed by the Bronze Age and the appearance of metal tools. One of the first minerals used by early man was flint, while ocher (an iron ore) and chalk were sought for use as pigments for coloring. By 3000 B.C., the Egyptians are mining copper on the Sinai Peninsula.

c. 600 B.C. · Thales makes first-known geological observation. The first-known geological observation is made by Greek philosopher Thales of Miletus (c. 625–c. 547 B.C.), who writes describing the effect of streams or moving water on the Earth. He also is the first to question what the universe is made of, and to try to answer this question without seeking a supernatural explanation. He says water is the fundamental or primary element from which everything is made. He also suggests that the Earth is a flat disk and floats on an infinite body of water.

c. 550 B.C. · Fossils are studied by Anaximander. The first person known to study fossils is Greek philosopher Anaximander (610–c. 547 B.C.).

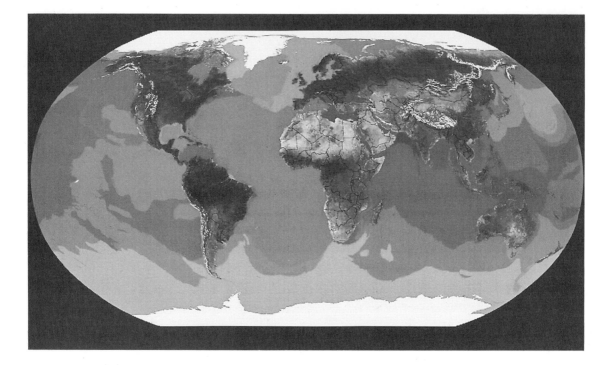

A view of Earth: its continents and oceans.

He theorizes that they are evidence of previous life forms. He states that life originated in the water and that humans developed from fish. He argues that all animals originated first in the water and later migrated to land, where they shed their outer coverings or shells and adapted to the new conditions. The first mention in China of fossils is by Chu Hsi, whose book, written around 1175, states that fossils were once living organisms.

c. 525 B.C. ▪ Pythagoras declares the Earth round. The first to teach that the Earth is spherical is Greek philosopher Pythagoras (c. 580–500 B.C.). As proof of this argument he offers the fact that it casts a round shadow on the Moon during an eclipse. He also says that the Earth's core is fire and that running water sculpts its surface. A Pythagorean quotation made famous by Roman poets is that, "Often seashells lie far from the beach, and men have found old anchors on mountaintops."

c. 400 B.C. ▪ Plato and the lost continent of Atlantis. The first mention of the lost continent of Atlantis is made by Greek philosopher Plato (c. 428–c. 347 B.C.), in his dialogue *Timaeus*. This moralistic tale mentions a submerged continent on the other side of the Pillar of Hercules (or the Strait of Gibraltar that lies between southernmost Spain and northwesternmost Africa). Although written as part of a fictional story, the legend of Atlantis persists and is believed by many a modern geologist. It is known, however, that around 1400 B.C., an island in the Atlantic Ocean did explode volcanically, and possibly inspired Plato's tale.

c. 325 B.C. ▪ Theophrastus studies minerals. The oldest-known written study on rocks and minerals is the *De lapidibus* (On stones) written by Greek botanist Theophrastus (c. 372–287 B.C.). He discusses about seventy different materials and attempts to classify them all, dividing them up into two groups he calls "stones" and "earths." He then classifies stones according to ten different qualities (color, density, texture, etc.), and discusses earths, which are substances used for coloring, cosmetics, and insecticides. This work remains the best study of minerals for almost two thousand years.

c. 300 B.C. ▪ Learning about tides. The first to closely observe and describe the tidal action of the sea is Pytheas, a Greek geographer and explorer. He speculates correctly that tides are influenced by the Moon. The first medieval statement that the tides are governed by the phases of the moon is made around 700 A.D. by English scholar Bede (673–735). Also called the Venerable Bede, he states correctly that high tides do not occur at the same time everywhere, and that tide tables have to be prepared separately for each different port. The first-known recording of tides for the purpose of prediction of floods is made around 1335 by English scholar Richard of Wallingford (c. 1292–1336). He later builds a mechanical clock that indicates low and high tide.

c. 240 B.C. ▪ Eratosthenes estimates the size of the Earth. Greek astronomer Eratosthenes (c. 276–c. 194 B.C.) is the first to estimate correctly the size of Earth. From his travels and experience he knows that on the summer solstice (the time of the year when the sun is at its highest point), when the sun is at the zenith (directly overhead) in Syene (Aswan, Egypt), at the same time it is 7 degrees from zenith in Alexandria, Egypt. He guesses that this difference can only be due to Earth's curvature. Knowing the exact distance between Syene and Alexandria, he then calculates the diameter of Earth by assuming it is a sphere with an equal curvature on its entire surface. His final circumference calculation of about 25,000 miles is almost correct. Centuries later, most learned men discount his calculation, considering it to be much too large, since it implies that most of the Earth is covered by water.

c. 20 B.C. ▪ Strabo's geographic theories. The first suggestion of the existence of unknown continents is made by Greek geographer, Strabo (63 B.C.–A.D. 19). He also discusses the land-forming activity of rivers, recognizes the long-dormant (inactive) Vesuvius as a volcano, and notes that earthquakes are less prominent when volcanoes are active. He is regarded the father of modern theories of mountain-making by volcano, and establishes the notion that volcanoes act as safety valves for pent-up subterranean pressures. He notes the presence of marine fossils in the desert and states that the sea had once covered certain portions of the land. He also teaches that entire continents can be moved over time and that probably all islands were at one time connected to larger continents.

c. A.D. 44 ▪ Description of Earth's weather zones. The first division of Earth into zones is made by Roman geographer Pomponius Mela. He uses five zones to divide the Earth: North Frigid, North Temperate, Torrid, South Temperate, and South Frigid. He says that only the two temperate (mild) zones are inhabitable, but that people in the north cannot reach those in the south because of the terribly hot Torrid Zone in between. He also says that the ocean surrounding Earth cuts into the land by means of four different seas, the most important of which is the Mediterranean. His divisions are generally used today.

c. 900 ▪ Animal, vegetable, and mineral classification. Persian physician and alchemist (a scientist who pursued the medieval quest to turn metals into gold) Rhazes (c. 865–c. 930) is the first to divide all substances into the grand classification of animal, vegetable, and mineral. He also subclassifies minerals into metals, volatile liquids (spirits), stones, salts, and others. This classification is still used.

1473 ▪ Establishment of geology. The first published use of the word "geology" is found in *Philobyblon* (The love of books), written by medieval writer Richard de Bury (1281–1345) more than a century before. This book uses the word geology to describe the science or law of the Earth, as opposed to the theology of the Earth, which is the science of the divine (and based on religion). Geology comes from the Greek words *ge* for Earth and *logos* for reason.

1546 ▪ Agricola writes about mineralogy. The first handbook on mineralogy is written by German mineralogist Georgius Agricola (1494–1555). Mineralogy is the branch of geology that studies the minerals from which rocks are made. In his *De natura fossilium* (On the nature of minerals), Agricola classifies minerals and other Earth materials in terms of their geometrical form (spheres, cones, and plates). This is the first mineral classification that is really empirically based (based on experiment and observation). In the same year, Agricola also considers the origins of mountains in his *De orta et causis subterraneorum* (On the origin and causes of things underground). He argues that there are many factors in mountain-building, but that the main mechanism is erosion caused by moving water, with mountains forming along the banks of ever-deepening river beds. In this work he also gives his ideas on the origin of ore deposits (rock containing metal) in veins, and correctly attributes them to being deposited by aqueous (watery) solution.

1556 • The study of geology. The first to base the study of geology on observation as opposed to speculation is German mineralogist Georgius Agricola (1494–1555). His opus, *De re metallica* (On metals), is published this year, one year after his death. This monumental work summarizes every aspect of mining and metallurgical processes to his time. Metallurgy is the extraction of metal from its ore and its refining and preparation. Agricola's book, which is the product of a lifetime of practical experience and takes him twenty-five years to complete, has 273 woodcut illustrations that show machinery and processes. The popular and definitive work earns Agricola the title "father of mineralogy."

1565 • Illustrations and study of fossils. The first illustrations of fossils are published by Conrad Gesner (1516–1565), a Swiss naturalist, in his *De rerum fossilium* (On the nature of minerals). He does not consider fossils to be the remnants of past living organisms, but discusses them along with other things he finds in the soil, such as minerals, ores, stalactites (long, icicle-shaped deposits that hang from the ceiling of a cave), and prehistoric stone tools. He also classifies minerals into fifteen categories.

1570 • Strata is observed. The first systematic observation on the range of strata is made by British geologist George Owen (1552–1613). Strata are the layers or bands of rock in the Earth formed by sedimentation (layers building up over time). As sediment builds up, its great pressure forms rock (by a process called compaction and cementation) which, in turn, provides us with a kind of calendar of Earth history. Owen makes the correct observation that masses of minerals found in the Earth are not simply thrown together in a haphazard manner but have their own regular

Visible strata in the Grand Canyon, Arizona.

order. Owen also traces bands of limestone for some distance. He is often called the father of English geology.

1667 · First law of crystallography. The first law of crystallography is stated by Nicolaus Steno (1638–1686), a Danish anatomist and geologist. Crystallography is the study of the structure and properties of crystals. Crystals are a solid form of a mineral with regular angles, smooth faces, and symmetrical corners. Crystal comes from the Greek word *krystallos* meaning "clear ice." Steno's principle states that the crystals of a specific substance have fixed characteristic angles at which the faces, however distorted they may be, always meet. He also argues correctly that the Earth is layered with the petrified remains (fossils) of once-living organisms, and that fossils are not the "practice-creations" of God as some believed. In his 1669 book, *De solido* (On a solid body), he distinguishes between marine and land fossils and states that some belong to extinct forms.

1680 · Leibniz distinguishes between igneous and aqueous rock. The first distinction between igneous rock and aqueous rock is made by German philosopher and mathematician Gottfried Wilhelm Leibniz (1646–1716). He states that certain rocks had cooled from a state of fusion (liquefaction by heat), and others had been formed by the action of water into more or less stratified (layered) masses. Igneous rock is rock that forms as molten magma or lava cools and hardens. Aqueous rock is rock that is formed by the influence of water.

1688 · Reading the Earth's past in fossils. The first to suggest that fossils can provide scientific evidence in revealing the historical past of the Earth is English physicist Robert Hooke (1635–1703). In his 1688 work on earthquakes, he states that the fossils of mollusks (clams) deserve to be regarded as historical objects, like old coins, that can give us valuable information about the past. He also concludes from the types of fossils he finds that the climate of England once had been much warmer. He attributes earthquakes and volcanoes to the existence of fires within the Earth.

1691 · Artesian wells. The first book on artesian wells is *De fontium mutinensium* (On the wonderful springs of Modena) written by Italian physician Bernardino Ramazzini (1633–1714). Artesian wells are wells dug into underground aquifers or basins that are like natural reservoirs. When an aquifer is reached and drilled into, water flows to the surface under natural pressure without pumping. The term is derived from the French province of Artois where naturally flowing wells were drilled as early as the twelfth century. Ramazzini's book contains diagrams and also explains how the wells originated. Later, in 1715, the first definitive statement on the origin of underground springs is made by Italian zoologist Antonio Vallisnieri (1661–1730). He says that spring water gushes from mountains because the rain and snow that had penetrated the ground earlier is now resurfacing.

1696 · First scientific interpretation of creation. The first attempt at a scientific interpretation of the Bible's six "days" of creation is made by William Whiston (1667–1752), an English mathematician and Anglican priest, in his book *A New Theory of the Earth*. In this work he attempts to explain Biblical accounts scientifically, and thus states that the great flood can be attributed to a passing comet. He also suggests that Earth is much older than most believe. Despite his religious orientation, he is one of the strongest advocates of the need to harmonize science and religion.

1725 · Writings on the sea. Italian soldier and oceanographer Luigi Ferdinando Marsigli (1658–1730), also called Marsili, publishes his *Histoire physique de la mer* (Physical history of the sea), the first complete book dealing with the sea. He also is the first to use a naturalist's dredge. With this machine that is dragged across the ocean bottom and scoops up earth, he is able to examine the contents of the sea floor. In 1691 the water cycle of the Earth had first been detailed by English astronomer Edmond Halley (1656–1742). He published a paper this year describing this cycle, stating that the sun evaporates sea water, which rises to mountain heights and is condensed into rain, which then falls and penetrates into the Earth to emerge in springs and rivers (which flow to the sea). Earlier, in 1663, Isaac Vossius (1618–1689), a Dutch scholar, published *De motu marium et ventorum* (On the motion of the sea and winds) in which he stated the correct theory that the overall ocean circulation of the North Atlantic region is essentially clockwise.

c. 1735 · Linnaeus attempts to classify minerals. The first to classify minerals according to their crystalline forms is Swedish botanist Carolus Linnaeus (1707–1778). This does not prove easy, however, since even crystals of the same compound may not resemble one another because of the various ways crystal faces may sometimes develop.

1743 · First geological maps. The first geological map is made by Christopher Packe (1686–1749), an English physician and geologist. He produces a chart that sketches the geology of East Kent, England, and begins the use of hachuring (shading) by drawing parallel lines in the direction of a slope to show the pattern of valleys. Hills and valleys are easily distinguishable with this new method as are the ranges of chalk, slate, and clay. The first true geologic or mineralogic map that ignores political boundaries is made a few years later in 1746 by French geologist Jean-Étienne Guettard (1715–1786). He declares that the mineralogical formations on the coasts of France and England that face each other are identical, indicating they were once part of the same geological system. Ignoring political boundaries, his maps instead show how the formations or great "bandes" of rock that appear to end at the English and French coasts are in fact connected underground beneath the Channel.

1752 · Modern statistical geography is established. Modern statistical geography is established by Anton Friedrich Büsching (1724–1793), a German geographer, who publishes the first of eleven volumes of his

Neue Erdbeschreibung. Six of these volumes focus on European geography. Altogether they help develop a scientific basis for the study of geography by stressing statistics (the collection and analysis of numerical data) over descriptive writing. Geography is distinct from geology in that it is the science that describes only the surface of the Earth. Geology is the science that studies the history, structure, and composition of the entire Earth.

1758 ▪ Analyzing ore with blowpipes. The blowpipe technique for analyzing ore (rock containing metal) is first introduced by Swedish mineralogist Axel Fredrik Cronstedt (1722–1765). The mouth blowpipe is a cone-shaped brass tube that allows a thin jet of air to be directed into the flame, making it hotter. By placing a piece of ore in the blowpipe flame, much can be learned by the changes the ore undergoes and by what is left after burning. With his device, Cronstedt systematizes and improves the well-known technique of observing color changes as a means of making a chemical analysis. The blowpipe remains a useful tool to the skilled user for more than a century, eventually to be replaced by the system of spectral analysis, which analyzes the colors in a spectrum of light. This same year, Cronstedt begins the classification of minerals not only according to their appearance but also according to their chemical structure—an important development.

1759 ▪ Three-part classification of rocks is established. Three-part classification of rocks of the Earth's crust is established by Italian mining engineer Giovanni Arduino (1714–1795). He originates the classification of Primary, Secondary, and Tertiary (pronounced ter'-she-air-e) rocks. Primary or "Primitive" rocks include the schists (rock formed when mudstone or shale is baked by magma) and the mass of rocks found at the core of mountains that contains no organic remains. Secondary rock is composed of limestones, marls or mudstone, shales (clay) and other stratified sedimentary materials (settled into layers), many of which are full of fossils. Tertiary rock is made up of generally looser detritus (rock debris caused by wearing away) and is sometimes full of the remains of plants and animals. Arduino also adds a fourth type—Quaternary or Volcanic—that consists of lavas and tuff (rock formed from volcanic ash deposits) accumulated by repeated eruptions and inundations of the sea. His categories are readily accepted.

1760 ▪ Earthquake theories. The first to suggest that earthquakes give off shock waves is English astronomer John Michell (c. 1724–1793) in

Catastrophism v. Uniformitarianism: A Seventeenth and Eighteenth Century Debate

James Hutton, the "father of geology"

In the mid-1600s, Irish Bishop James Ussher proclaimed the time of Earth's creation to be on the evening of October 22, 4004 B.C. based upon a count of the ages of the people in the Bible. He also set the date of the Great Flood and Noah's ark at 2349 B.C. For many years Western scientists used this reading of the Bible as a scientific principle. Catastrophism, the belief that the Earth's features were created by sudden catastrophes, was directly linked to the biblical accounts of creation and the flood.

In 1784 Scottish geologist James Hutton published his *Theory of the Earth,* in which he argued his uniformitarianism theory that the Earth is much more than 6,000 years old and that many forces have shaped and reshaped the planet's surface over vast amounts of time. Rivers, for example, carried silt and formed it into rocks, while wind and rain wore away at exposed surfaces. The primary force, however, was volcanic activity. Hutton viewed the Earth's inner core as a "heat engine" capable of fusing together sedimentary rock, causing upheavals in strata and creating mountains. This Vulcanist theory contradicted the catastrophists, who generally believed in the Neptunist theory that sediment from the Great Flood and other oceanic activity was responsible for the Earth's strata.

James Hutton's views were not accepted for some time, but by the nineteenth century catastrophism had fallen out of scientific favor. Current research estimates Earth to be 4.5 billion years old; and uniformitarianism paved the way for evolution theories to come.

a long article presenting many theories on earthquakes. Michell suggests that one can calculate the center of a quake by noting the time at which the motions are felt. His work is ahead of its time as he states that earthquakes are partly tremulous (a shaking motion), but that they also move the Earth by waves or vibrations that succeed one another. He considers all the known ideas about earthquakes and evaluates each according to known facts. Because of his pioneering work on vibrations and waves, he is called the father of seismology (the study of earthquakes).

1763 · Mason-Dixon Line survey begins. The first work on what becomes known as the Mason-Dixon Line begins. Two English astronomers, Charles Mason (1728–1786) and Jeremiah Dixon, are hired to begin a survey of the Pennsylvania-Maryland border in order to settle a boundary dispute. It takes them five years to survey the 233-mile line. The result is the creation of the Mason-Dixon Line. This line becomes famous in American history as the boundary between the free states and the slave states during the Civil War (1861–1865). After the war it comes to serve as the political boundary between the North and the South.

1769 · Benjamin Franklin publishes a chart of the Gulf Stream. Benjamin Franklin (1706–1790), American statesman and scientist, develops the first published chart of the Gulf Stream. The Gulf Stream is the warm ocean current that flows northeast up the Atlantic coast of North America between Cape Hatteras, North Carolina, and Newfoundland, Canada. Franklin uses temperature measurements and observations of water color to track the Gulf Stream's course. He suggests that ships going to Europe stay in its current, and that those returning to America avoid it. The first written description of the Gulf Stream in the North Atlantic was given in 1513 by Juan Ponce de Léon (c. 1460–1521), Spanish explorer.

1774 · New methods for classifying minerals. German geologist Abraham Gottlob Werner (1750–1817) publishes his *Von den Ausselichen Kenneichen der Fossilien* (On the external characteristics of minerals), in which he establishes a new language and new methods for classifying minerals. Placing little emphasis on crystal shape and chemical composition, Werner bases his classification on the external characteristics of the minerals themselves, such as color, external shape, fracture (how it breaks), transparency, hardness, specific weight, etc. Werner later becomes known for his principle that all strata (layers or beds of rock) were laid down as sediment by the action of water. Followers of this theory belong to what is called the Neptunist school (after Neptune, the Roman god of freshwater), and they strongly resist the opposing school (called Vulcanists after Vulcan, the Roman god of fire) that believes that the action of heat and volcanoes formed all strata. **(See also 1787)**

1779 · Scientific investigations of mountains. The first person to climb mountains in order to investigate them scientifically is Swiss physicist Horace-Bénédict de Saussure (1740–1799). This year he publishes the first part of his four-volume *Voyages dans les Alpes* (Voyages in the Alps), in which he summarizes his findings and regularly uses the word "geology." Until Saussure, the high regions of the Swiss Alps were regarded fearfully as *montagnes maudit*—evil mountains. Saussure not only provides accurate observations on mountains and glaciers, but also describes their beauty. The first major classifier of mountains was German mineralogist Johann Gottlob Lehmann (1719–1767). In his *Versuche einer Geschichte von Flotz-Gebrungen* (Essay on a history of secondary mountains) published in 1756, he classified mountains according to three types, often based on their strata (layers of rock), and also offered a theory of their origins.

1784 · Crystal structure theory. A mathematical theory of crystal structure is offered by French mineralogist René-Just Haüy (1743–1822). This year he publishes his *Essai d'une théorie sur la structure des cristaux* (Attempt at a theory on the structure of crystals), in which he joins mathematics and mineralogy (the study of the minerals from which rocks are made) and lays the foundation for a new way of understanding crystals. His law of crystal symmetry states that crystals are the result of the stacking together of tiny, identical units (and that if a line is drawn through a crystal's center, it would divide into two identical halves). This new revelation about crystal structure lays the groundwork for the science of crystallography, founded in 1801 when Haüy publishes his five-volume masterpiece, *Traité de minéralogie* (Treatise on mineralogy). In this work he explains that if crystalline forms are identical, or if they are different, then that identity or difference is found in their chemical composition. Crystallography will become highly significant to physics with the eventual development of X-ray techniques.

March, 1785 · Uniformitarianism theory is proposed. Uniformitarianism is first proposed by Scottish geologist James Hutton (1726–1797) in a paper, "Concerning the System of the Earth," that he presents to the Royal Society of Edinburgh. Out of this brief paper geology

Igneous rocks granite
and obsidian, both
found in the Sierra
Nevada Mountains
in California.

has its beginnings as a real science and an organized field of study. Hutton's theory of "uniformitarianism" contains one of the most fundamental principles of geology—that relatively gentle, natural processes have been constantly (and uniformly) at work, gradually shaping the Earth over an enormously long time. Hutton says that the prime force behind this shaping is the internal heat of the Earth. His theory of geologic gradualism gets its very long name because it views the geologic evolution of the Earth as a slow, continuous transformation that is only rarely marked by sudden, catastrophic change. These ideas meet considerable resistance, but Hutton eventually prevails and comes to be known as the father of geology.
(See also 1830)

1787 ▪ Geologic formation theory. The first systematic study of geologic formations is written by German geologist Abraham Gottlob Werner (1750–1817). In his *Kurze Klassifikation* (Brief classification), he classifies rock types according to his theory that from the earliest times an ocean covered the entire Earth and deposited layer upon layer of sediment; the sediment eventually turned into rock. In this work Werner also says that basalt rock (a dark, fine-grained rock we now know to be formed when lava cools) is aqueous (formed by the action of water) and not volcanic in origin (formed by the action of heat). Unlike Scottish geologist James Hutton (1726–1797), who recognizes the important geologic role of heat and volcanic action (and is therefore called a Vulcanist), Werner incorrectly believes along with other Neptunists that virtually all strata (rock layers) had been laid down as sediment by the action of water. Werner's ideas dominate all of Europe, possibly because they fit so well with the Biblical story of the Great Flood.

1792 ▪ Volcanic rock observations. The first to study volcanic rock experimentally is Lazzaro Spallanzani (1729–1799), an Italian naturalist and biologist. This year he publishes the first volume of his six-volume work, *Viaggi alle due Sicilie e in Alcune Parti dell'Appenine* (Travels in the two Sicilies and other parts of the Appenines), in which he describes his observations of the volcanoes Vesuvius, Stromboli, Vulcano, and Etna. Trying to observe active volcanoes, Spallanzani suffers burns while descending into a volcano and measuring the flow of red-hot lava. He is also overcome by gas at Etna. His studies earn him the status of pioneer in volcanology or vulcanology (the study of volcanoes). In 1827 the first extensive study of the nature and effects of volcanic action is made by English geologist George Julius Poulett Scrope (1797–1876) in his *Memoir on the Geology of Central France*. His astute observations on the age of the dormant (nonactive) volcanoes in the Auvergne region of France play a major role in deposing the Neptunist theory that all rocks were formed by sedimentation from the oceans.

1796 ▪ Fossils are classified. French anatomist Georges Cuvier (1769–1832) is the first to extend a system of classification to fossils. He notes that although many fossils are different from living animals, they nonetheless belong to one of the four phyla (branches) he had established (Vertebrata, Mullousca, Articulata, and Radiata). A phylum (the singular form of phyla) is one of the largest and broadest classification groups, just below a "kingdom." The order of classification, from the smallest to the largest, is species, genus, family, order, class, phylum, and kingdom. Despite his awareness that the deeper the fossil is found, the older the rock (and the more the fossil differs from the life forms he knows), Cuvier refuses to make any judgments about an evolutionary theory. He suggests, rather, that the world was subjected to several catastrophic events.

1798 ▪ Density of the Earth is determined. The first accurate determination of the Earth's mean (average) density is made by English chemist and physicist Henry Cavendish (1731–1810). Density is the mass of a substance compared to its volume. The volume of two objects can be the same (as in the example of an airplane model made of balsa wood and one of metal) and still have a very different mass (since, in that instance, the atoms of metal have a different and heavier mass than those of wood). Aware that the Earth's mass can be calculated if the value of the force of gravity (gravitational constant) is known, Cavendish devises an experiment to determine what that constant is for smaller bodies, from which he will extrapolate (project) a constant for the entire Earth. Using a torsion balance (a twisted wire) to which he attaches a suspended beam with two lead balls, he measures the period of oscillation (the duration of its back-and-forth motion) and is able to calculate the gravitational force between the two pairs of balls. Using this value, he is able to calculate the Earth's mass and arrive at a mean density for the Earth itself, which he says is 5.48 times that of water. This is very near today's accepted value of 5.517.

1798 · Start of experimental geology. Experimental geology is founded by Scottish geologist and chemist James Hall (1761–1832) when he begins a series of papers in which he provides experimental evidence for the geological theories of his colleague, Scottish geologist James Hutton (1726–1797). By melting minerals and cooling them at a controlled rate, Hall proves that he can obtain different kinds of rocks. He continues to experiment extensively with igneous rocks (formed from molten lava) and shows that they are produced by intense heat. He is also known as the founder of geochemistry, the study of the chemical makeup and the various chemical changes of the Earth.

1799 · Geologic map is begun. The first geologic map based on scientific principles is begun by William Smith (1769–1839), an English geologist. After extensive observations of his native land, Smith discovers that each successive layer of strata (layers of rock) has its own characteristic forms of fossils, and that with study one can tell one layer from another by knowing what fossils are in them. He then makes a map using different colors to indicate the succession of sedimentary beds or groups of beds. Eventually, in 1815 he publishes his landmark map, *A Delineation of the Strata of England and Wales with Part of Scotland*, which illustrates the principles of paleontological stratigraphy. (Paleontology is the study of life in past geological eras through the examination of fossil remains.) This map links the study of fossils (paleontology) with the study of the distribution and order of rock layers (stratigraphy). His color-keyed geologic map, roughly 6 by 9 feet, is very easy to understand.

The July 22, 1980, eruption of Mount St. Helens in southern Washington. A volcano is a hole in the Earth's surface through which molten rock and hot gases escape from deep within the Earth.

1803 • Ocean theories and studies. German naturalist Friedrich Wilhelm Heinrich Alexander von Humboldt (1769–1859) writes an article in which he states that the Atlantic Ocean is a valley dug out by a torrential current. He also studies the oceanic current off the west coast of South America that is originally named after him but is later called the Peru Current. Before Humboldt, James Rennell (1742–1830), an English geographer, began his scientific study of winds and currents in 1790, and made the first comprehensive study of the Atlantic Ocean currents. Earlier, in 1772 Antoine-Laurent Lavoisier (1743–1794), a French chemist, made the first quantitative analysis of seawater, and in 1768 English navigator James Cook (1728–1779) began the first of three ocean voyages during which he was the first to take the subsurface temperature of the ocean.

1809 • Beginnings of scientific paleontology. Principles of scientific paleontology are first offered by English geologist William Martin (1767–1810). This links the study of fossil remains (paleontology) with the study of the distribution and order of rock layers (stratigraphy). In his work, *Outlines of an Attempt to Establish a Knowledge of Extraneous Fossils on Scientific Principles*, Martin offers the sound beginnings of a science of past plants and animals that is based on fossil evidence. Two years later, two French scientists make a color geologic map to demonstrate how fossils can be used to determine accurately the geological chronology of a particular area. In 1811 French mineralogist Alexandre Brongniart (1770–1847) and French anatomist Georges Cuvier (1769–1832) publish their *Essai sur la géographie minéralogique des environs de Paris* (Essay on the mineral geography of the surroundings of Paris) in which they offer a table of stratigraphical succession linking fossils and geological chronology. This work places paleontology on a more accurate, scientific basis. It is based largely on the work of Brongniart.

December 16, 1811 · Earthquakes alter flow of Mississippi River. The first major shift of the Mississippi River occurs during a series of earthquakes centered in New Madrid, Missouri. Continuing into January and February 1812, these major quakes alter much of the Midwest topography (natural features) and are considered the strongest in U.S. history (estimated at 8.0 on the Richter scale) because they affect a large area of about a million square miles. Some lake bottoms are raised as much as 15 feet, streams change direction, and the Mississippi and Ohio Rivers flow backwards.

1812 · Mohs scale of hardness. Mohs hardness scale is first proposed by German mineralogist Friedrich Mohs (1773–1839). He devises a decimal scale to measure the resistance of a mineral to scratching or abrasion. This is measured by scratching the mineral's surface with a substance whose hardness is known. The Mohs scale is composed of ten minerals that have been given values. In order from softness to hardness, they are: (1) talc, (2) gypsum, (3) calcite, (4) fluorite, (5) apatite, (6) orthoclase, (7) quartz, (8) topaz, (9) corundum, (10) diamond. If a mineral is scratched by topaz but not by quartz, its Mohs hardness is 7.5–8.

1816 · Glacier theories are offered. The first to propose that glaciers once covered most of Europe is Swiss civil engineer Ignatz Venetz (1788–1859). A glacier can be described as a river of slowly moving ice that forms in mountains and creeps down a valley until it melts. Venetz's 1816 article on glaciers and their movement influences German-Swiss mining engineer Johann von Charpentier (1786–1855), who, in turn, persuades

Swiss-American naturalist Jean Louis Rodolphe Agassiz (1807–1873) of this fact. Charpentier is the first to propose the idea of the extensive movement of glaciers. In 1834 he suggests that the huge erratic boulders found scattered throughout the Alpine regions have been brought there by ancient glaciers. He precedes Agassiz in this notion of glacial geology and actually takes Agassiz into the field to demonstrate that the valley glaciers in the Alps once extended to the lower levels, indicating that the glaciers of recent past geologic ages were more extensive than at present. **(See also 1840)**

1818 ▪ Ocean floor studies. The first deep-sea study of the ocean floor is conducted by English explorer John Ross (1777–1856). He leads an expedition into Baffin Bay (in the Atlantic Ocean between west Greenland and the Canadian Arctic Islands) and succeeds in bringing up muddy sediments and worms using a "clamp" of his own design. His findings are ignored, however. In 1841 English naturalist Edward Forbes (1815–1854) pioneers the use of a dredge in the scientific study of shallow water. As one of the first to consider the sea as an entity and to divide the ocean into natural zones on a scientific basis, he is regarded—along with American oceanographer Matthew Fontaine Maury (1806–1873)—as the cofounder of the science of oceanography. **(See also 1855)**

1819 · Oxford appoints first professor of geology. The first "Reader in Geology" at Oxford University is William Buckland (1784–1856), an English geologist. Although already a professor of mineralogy at Oxford, Buckland is appointed to a teaching position in geology. This is the first such appointment in a major English university and contributes to the public recognition of geology as a science. Buckland has the distinction of publishing in 1836 the last major geological textbook to be written from the diluvialist (Great Flood) point of view. It is titled *Geology and Mineralogy Considered with Reference to Natural Theology.* In 1866 Othniel Charles Marsh (1831–1899), an American paleontologist, is appointed professor of vertebrate paleontology at Yale University, the first such professor in the United States. He makes many major fossil discoveries in the American West and discovers the remains of pterodactyls, the flying lizards of the Cretaceous Period.

1822 · Dinosaur fossil is discovered. The first fossil to be recognized as that of a dinosaur is discovered by Gideon Algernon Mantell (1790–1852), an English physician, and his wife, Mary Ann Mantell. While the couple is searching for fossils around the quarries of Sussex, England, Mrs. Mantell discovers large fossil teeth unlike anything seen before. This eventually proves to be the remains of a dinosaur. By the time of his death, Gideon Mantell had discovered four out of the five genera of dinosaurs known during his time. From his work, the dinosaurian reptiles known as *Iguanodon, Hylaeosaurus, Pelorosaurus,* and *Regnosaurus* are known and described. Mantell's fossil collecting gets out of hand, however, and as it takes over his home (which swarms with sightseers) and ruins his medical practice, his wife eventually takes the children and moves out.

1822 · Naming of Cretaceous Period. The Cretaceous Period is named by the Belgian geologist Jean-Julien d'Omalius d'Halloy (1783–1875). As part of the Mesozoic Era, it is the interval of geological time that began about 136 million years ago following the Jurassic Period and preceding the Tertiary (pronounced ter'-she-air-e) Period. Its name refers to chalk (*creta* in Latin), which was the characteristic rock formed in most of Europe during this time. It was during this period that the Earth assumed many of its present features. In 1829 the Jurassic Period is named by French mineralogist Alexandre Brongniart (1770–1847) and German naturalist Friedrich Wilhelm Heinrich Alexander von Humboldt (1769–1859). They name this part of the Mesozoic Era—between the Triassic and Cretaceous Periods—after the Jura Mountains, which are along the border of France and Switzerland, and for the chalk sequence in the strata or layers of rock in these mountains.

1827 ▪ Minerals are distinguished from rocks. The first to distinguish minerals from rocks is French mineralogist Alexandre Brongniart (1770–1847). Rock is made up of one or more minerals and is divided into one of three types according to how it was formed. A mineral is a naturally occurring substance with a definite chemical composition. It is often found in crystal form. A mineral can also be identified by its having a number of certain key properties.

1829 ▪ Invention of polarizing microscope. The polarizing microscope is invented by Scottish physicist William Nicol (1768–1851). Using plane-polarized light (which vibrates in only one plane as opposed to ordinary light which vibrates in all directions), this new device illuminates the specimen being examined, and the specimen appears bright against a dark background. Nicol also develops a method of making very thin sections of minerals and fossil wood so he may examine them with his new microscope. It is not until the work of English geologist and chemist Henry Clifton Sorby (1826–1908) in 1851 that microscopic petrography actually comes into being. Petrography is the description of rocks and their grouping into classes. Convinced of the value of the microscope as a tool in all sciences, Sorby prepares thin sections of rocks (1/1000th of an inch) and gives the first description of their microscopical structure. His subsequent findings establish the value of this new technique, and he becomes known as the father of microscopical petrography (the study of rocks in thin sections, based on the different optical properties of their mineral makeup).

1830 ▪ Uniformitarianism is validated. Uniformitarianism is first successfully popularized by Charles Lyell (1797–1875), a Scottish geologist, in his classic work, *The Principles of Geology*. Written in three volumes, this landmark work is very well received and serves to validate the gradualist ideas of Scottish geologist James Hutton (1726–1797), concerning what the proper time scale of geology should be. Lyell argues that most of Earth's history is made up of gradual, everyday events such as the regular movement of a stream, and that such major, dramatic events as earthquakes and floods are the exception. He also estimates the age of some of the oldest fossil-bearing rocks to be 240 million years. He achieves his goal of writing a book "to establish the principle of reasoning" in geology, and dismisses religious explanations of natural phenomena that are not supported by hard evidence. This work greatly influences English naturalist Charles Robert Darwin (1809–1882), who said, "I always feel as if my books came half out of Lyell's brain." **(See also March 1785)**

1834 ▪ Triassic Period is named. The Triassic Period is named by German geologist Friedrich August von Alberti (1795–1878). As the earliest period of the Mesozoic Era (beginning around 230 million years ago), it is named after the "Trias," which is a sequence of strata (layers of rock) in central Germany. The name refers to the threefold division of the strata of rocks formed by the pressure of water. The Cambrian geologic period is named by Adam Sedgwick (1785–1873), an English geologist, in 1836. During his investigations of ancient Welsh rocks, Sedgwick gives the name Cambrian (from the ancient name for Wales) to the oldest fossil-bearing rocks. The Cambrian geological period was the earliest period of the Paleozoic Era and is considered to be from 570 to 500 million years ago.

1837 ▪ Study of human fossils is founded. Human paleontology (the study of human fossils) is founded by French paleontologist and archeologist Édouard-Armand-Isidore-Hippolyte Lartet (1801–1871) when he discovers the jawbone of a fossil primate (an order of animals that includes monkeys, apes, and humans) and turns his attention fully to the origins of mankind. In 1852 he finds evidence that man coexisted with now-extinct animals. Lartet also discovers some of the earliest-known art, and goes on to show that the Stone Age was comprised of a succession of phases in human culture.

1838 ▪ Coining of term *geochemistry*. Geochemistry is coined by Christian Friedrich Schonbein (1799–1868), a German physical chemist, when he first uses the word "geochemistry" in an article to describe the study of the chemical and physical properties of rock formations. As it comes to be realized that the Earth is a complex system in which everything that happens involves chemical elements, geochemistry comes to be regarded as the chemistry of the distribution of the elements in various parts of the Earth. **(See also 1798)**

1838 ▪ Foundation for study of microfossils is laid. Micropaleontology, the study of microfossils, is founded by German biologist Christian

Gottfried Ehrenberg (1795–1876). Microfossils are fossils that can only be seen with a microscope. Ehrenberg founds micropaleontology after discovering many microscopic fossil organisms are contained in various geological formations and realizing that such single-cell fossils make up certain rock layers.

1839 · Pleistocene Epoch is identified. Charles Lyell (1797–1875), a Scottish geologist, first identifies the Pleistocene Epoch in the history of the Earth. Spanning a time period from about 2.5 million to 10,000 years ago, this epoch includes several advances and retreats of ice sheets and glaciers. It is during this time that humans are believed to have evolved as a species.

1839 · Murchison and the Silurian Period. The Silurian geologic period is named by British geologist Roderick Impey Murchison (1792–1871) in his eight hundred-page work, *The Silurian System.* Recognition of the period establishes for the first time the stratigraphic sequence (order of rock layers) of early Paleozoic rocks. This enables geologists to accurately trace the Earth's history backward across an increasingly long span of time. Murchison names his system after the Silures, an old British tribe that in Roman times inhabited the areas he explores. In 1839 Murchison, with English geologist Adam Sedgwick (1785–1873), co-names the Devonian Period of geologic time after studying the deposits in Devon and Cornwall in southwestern England. The order of the periods of the Paleozoic Era (from 620 to 230 million years ago) from the earliest to the most recent is: Cambrian, Ordovican, Silurian, Devonian, Mississippian, Pennsylvanian, and Permian.

1840 · Ice Age theory. A theory of the Ice Age is put forth by Swiss-American geologist Jean Louis Rodolphe Agassiz (1807–1873) in his *Études sur les Glaciers* (Studies on the glaciers). After spending five summers among the glaciers of his native Switzerland, Agassiz states his theory of glacier movement, demonstrating by way of experiment the fact that glaciers did and still do actually move. A glacier can be described as a river of slowly moving ice that forms in mountains and creeps down a valley until it melts. Agassiz also explains the power of glaciers to move things, which explains much about modern geological configurations. His ideas will not be accepted for another twenty-five years.

1841 · Murchison names Permian Period. The Permian Period of geologic time is named by British geologist Roderick Impey Murchison

Measuring an Earthquake: A Timeline of Breakthroughs in Seismology

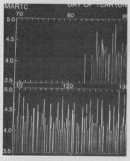

A seismogram.

In the second century A.D. Chinese astronomer and mathematician Chang Heng invented a simple seismoscope by suspending a metal pendulum inside a jar that held metal balls on its outer rim. When an earth movement occurred, the pendulum swayed back and forth, causing the release of one or more balls into the mouths of bronze toads resting at the base of the jar. The number of balls released and the direction in which they fell told the magnitude and location of the earth movement. Further breakthroughs in detecting and recording earthquakes occurred many centuries later. Some important ones are listed below:

1703	Jean de Hautefeuille built a seismoscope using mercury to sense motion.
1760	John Michell theorized that earthquakes move the earth by waves that succeed one another.
1846	Robert Mallet compiled the first catalog of recorded earthquakes from 1606 B.C. to 1850.
1880	John Milne invented the first seismograph to record earthquakes.
1935	The Richter scale was introduced to measure the magnitude of earthquakes.
1940	J-B tables became the standard tables of travel times for earthquake waves.

(1792–1871). This is the only name not based on a type of rock found in Europe. On the invitation of the czar, Murchison goes to Russia where he recognizes a sequence of beds that prove to be younger than rocks of the Carboniferous period Murchison knows to exist in England. He names them Permian (after the Russian district of Perm where they are found) to distinguish them from the rocks of the older Carboniferous Period.

1842 ▪ "Terrible lizards" given name and face. English zoologist Richard Owen (1804–1892) coins the word "dinosaur." It is derived from the Greek for "terrible lizard," and refers to the gigantic proportions of these beasts. In 1854 Owen prepares the first full-sized reconstruction of dinosaurs for display at the Crystal Palace in London. Although quite inaccurate, these large exhibition models generate enormous interest in dinosaurs that remains high today.

1846 ▪ Dynamics of earthquakes. English engineer Robert Mallet (1810–1881) publishes an article on the dynamics of earthquakes. During his career, he compiles the first modern catalog of recorded earthquakes and the first seismic (earthquake) map of the Earth. He also coins the word seismology (the study of earthquakes). His earthquake catalog records all known quakes from 1606 B.C. to 1850. After a massive earthquake in Naples, Italy, in 1857, Mallet conducts his own experiments by exploding gunpowder and measuring the rate at which shock travels through different kinds of material.

1846 ▪ Forbes founds biogeography. Biogeography is founded by English naturalist Edward Forbes (1815–1854). In this year he publishes a paper detailing the migration of most of the plants and animals of England from the European mainland during one of three separate episodes of the glacial epoch. This pioneering work becomes the starting point of biogeography—the study of the distribution and dispersal of plants and animals throughout the world.

1855 ▪ First oceanography textbook. Matthew Fontaine Maury (1806–1873), an American oceanographer, publishes *The Physical Geography of the Sea*, the first textbook on oceanography (the study of the oceans). Along with Edward Forbes (1815–1854), the English naturalist and cofounder of oceanography (see 1818), Maury spends years studying the physical and mechanical aspects of the sea. He also promotes and directs the first program of sounding (determining the depth) of the North Atlantic and publishes the first chart of the depths of the Atlantic Ocean.

1870 ▪ Cretaceous Period dinosaur remains are found. The first complete remains of the dinosaurs of the Cretaceous Period (between 160 and 70 million years ago) are discovered by American paleontologist Edward Drinker Cope (1840–1897). This begins his lifelong writings about the rich fossil fields of the American West. His discovery establishes that the Age of Mammals began much earlier than most thought.

1874 ▪ Paleocene Epoch is proposed. The Paleocene Epoch of geologic time is proposed by Alsatian (from Alsace, a region in France) botanist Wilhelm Philipp Schimper (1808–1880). Beginning approximately sixty million years ago, it is a part of the early Tertiary (pronounced ter'-she-air-e) Period that precedes the Eocene Epoch and follows the (older) Cretaceous Period. In North America, this epoch is characterized by a general warming trend in climatic conditions, the absence of dinosaurs, and the expansion and evolution of mammals.

1875 ▪ Colorado River is explored. Results of the first river-borne exploration of the Colorado River are published by American geologist John Wesley Powell (1834–1902). His work, *Exploration of the Colorado River of the West and Its Tributaries* originates and formalizes a number of concepts that become part of the standard working vocabulary of geology. After the American Civil War (1861–1865), the canyon of the Colorado River was the last unexplored region of the United States. The one-armed Powell led four boats (only two of which survived) on his first river trip in 1869. His party left from Green River, Wyoming, and traveled through the Grand Canyon down "the great unknown." He made another trip down the canyon in 1871, experiencing and documenting the carving power of rivers and setting the stage for the systematic survey of this canyon country.

1878 ▪ Mountain building. Albert Heim (1849–1937), Swiss geologist, publishes his *Untersuchung Uber den Mechanismus der Gebirgsbildung* (Inquiry into the mechanism of mountain building). Heim is the first genuine European geological artist. His talent lies in his power to describe accurately the most complex geological structures and to then illustrate them in brilliant drawings. His studies of the Swiss Alps greatly advance knowledge of the dynamics of mountain building and of glacial effects on rocks and surface features.

1879 · Founding of the U.S. Geological Survey. The U.S. Geological Survey is first established under the direction of American geologist Clarence Rivers King (1842–1901). The survey's mission is to conduct investigations and research of the geology of the United States for scientific purposes and for a practical awareness of its material resources.

1879 · Establishment of the Ordovician Period. Ordovician Period of geological strata (rock layers) is established by English geologist Charles Lapworth (1842–1920). He proposes that a complex series of strata exists between the Cambrian and the Silurian Periods that is in fact a separate system with its own geologic period. Lapworth's suggestion is accepted almost immediately by the geological community.

1880 · Milne devises first precise seismograph. The first precise seismograph is invented by English geologist John Milne (1850–1913). His device senses motion with a horizontal pendulum whose movement is recorded on a drum, usually by a pen. He uses his device to record several distant earthquakes (in Japan) and soon establishes a chain of seismological stations around the world, marking the beginning of modern seismology (the study of earthquakes). The first instrument built to study an earthquake's shocks had been designed in 1703 by French physicist Jean de Hautefeuille (1647–1724). He built a rudimentary seismoscope that used drops of mercury to sense and indicate motion. Although fairly crude, it is considered the earliest of its kind.

1881 · First geophysics textbook is written. The first textbook in geophysics is written by English geologist Osmond Fisher (1817–1914) . Geophysics is concerned with the structure, composition, and physical properties of the entire Earth, including its origins. In his *Physics of the Earth's Crust*, Fisher states that the Earth's fluid interior was subjected to convection currents (the transfer or movement of heat) rising beneath the oceans and falling beneath the continents. This modern view is mostly ignored during his life. **(See also 1906)**

August 26, 1883 · Eruption of Krakatoa. The first of a series of violent explosions occurs on the island volcano of Krakatoa. The ensuing eruption on this Indonesian island is one of the most catastrophic in history. The following day, explosions that propel ash to a height of 50 miles are heard 2,200 miles away in Australia. A series of tsunamis (pronounced sue-nah'-mees) or tidal waves are triggered, the greatest of which is 120 feet high. The tsunamis kill some thirty-six thousand people in the coastal towns of Java and Sumatra. All life on what remains of Krakatoa is buried under a thick layer of sterile ash, and plant and animal life is not reestablished for five years.

1885 ▪ Naming earthquake waves. Rayleigh (seismic or earthquake) waves are first proposed by English physicist John William Strutt, Baron Rayleigh (1842–1919). Caused by an earthquake, these are a type of surface or ground-level wave that move in an up and down motion like waves in the sea. Their motion is a combination of longitudinal and vertical vibration that gives a rolling movement to the ground. Of all the seismic waves, these slow and powerful waves have the strongest effect on a seismograph and do the most damage. Rayleigh waves are later distinguished from Love waves, named after English mathematician and geophysicist Augustus Edward Hough Love (1863–1940), which are another type of surface wave that moves from side to side. In 1940 "J-B tables" are first proposed by English astronomer Harold Jeffreys (1891–1989) and New Zealand mathematician Keith Edward Bullen (1906–1976). These tables become accepted as the standard tables of travel times for earthquake waves.

1885 ▪ Gondwanaland: a hypothetical supercontinent. Gondwanaland is first named by Austrian geologist Eduard Suess (1831–1914) in his massive, four-volume work, *Das Antlitz der Erde* (The face of the Earth). In this work he refers to Gondwanaland, a hypothetical, former supercontinent in the Southern Hemisphere that he argues broke up and gradually drifted apart during the early Mesozoic Era. Suess says its pieces formed Africa, Antarctica, Australia, India, and South America. He argues that the fossils of a certain fern unite all these places. He names this supercontinent after the Gondwana (land of the Gond peoples) region of India, an area known for this fern. This marks the beginnings of the modern theory of continental drift. **(See also 1915)**

1889 ▪ Isostacy principle is established. The principle of isostasy is established by American geologist Clarence Edward Dutton (1841–1912). He proposes the principle and the name to describe the equilibrium between the lighter (surface) and denser (underground) parts of the Earth's crust. The crust is the hard, outer shell of the Earth and it floats upon the softer, denser mantle. His principle states that just as a boat with a heavy cargo floats lower in the water, so the Earth's crust floats lower in its mantle if it has a heavy mountain above it. When this balance (isostasy) is disturbed by erosion or other forces, a compensating movement occurs and the mountain floats upward.

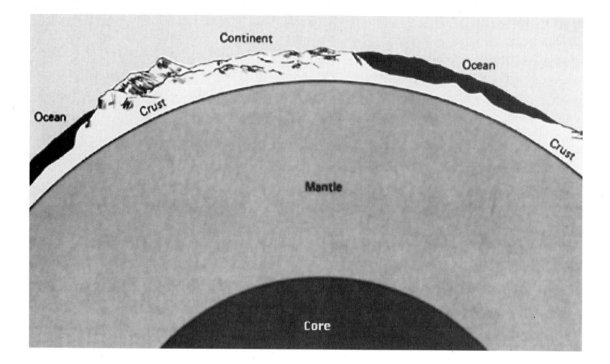

The Earth's interior.

1905 · Meteorite theory is proposed. American mining engineer and geologist Daniel Moreau Barringer (1860–1929) proposes that the well-known, mile-wide crater in Arizona is not an extinct volcano but was formed by the impact of a large meteorite. Discovered in 1891, this rimmed, bowl-shaped pit is located in the rolling plain of the Canyon Diablo region. Although Barringer's meteor idea is derided, most modern evidence seems to indicate he is correct. In 1960 the discovery of a type of silica formed only under extremely high pressure confirms that the name Meteor Crater is an appropriate one.

1906 · Evidence of Earth's core. The first clear evidence that the Earth has a central core is provided by Irish geologist Richard Dixon Oldham (1858–1936). Studying the waves that reach a seismic instrument from a distant earthquake, Oldham focuses on the two waves (compression and shear waves) that follow a path deep through the Earth's interior. When he finds that at one point the shear wave is deflected, he realizes that it is because shear waves cannot pass through a liquid. This is proof that the Earth has a central core of dense, molten fluid. Oldham becomes a pioneer in the application of seismology (the study of earthquakes) to the study of the interior of the Earth.

1907 · Determining the age of the Earth. The first method of dating the Earth is suggested by Bertram Borden Boltwood (1870–1927), an American chemist and physicist. Basing his ideas on the notion that lead is always found in uranium minerals, and that lead might be the final, stable product of uranium disintegration, he suggests that a method of determining the age of the Earth's crust might be possible. This method would be based on the quantity of lead found in uranium ores, which would then be directly related to the known rate of uranium disintegration. Boltwood's idea that the Earth has a uranium "clock" in it is proven correct when radioactive dating is eventually perfected. **(See also 1929)**

1909 · Discovery of Mohorovičić discontinuity. Mohorovičić discontinuity is discovered by Croatian geologist Andrija Mohorovičić (1857–1936). Based on his analysis of different types of earthquake wave speeds and arrival times, he is able to calculate the depth of the boundary where material changes from the Earth's crust to its mantle. The crust is the hard, outer shell of the Earth and it floats upon the softer, denser mantle. Mohorovičić states that the separation between these top two layers is not gradual but sharp, and lies from ten to forty miles below the surface. This separation or boundary comes to be called the Mohorovičić discontinuity. The Gutenberg discontinuity is discovered in 1913 by German-American geologist Beno Gutenberg (1889–1960). He is the first to explain satisfactorily the existence of the "shadow zone" inside the Earth where earthquake waves are not felt. Gutenberg postulates the existence of a liquid core at the center of the Earth that refracts (bends) waves. He knows that it is liquid because transverse (seismic) waves do not penetrate it. The sharp boundary between the core and the rocky mantle above it is later called the Gutenberg discontinuity.

1911 · Founding of modern geochemistry. Modern geochemistry is founded by Swiss-Norwegian geochemist Victor Moritz Goldschmidt (1888–1947). Geochemistry is the study of the chemistry of the distribution of the elements in various parts of the Earth. This year Goldschmidt publishes *Die Kontaktmetamorphose im Kristiania-Gebiete* (Contact metamorphism in the Kristiana region), in which he studies rocks altered by heat and is able to connect the mineralogical and chemical composition of certain rocks. In 1923 he publishes the first volume of an eight-volume study, *Geochemische Verteilungsgesetze der Elemente* (The geochemical laws of the distribution of the elements). In this book he works out the chemical consequences of the properties of the elements and, using the new discoveries of nuclear physics, is able to predict which elements will appear in certain minerals. This transforms mineralogy from a purely descriptive science to one capable of prediction. Now recognized as the founder of modern geochemistry and inorganic crystal geochemistry, Gold-schmidt was placed in a concentration camp by the Nazis but managed to escape to England by way of Sweden in 1942.

1911 · Principles of echo-sounding are discovered. German physi-cist Alexander Karl Behm (1880–1952) discovers the principles of echo-sounding. Sounding is the measurement of the depth of a body of water. Behm's experiments in an aquarium show that it is possible to measure the sea's depth by timing the echo of an underwater explosion. In 1917, French physicist Paul Langevin (1872–1946) first succeeds in using sound waves or an acoustical echo as an underwater detector. His system uses piezoelec-tricity (electricity produced when a crystal is squeezed or made to vibrate) to create ultrasonic waves (sound too high in frequency to be heard by human ears). This employs the principle that certain sound vibrations can cause an electrical effect. By World War II (1939–45), the echolocation sys-tem called "sonar" (*so*und *na*vigation and *r*anging) is perfected. Modern sonar, which employs a transducer (a device that converts energy from one form to another), is used for mapping ocean bottoms for fish or wreck locations as well as for submarine detection.

1913 · Metamorphic rock theory. Friedrich Johann Karl Becke (1855–1931), a German mineralogist, offers the first comprehensive theory of metamorphic rocks: Metamorphic rock is rock that has been formed by the alteration of other rocks (by heat or pressure). These rocks can be igneous (formed when molten magma or lava cools), sedimentary (formed from the debris of both other rocks and living matter), or metamorphic (formed from other rocks) and are the result of the alteration of preexist-ing rock by extreme temperatures or pressures.

1915 · Continental drift theory. Continental drift theory is proposed by German geologist Alfred Lothar Wegener (1880–1930). He publishes his *Die Entstehung der Kontinente und Ozeane* (The origin of the continents and oceans) which offers geology the revolutionary theory of continents in motion. Wegener argues that all the continents were originally part of a sin-gle, original landmass he calls "Pangea," which slowly separated and gradu-ally drifted apart. Although others had noticed the puzzlelike fit of the conti-nents and some had even speculated that the continents had come apart in a sudden, catastrophic splitting, no one had ever offered the startling idea

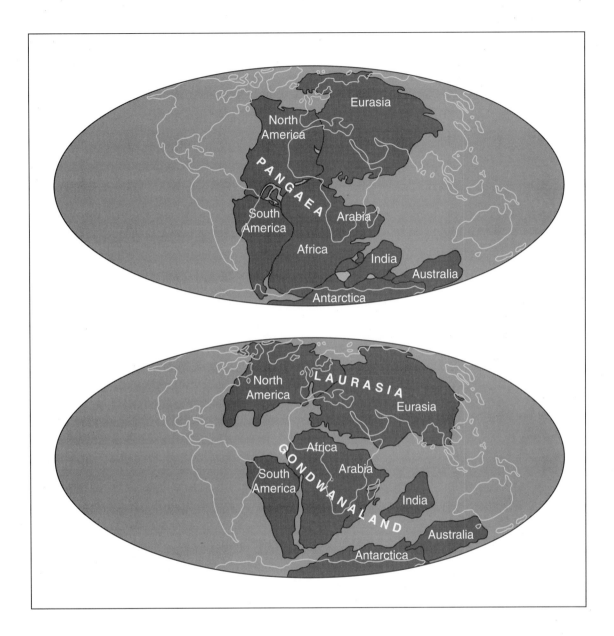

of a gradual, continuous drifting apart. Wegener is at a loss, however, to suggest a cause or explanation as to how this movement could actually occur. Current plate tectonics has its origins in Wegener's theory. **(See also 1965: First geological use of the term "plates")**

1924 ▪ Seismic refraction method is put to use. A petroleum deposit is discovered by using the seismic refraction method. This discov-

A map showing the Continental Drift. The Panganea supercontinent (top) and its break up into Laurasia and Gondwanaland.

283

ery made at Orchard Dome, Texas, proves the usefulness of seismic surveys in subsurface geology. The technique called refraction seismology is an excellent method of studying the rocks below the Earth's surface. It is based on calculating the time it takes between the start of a sound wave and its arrival at a detector placed in a certain spot. This, in turn, is based on the knowledge that different materials with differing densities have unique effects on seismic waves, and that each gives off its own special signature. The method involves setting off an explosive on the surface which produces waves that pass down into the Earth. Surface devices called "geophones" record the refracted waves (their paths are bent) and give information about subsurface conditions.

1929 · Calculating mineral age. The first calculation of mineral age from lead found in uranium ore is achieved by American geologist Clarence Norman Fenner (1870–1949) and American chemist and geophysicist Charles Snowden Piggot (1892–1973). Called "radiometric dating," this method is able to date rocks and minerals by measuring the amounts of radioactive elements in them. It is accomplished by using a mass spectrometer. This instrument is able to detect the different atoms that make up a substance by bombarding it with electrons. This creates ions or charged atoms that are then passed through a magnetic field. The field bends or changes the paths of the ions depending on how much mass they have. This allows them to be identified. This mass spectrometer allows them to put into actual practice the ideas of American chemist and physicist Bertram Borden Boltwood (1870–1927) who stated in 1907 that the quantity of lead in a mineral was directly related to uranium disintegration, and that knowledge of the rate of its disintegration would provide science with a geologic "clock." **(See also 1907)**

1935 · Seismic measurements of the ocean floor. The first seismic measurements obtained in open seas are made by American geophysicist William Maurice Ewing (1906–1974). Ewing's work initiates the seismic study of the ocean floor by the use of explosives. He studies the structure of the Earth's crust and mantle in the Atlantic Ocean basins and in the Mediterranean and Norwegian seas, and proposes that earthquakes are associated with the central oceanic rifts (a fault or crevice) that encircle the globe. These rifts are the openings of potentially active lava flow. In 1939 Ewing takes the first deep-sea photographs. Combining these photos with the seismic data he obtained, he suggests that the sea-floor spreading (caused by active undersea volcanoes) that he detects may be worldwide.

Ewing makes fundamental contributions to an understanding of the ocean floor and brings this field into the twentieth century by his use of ultrasound reflection (bouncing sound waves), gravity measurements, and core sampling (drilling). **(See also 1956)**

1935 ▪ Introduction of the Richter scale. The Richter scale is introduced by American geophysicist Charles Francis Richter (1900–1985). This new scale becomes a widely used method of measuring the magnitude of earthquakes. Magnitude is the amount of energy released by an earthquake. Richter uses a torsion pendulum seismograph that has a small copper cylinder attached to a stretched, vertical wire that can swing horizontally. This registers earth movement, which is then compared to readings taken from other locations, and an average magnitude is calculated from all the readings. The results are plotted on a logarithmic scale, in whole numbers and tenths, from 1 to 9. This scale of numbers is arranged so that each increase of one unit represents a tenfold increase in the magnitude of the earthquake. Thus an earthquake with a reading of 6.5 has ten times the force of one with a 5.5, and a 7.5 quake has 100 times the intensity of a 5.5. The strongest earthquakes so far recorded have reached 8.9 on the Richter scale.

1936 ▪ Ocean bottom core samples are acquired. The first core samples of the ocean bottom are obtained by Charles Snowden Piggot (1892–1973), an American chemist and geophysicist. At this time he is an investigator at the Geophysical Laboratory of the Carnegie Institution. He measures the radioactivity of the rocks he finds with his deep-sea drilling. This allows him to study the distribution of radium in the Earth as well as to date the samples he obtains.

1947 ▪ Discovery of carbon-14 dating technique. The carbon-14 dating technique is first developed by American chemist Willard Frank Libby (1908–1980). Using the knowledge that the isotope carbon-14 is taken in by all living things, and that after an organism dies the carbon-14 inside it decays at a constant rate (since it begins to break down and undergo radioactive decay), Libby realizes that he has discovered a practical dating technique. Using an improved Geiger counter (that detects and measures radioactivity), he is able to date roughly the age of an ancient piece of organic matter by measuring how much carbon-14 is left in it (since he knows exactly the rate at which it breaks down). The carbon-14 dating method enables geologists to learn a great deal about the Earth's recent history.

1956 · Mid-Oceanic Ridge is discovered. The Mid-Oceanic Ridge is discovered by American oceanographer and geologist Bruce Charles Heezen (1924–1977) and American geophysicist William Maurice Ewing (1906–1974). Using sonar (a kind of echolocation), they are able to measure and record this gigantic, undersea mountain chain that encircles the Earth and runs continuously for 40,000 miles. They also postulate the Heezen-Ewing theory that an enormous central rift (a crack or fissure)—which at some points is double the size of the Grand Canyon—exists along the ridge and may be subject to underwater earthquakes. Their discovery sparks further undersea investigations and eventually leads to the discovery that these ridges occur where the great tectonic plates of the Earth are pulling apart. Tectonic plates are the separate pieces that comprise the Earth's outer shell. **(See also 1965: First geological use of the term "plates")**

1962 · Sea-floor spreading theory. A theory of sea-floor spreading is first proposed by American geologist Harry Hammond Hess (1906–1969). In this year he presents evidence for his theory, stating that the sea floors crack open along the crest of the mid-ocean ridges and that new sea floor forms there. This new floor forms when hot molten magma wells up through a ridge (which is a crevasse or crack), runs down its sides, and solidifies into new floor. This formation of new oceanic crust and the gradual widening of the oceans is also called "constructive margin" or sea-floor spreading. This theory becomes central to the new science of plate tectonics (the pulling apart and colliding of pieces or plates of the Earth's shell) and helps explain why the continents may have pulled apart.

1965 · First geological use of the term "plates". The first to use the term "plates" geologically is Canadian geologist John Tuzo Wilson (1908–1993). He uses this simple word to describe the rigid pieces—separated by mid-ocean rifts (faults or crevasses) and major mountain chains—that make up the Earth's rigid shell and move with respect to one another. He also offers a model of their behavior and establishes global patterns of faulting (fractures in rocks where movement occurs). "Plate tectonics" is first used as a geologic term in 1967 by D. P. Mackenzie of England and R. L. Parker of the United States. They propose that the Earth's surface is divided into at least six major and seven minor plates or large rock segments that are moving in respect to one another. It compares the continents to huge icebergs carried along by the currents underneath them.

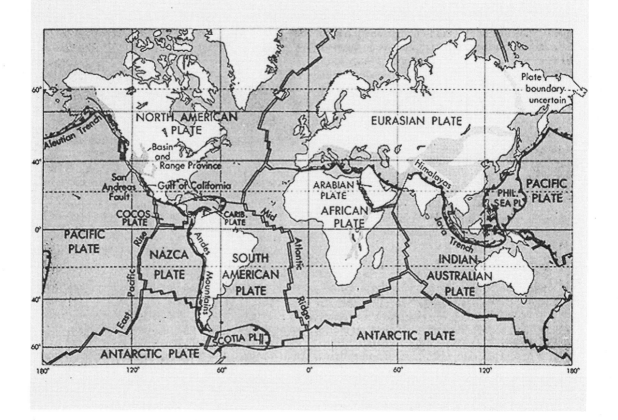

Plate tectonics helps explain continental drift as well as volcanoes, earthquakes, and sea-floor spreading. More recent information suggests that the Earth's shell or lithosphere is split into nine large plates and as many as twelve smaller ones.

A map of the major plates that make up Earth's crust.

1965 • Photogeology comes into use. Photogeology is first practiced

seriously by American geologist Harold Rollin Wanless (1898–1970) with his publication of *Aerial Stereo Photographs*. In this work he uses aerial photographs to interpret the exposed geological features on the Earth's surface. This early photogeology is eventually followed by aircraft using infrared film and later Earth-orbiting, remote sensing satellites that reveal a wealth of extremely varied geological information. Using false color film that is sensitive to red (infrared) light provides geologists with pictures whose colors have shifted. Green looks blue, red objects look green, and heat-emitting objects look red. This can easily identify land masses and bodies of water as well as rocks, vegetation, and even people.

July 24, 1969 ▪ First up-close look at Moon rocks. The first samples of Moon rocks are brought back to Earth. The U.S. spacecraft, *Apollo 11*, splashes down on Earth after its historic eight-day voyage to the Moon. Later radiation tests show the age of these rocks to be between 2,700 and 4,700 million years. The oldest Earth rocks to date are about 4,500 million years. Further study of these Moon rocks suggests that the Moon's geology is simpler than that of the Earth. The Moon has a crust or outer shell of about 65 kilometers (40 miles) thick and is composed chiefly of an orthosite, a relatively rare, silica-like rock. Its mantle (below the crust) is believed to consist of denser rocks that are rich in iron and magnesium.

July 23, 1972 ▪ Launch of *ERTS 1*. The first Earth resources technology satellite, *ERTS 1*, is launched by the United States. This infrared camera-in-space works on the principle that all living and nonliving objects

An illustration of hydrothermal vents on the ocean floor emitting dark clouds of sulfurous hot water.

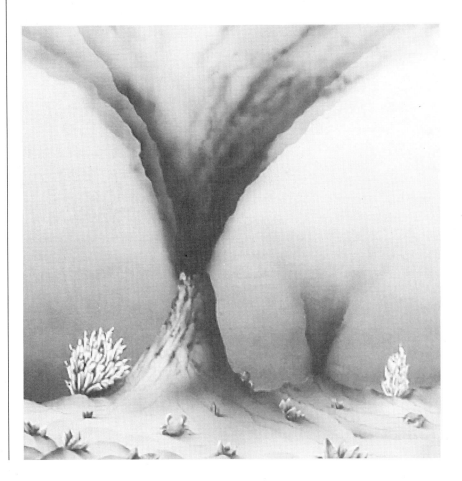

on the Earth absorb, give off, and reflect electromagnetic radiation in their own "signature" manner or distinctive way. This satellite and its several follow-ons scan the Earth from space and provide photographic information that proves valuable to such diverse fields as agriculture, geology, cartography, urban planning, and oceanography among others. The satellite is later renamed *Landsat 1*.

1974 · Discovery of deep-sea vents. The first deep-sea vents are discovered by American oceanographers. These hydrothermal (hot water) vents or "hot spots" are found on the floor of some of the ocean's deepest waters where no light reaches. They are milky-blue plumes of mineral-rich hot water pouring out of chimneylike openings in the ocean floor. The oceanographers also find indications of some forms of marine life that appear to flourish in absolute darkness. **(See also 1986)**

September 3, 1976 · Pictures of Mars are transmitted to the Earth. The first pictures of the surface of Mars are transmitted to the Earth. U.S. unmanned spacecraft *Viking 2* touches down on Mars and transmits images of its rocky surface and planetary geology. The pictures also show a deeply pitted surface covered by very fine soil. Surface temperatures range from -114° F to -23° F. Analysis of the photos reveal that massive flows of water have at one time flowed across the Martian surface.

June 26, 1978 · Oceanic data satellite is launched. The first satellite dedicated to the gathering of oceanic data, *Seasat 1*, is launched by the United States. Using remote sensing technology (recording information from a distance with a camera), its mission is to measure global ocean dynamics and physical characteristics. Despite a power loss that limits its life to only ninety-nine days, it achieves 80 percent of its objectives. It obtains data on ocean surface wind speeds, wave heights, rain, surface temperature, and swell lengths.

1980 · Dinosaurs and asteroids. Asteroids and dinosaur extinction is first linked. American physicist Luis Walter Alvarez (1911–1988) and colleagues discover an unusually high concentration of iridium (a very rare platinum metal) in a sedimentary layer that marks the Cretaceous-Tertiary boundary of geologic time (about one hundred million years ago). Since iridium is rare on Earth but occurs in asteroids and meteorites, and since this time frame coincides with the disappearance of the dinosaurs, Alvarez speculates that a giant asteroid collided with Earth, causing a prolonged dust-blackout and mass extinctions.

1983 · Linking of plate tectonics and climate. Plate tectonics and climate are first linked by American geochemist Robert A. Berner (1935–), Cuban-American chemical physicist Antonio C. Lasaga, and American geologist Robert Minard Garrel (1916–1988). Plate tectonics describes the pulling apart and colliding of pieces or plates of the Earth's shell that allows molten rock to rise up from the Earth's interior. These scientists publish a computer model indicating that the carbon dioxide content of the atmosphere is highly sensitive to changes in the rate of sea-floor spreading (formation of new sea floor by the eruption of lava) and the loss or gain of land area. Carbon dioxide is an important gas in our air and is used by plants. It also keeps some of the heat energy received by the Earth from being radiated back into space.

1986 · Documenting of life-forms on deep-sea vents. The first documented life-forms on deep-sea vents are described by American oceanographer Laverne Duane Kulm and colleagues. They publish a detailed report about an area of deep-sea vents located at a depth of about 2,000 meters near where the Pacific Plate is sinking below Oregon. They find mineral precipitates (chemical sediments) that are being vented (released) as fluids. This demonstrates that fluids and gases emerge not only from the Earth's surface but also from the ocean floor. **(See also 1974)**

1989 · Discovery of oldest-known rocks. Rocks that are 3.96 billion years old—taken from near Canada's Great Slave Lake—replace rocks from west Greenland, about one hundred million years younger, as the world's oldest-known rocks. Their age is determined through measurements of the uranium and lead contents of the mineral zircon in granite rocks. This discovery supports the idea that even older rocks, from the original crust of the Earth, must have existed because these rocks are a kind of granite, and granites are formed from preexisting rock.

1991 · Earth's orbit and climate cycles are linked. The first demonstrated link between periodic changes in the Earth's orbit and its longer climate cycles is obtained by American geologists Dennis Kent and Paul Olsen. They extract 4-mile-deep sample cores drilled from an area beneath New Jersey. Besides being able to learn more about fluctuating climates two hundred million years ago, they find that many climate changes mirror known periodic changes in the Earth's rotation (spin on its axis) and orbit (the path it takes around the sun). This information has implications for astronomers as well as geologists. Because we know that the orbits of other planets determine the Earth's longer climate cycles, knowledge of the cycles themselves can indicate how these planets were behaving two hundred million years ago.

1993 ▪ Water-vapor rivers are found in Earth's atmosphere.

Rivers of water vapor in the Earth's atmosphere (the mass of air surrounding the Earth) are first identified by American climatologist Reginald Newell. He creates a map using balloon measurements and satellite readings. He finds these rivers of water vapor all over the globe, the longest of which runs about 4,000 miles. They are generally 150 miles wide and only 1 mile deep, with 350 million pounds of vapor flowing past a given spot each second. Although these rivers are not permanent, there are at least a few of them in the atmosphere at any given time. Newell believes the rivers form when two air masses, thick with evaporated water from the oceans, collide. The air at the edge has nowhere to go but up, and as it rises it cools. As it cools, its capacity to hold water vapor diminishes, and the bands of water-saturated air that result are the rivers. Clouds eventually develop from them and rain results.

December 1994 ▪ New dinosaur extinction theory.

A new hypothesis on dinosaur extinction is offered by an international team of American geologist Kevin O. Pope, American atmospheric physicist Kevin H. Baines, American planetary geologist Adriana C. Ocampo (1955–), and Boris A. Ivanov of Russia. Their hypothesis, like earlier ones, connects the mass extinctions with asteroid impact sixty-five million years ago. They find that the impact site is unusually rich in sulfur, and suggest that the vaporization (turning into a vapor or gaseous state) of more than 100 billion tons of its sulfur may have filled the atmosphere with life-killing sulfur dioxide and sulfuric acid for decades, poisoning all life forms.

1995 ▪ Discovery of new tectonic plate boundary.

A new type of tectonic plate boundary is discovered in the Indian Ocean. Until now, the several known plates were classified as one of three types: mid-ocean ridges where plates are moving apart (divergent); deep-sea trenches where two plates come together and one dives under the other (convergent); and transform faults where plates slide past each other (such as the San Andreas fault of California). This new type of plate boundary is both convergent and divergent at the same time. Scientists find that the Indo-Australian plate has actually been breaking apart for several million years. The Australian plate is pivoting counterclockwise around a point 600 miles south of the tip of India, pushing into the Indian plate to the east, and pulling away from it to the west.

January 1996 · Evidence supports movement of Earth's crust.

The first evidence for the deep recycling of the Earth's crust is obtained by scientists from South Africa and Scotland. They find a speck of the silicate mineral staurolite encased in a diamond. This suggests that at least part of the Earth's crust plunged down through a subduction zone (the region where one tectonic plate is forced beneath another) and into the mantle, then to be carried back to the surface. Scientists have long suspected that over billions of years of geologic time, much of the Earth's surface gets pushed down into the planet's hot interior, undergoing great changes before reappearing at the surface. It seems likely that the staurolite crystal, which is a common mineral of clay sediments—considered a blemish when found in a diamond—was formed on the Earth's crust by pressure and was later carried into the mantle where diamonds are formed.

Energy, Power Systems, and Weaponry

c. 50,000 B.C. ▪ Introduction of bow and arrow. The bow and arrow is introduced sometime between 50,000 B.C. and 30,000 B.C. This is probably the first composite mechanism invented by man. The bow consists of a stave (narrow strip) of wood that is bent and held in tension by a string or cord. The arrow is a wooden shaft tipped by a pointed stone, usually flint. It enables the energy stored by drawing the bow (holding it in one hand and pulling back on the cord with the other) to be rapidly released. Although used later as a military weapon, the bow and arrow's primary importance to early man is as a hunting weapon.

c. 1000 B.C. ▪ China sees first use of crossbows. Crossbows are first used in China. This mechanized bow and arrow system increases the user's ability to draw back the bow with great tension. It is designed to catch the bowstring in a hook when drawn back, and the arrow is laid in a groove before shooting. The fully mechanized crossbow does not appear in Europe until the tenth century. This system employs a winch (a cord wrapped around a small drum that is turned by a handle) controlled by a wheel with notches and uses a ratchet to turn the wheel. It is a fearsome weapon that shoots heavy bolts that are shorter than arrows. Although it is outlawed for use in war in 1139 by the Lateran Council (except against infidels or non-Christians), this law has little effect on actual practice and it remains the supreme hand-missile weapon until the introduction of firearms.

c. 500 B.C. ▪ Toothed gearwheel known to be used. The first-known use of a toothed gearwheel occurs about this time. Gears are toothed wheels that are connected so that one wheel turns another. Gears transmit rotary motion and turning force or torque. The teeth of one gear engage the teeth on a mating gear, and when attached to a rotating shaft, it can power such devices as a pulley or a waterwheel.

c. 500 B.C. ▪ Rotary mills make first appearance. Rotary mills driven by donkeys or slaves first appear in the Mediterranean world. Used to grind grain to make flour for baking, the rotary mill uses a grinder shaped like an hourglass that rests on top of a fixed lower stone. The grain is poured in from above, and the top (grinder) stone is turned by pushing or pulling a long wooden pole attached to it.

c. 400 B.C. ▪ Catapults are used in wars. Catapults are first used by the Chinese in warfare. This ancient military device operates by the sudden release of tension on wooden beams or twisted cords of rope, which forcefully propels stones and other large projectiles for some distance. Although known by the Greeks at this time, it is the Romans who make improvements to its basic design and perfect its use in battle.

c. 250 B.C. ▪ Archimedean screw is used to pump water. Archimedes (c. 287–212 B.C.), a Greek mathematician and engineer, invents the Archimedean screw for raising water. This pump is essentially a metal pipe made in a helix or corkscrew shape that draws water upwards as it is turned or revolved. When it is rotated, this hollow, helical cylinder can scoop up water from a lake or pond and deliver it to a higher level. The Archimedean screw is also used to remove water from the hold of a ship.

c. 100 B.C. ▪ Drawing water with wheel-of-pots. Wheel-of-pots driven by the river current first appears in Egypt as a method of drawing water. Also called a waterwheel, this large wooden wheel has a series of receptacles or pots on it. The pots are slowly immersed in the river where they collect water and then pour it over the Earth (usually for irrigation canals) as the wheel is turned by the current. It is thought that an earlier system of a pulley and chain-of-pots was used to water the Hanging Gardens of Babylon around 700 B.C. The Chinese were probably the first to use such a water delivery system.

c. 100 B.C. · Chain mail is introduced. Romans first introduce chain-mail armor, consisting of interlinked metal rings sewn directly to fabric or leather. This form of body armor for soldiers is used until medieval times when armorers improve on this early version and are able to make chain mail independent of cloth or leather in the form of both a shirt and a coat. Chain mail forms the main armor of western Europe until the fourteenth century when it is replaced by plate armor made from thin sheets of metal.

c. 85 B.C. · Windmill is written about. The earliest-known written reference to the use of a windmill is made by Antipater of Thessalonica (northern Greece). A windmill converts natural wind energy into rotary motion to do work, and becomes one of the prime movers that replaces animal or human muscle as a power source. It is believed that this windmill is of the primitive, horizontal type in which the paddle wheel revolves in a horizontal plane. Windmills were used in China and Japan as early as 2000 B.C. The windmill reaches Europe via the Arabs near the end of the twelfth century in the form of "post mills" with sails to catch the wind.

c. A.D. 75 · Oil is used for lighting purposes. Pliny (23–79), a Roman scholar, is the first to record the use of oil for lighting purposes. Although the burning of grease or oil was known by very early man, the Greeks introduce sophisticated lamps with handles, spouts, and nozzles used for receiving oil and holding wicks. Roman metal workers also create elaborate bronze and iron oil lamps.

c. 650 · Forging of blades of Damascus. The blades of Damascus first come into demand as far away as Europe. These weapons are made following the ancient method from India. Starting with round ingots of iron—weighing about 1 kilogram and measuring about 13 centimeters in diameter and 13 millimeters thick—these are hammered together in one or more directions to make blades that are then forged (formed), cooled, and tempered (toughened). This process, which involves repeated heating and hammering together of strips of iron, results in the addition of small amounts of carbon. The finished sword blade is exceptionally hard and has a characteristic streaked appearance because of the varying carbon content of the iron strips. It becomes a fearsome weapon.

670 · Origins of Greek fire. "Greek fire" is invented by Callinicus of Egypt. This flammable mixture is able to burn on water and is used in naval battles to burn wooden boats. The Byzantine Greeks throw the incendiary mixture in pots at enemy ships or launch the deadly compound from tubes mounted on the prows of their ships. In 673 they effectively use it to destroy the Arab fleet attacking Constantinople. The first detailed description of Greek fire is written around 1100 by Marcus Graecis in his *Liber ignium ad comburendos hostes* (Book of fire for burning enemies). Although its exact composition is still unknown, Greek fire appears to have been a petroleum-based mixture. Other writers also mention such ingredients as saltpeter (potassium nitrate), pitch, naphtha, sulfur, and charcoal.

The waterwheel of an old mill. Until the invention of the steam engine, large factories had to be located near a source of moving water.

c. 950 · Invention of gunpowder. Black powder or gunpowder is believed to be invented in China at this time, although some Chinese texts make the first reference to fireworks as early as 600. A mixture of saltpeter (potassium nitrate), sulfur, and charcoal, it burns rapidly when ignited and can propel missiles when exploded in a confined space. As the first explosive invented, it comes to Europe around the thirteenth century and is used in firearms. English scholar Roger Bacon (c. 1220–1292) publishes his *De mirabile potestate artis et naturae* (On the wonderful power of art and nature) in which he lists the ingredients for making gunpowder. This knowledge may have reached the West from the Orient during the Mongol invasion a few years before. Not used for peaceful purposes, such as mining or road building, until the seventeenth century, it remains the only available explosive material until the mid-nineteenth century discovery of nitroglycerine.

1288 · Making of the first-known gun. The first-known gun is made in China. It is like a hand cannon that uses black powder or gunpowder, and is small enough to be used by one person. The Chinese initially use bamboo to house the explosion and the projectile, but soon switch to a metal tube. The first Western account of a gun or firearm is a German description in 1313 of an "iron pot" or "vase." These primitive guns use black powder or gunpowder and are thought to be made of wooden or iron staves (narrow strips) bound together with hoops. They are more like hand cannons than small arms. Some attribute this invention to the German monk Berthold Schwarz.

c. 1290 · First use of the longbow. The longbow first comes into use in England. With an effective range of 240 yards, this bow and arrow proves to be the dominant weapon used by the English into the sixteenth century. Probably of Welsh origin, it plays an important role in the battles of Crecy, Poitiers, and Agincourt. Averaging 5 feet in length and requiring a 60- to 90-pound pull as well as proper training to use, it proves to be a devastating weapon against the slow-firing crossbows and even slower early firearms. A skilled archer can fire six of these arrows per minute.

1324 · Cannons are used in battle. Cannons are first used in the West at the siege of Metz in northeastern France. These early cannons are made of bronze or welded wrought-iron strips and can fire cast-iron balls. Gunpowder cannons play no decisive part in this battle or any other for another century, but large cannons will eventually replace medieval siege engines that were more like ancient catapults.

c. 1425 · Introduction of matchlock guns. The first "matchlock" small arms are introduced. These are hand-carried long guns that ignite the powder charge by lighting a match when the trigger is pulled. With this "serpentine" fuse method, the shooter can stand and take aim, knowing that firing depends only on pressing a lever. These early shoulder muskets are heavy and must be supported by a forked rest. This is the first great small-arms invention. It allows soldiers to concentrate on their targets (and not have to look to ignite the fuse), even at moving targets. The matchlock firearm is eventually replaced by the wheel-lock musket. With this gun, the charge or powder is ignited by sparks produced when a notched wheel is spun against iron pyrite. This eliminates the need for a dangerous burning fuse. The wheel-lock musket also can be loaded and readied ahead and then fired immediately. They are not as reliable as the matchlock in firing, and have to be kept very clean. Wheel locks are also expensive and more likely to need repairs, but they can penetrate the best armor. **(See also 1630)**

c. 1450 · New type of windmill. A type of windmill called the *wip-molen* is invented by the Dutch. As a kind of post mill, its top can be turned manually so that its sails can face and catch the prevailing wind. Although used for grinding corn and some industrial purposes, these windmills are mainly used for draining marshy areas. The vanes or sails catch the wind and drive a vertical shaft that moves a valve wheel at the bottom. The windmill becomes a permanent part of the Dutch landscape in areas lying at or below sea level.

1525 ▪ Development of rifled gun barrels. Rifled gun barrels are invented. These spiral cuts or grooves in a gun's barrel make the bullet leave with a spinning action that provides greater accuracy and stability to its flight. The invention of rifling has been attributed to a German gunsmith named Kutter or Kotter. In 1631 the first military use of weapons with rifled barrels is made by the Landgrave of Hesse who equips his troops with small arms that are grooved. Although rifling improves the trueness of a bullet's flight and consequently helps the shooter's aim, the use of round balls or bullets detracts from that accuracy.

1630 ▪ Modern flintlock is created. A modern form of the flintlock gun is invented. Its new ignition system using flint against steel replaces the matchlock and the wheel lock. The new flintlock gun has a frizzen (striker) and pan cover that are made in one piece. Its barrel is smooth and it fires small, round lead bullets. Cheaper and requiring less maintenance than a matchlock, it is militarily practical and becomes the firearm of choice, widely used until early in the nineteenth century.

1659 ▪ Discovery of natural gas. Natural gas is discovered in England but not put to any practical use for some time. Usually a mixture of methane and ethane—both of which are gaseous under atmospheric conditions—it usually occurs geologically in association with petroleum deposits. The Chinese were the first to use natural gas. As early as 940 B.C. they piped it through bamboo poles to the seashore where they burned it to boil down seawater for salt. The Japanese also were using it by 615 B.C. In 1670 gas distilled from coal is discovered in Europe. It is found that heating bituminous coal in the absence of air (called destructive distillation) results in a gas very useful for burning, especially for heating purposes. Coal tar and charcoal-like coke are also obtained as by-products of this process.

1663 ▪ Building of the steam engine. Edward Somerset, Marquis of Worcester (1601–1667), an English inventor, builds what many consider to be the first steam engine. His apparatus can lift water through a pipe by using steam power. His machine contains alternating vessels filled with cold and heated water and can shoot a stream of water 40 feet into the air. The British Parliament grants him a patent this year. Although this is the first serious attempt to make practical use of steam power, Worcester is unable to form a company and cannot exploit his invention. **(See also 1698)**

1698 ▪ Steam-powered water pump is patented. English engineer Thomas Savery (c. 1650–1715) patents a steam-powered water pump. It works by the expansion and suction effects caused by generating and then condensing steam (changing from a gas to a liquid). Called the Miner's Friend, it is a one-cylinder suction pump that drains water from mines and is based on principles established in 1687 by French physicist Denis Papin (1647–1712). It is slow, noisy, expensive, and dangerous since it uses steam under high pressure. In 1707 Papin designs a pump with a piston (a plug that fits tightly in a cylinder and can slide up and down) that moves under the effect of steam. It works by means of a piston sliding into a vertical cylinder whose base is underwater. The water is heated and the piston is pushed up by the force of the steam. When the steam condenses (changes from a gas to a liquid), the piston moves down and lifts a weight by means of a pulley. **(See also 1712)**

1709 · Smelting iron ore with coke. English ironmaster Abraham Darby (c. 1678–1717) successfully smelts iron ore with coke. Discovered in England in 1603, coke is the solid residue of carbon that remains after certain types of bituminous coal are heated to a very high temperature. A charcoal-like substance, it burns hotter than coal. Darby finds that coke can be used in a larger furnace than charcoal can and therefore coke can create a hotter fire (which produces iron at a faster rate). This solid substance is also used for heating purposes and is called oven coke.

1712 · Newcomen steam engine is an improvement. Thomas Newcomen (1663–1729), English engineer, devises an improved version of the Savery steam engine. Unlike the machine built in 1698 by English engineer Thomas Savery (c. 1650–1715), Newcomen's steam engine does not use steam under high pressure but rather allows air pressure to do all the work. For this reason it is called an atmospheric engine. This is the first really practical steam engine as well as the first to use a piston (a plug that fits tightly in a cylinder and can slide up and down) and cylinder for practical purposes. It is used for nearly fifty years in England and Europe to pump out flooded coal and tin mines. In 1755 the first atmospheric steam engine in the American colonies is a Newcomen machine sent from England. **(See also 1698 and 1765)**

c. 1740 · Crucible process of steelmaking is invented. Benjamin Huntsman (1704–1776), an English inventor, invents the crucible or cast process of making steel. Steel is stronger and lighter than iron. Huntsman's steel is more uniform in composition and more free from impurities than any steel previously produced. He heats small pieces of carbon steel in a fire-clay crucible (like a pot) placed in a coke fire. Coke is a charcoal-like

Iron and Steel Production and the Industrial Revolution

From about 1730 to 1850 Great Britain's economy underwent a profound change that is commonly called the Industrial Revolution. Advances in technology and new ways of producing goods brought the onetime agrarian society into an industrial age. Along with the textile and transportation industry, new ways of producing iron and steel transformed the nation by introducing large factories requiring many workers to live in areas where coal resources were available.

For centuries England had converted iron ores to iron and steel by heating the raw materials with charcoal, which is made from trees. By the mid-eighteenth century, however, British timber was in short supply from many years of overuse. Iron and steel producers had to look for another fuel, and they found it in coke, which is what coal turns into when it is heated in the absence of air. Coke was far superior to charcoal in converting iron ore, and it eventually was cheaper to produce as well. Coke was also more efficient than charcoal, because it could be packed more tightly into a furnace, therefore allowing a larger volume of iron to be heated.

The only trouble with coke was that it required a more intense flow of air through the furnace. This problem was alleviated in 1763 when James Watt's steam engine provided the means to force the air through the furnace. The iron and steel producers' new methods and technology produced a thriving new industry.

substance that burns hotter than coal. Since Huntsman is able to reach temperatures of 2,900° F, he is able to melt steel for the first time, thus producing a highly desirable metal that is all of a similar, uniform nature. He does not patent his process. He attempts to keep it a secret, but it is eventually copied by others.

1751 · Invention of the iron-planing machine. Nicolas Focq of France invents the iron-planing machine. A plane smooths and shapes a surface by removing very thin layers. This device marks the beginnings of the production of machine tools. Operated by a hand-crank, Focq's machine allows the cutting tool to travel across the surface to be planed, achieving an even and much more precise cut than can be made by hand. In 1817 Richard Roberts (1789–1864), an English inventor, builds a small planing machine for smoothing metal. This is the first improvement of a metal-planing lathe since Focq, and it significantly advances the manufacture of precision tools and specialized machines.

1752 · Fantail invention improves windmills. English civil engineer John Smeaton (1724–1792) invents the fantail for windmills. This device keeps the main sails facing the wind at all times. As the first person to investigate scientifically the design of windmill sails and waterwheels, Smeaton proposes five sails instead of the traditional four and also introduces cast iron into millwork.

1765 · Watt makes improvements to steam engine. Scottish engineer James Watt (1736–1819) introduces a separate chamber to the Newcomen steam engine and produces a machine that is much more efficient in its use of fuel and also significantly quicker in the work it performs. In the Newcomen engine, a single steam chamber was cooled to condense the steam and produce a vacuum, which then had to be heated up again. Watt's second, separate chamber can be kept constantly cold while the other is kept hot. This eliminates long pauses to reheat the chamber. In 1769 Watt obtains his first steam-engine patent for his new system. The steam engine turns into a "prime mover" and more than just a pump. Because of Watt, steam engines powered by burning coal can deliver large quantities of power to any needed spot. This means that the location of large factories no longer has to be near a source of moving water. It also means that the Industrial Revolution is under way. **(See also 1712)**

c. 1771 · Automated cotton mill is constructed. The first automated cotton mill is built by English inventor Richard Arkwright

A train powered by a steam engine.

(1732–1792). His waterwheel-operated mill powers his new spinning machine that can spin thread by mechanically reproducing the motions ordinarily made by the human hand. Arkwright's machinery eventually replaces many other manual steps of textile manufacture, and he converts his power source from water to steam. His cotton mill can be considered the first factory, since it uses a single energy source to power scores of machines.

1775 ▪ Boring machine for metal is assembled. English industrialist John Wilkinson (1728–1808) builds a boring machine for drilling holes in metal, considered to be the first modern machine tool. Wilkinson's new machine can drill precise, round holes whose accuracy is essential for boring cylinders for the newly invented steam engines. Precise holes mean less leakage. Wilkinson also becomes a master working with iron, building the first iron furnace at age twenty and the first iron bridge in 1779. Fittingly, he chooses to be buried in a cast-iron coffin of his own design.

1781 ▪ Watt continues to enhance steam engine. Scottish engineer James Watt (1736–1819) begins a series of major improvements to the steam engine that make it the primary power source of the Industrial Revolution. This year he invents the sun-and-planet gear which adapts the back-and-forth, rocking action of a steam engine to a rotary (revolving) motion. In 1782 Watt patents the parallel-motion, double-acting steam engine that admits steam to both sides of the piston (a plug that fits tightly in a cylinder and can slide up and down), allowing the piston to both push and pull. In 1784 he is the first to use steam to heat a building. In 1788 Watt invents a centrifugal governor that automatically controls an engine's output of steam, never allowing it to grow too large or too small. This consists of two metal spheres that are spun outward (centrifugally) by the engine's output of steam. The farther the two spheres spin outward, the more they choke off the steam output. As the steam decreases, the spheres rotate more slowly and reverse the process. This could be considered the first practical example of automation, since it is a device that allows a machine to control itself. In 1790 Watt invents a pressure gauge or indicator that shows the amount of steam pressure in the engine cylinders. **(See also 1765)**

1783 ▪ Horsepower, a unit of work. "Horsepower" is introduced by Scottish engineer James Watt (1736–1819) as a unit of work. Seeking a means to measure the power of his steam engine, Watt tests a strong horse and decides it can raise a 150-pound weight nearly 4 feet a second. He then defines 1 horsepower as 550 foot-pounds per second (33,000 foot-pounds per minute). This unit of power is still used.

1784 · Wrought iron is produced with puddling method. Henry Cort (1740–1800), an English inventor, first patents his "puddling process" for converting pig iron (crude iron) into tough, malleable wrought iron. By stirring molten pig iron in a reverberating furnace (one in which flames and hot gases swirling above the metal provide the heat so that the metal does not come in contact with the fuel), Cort is able to separate carbon from the iron. This process combined with his earlier iron bar breakthrough (a method of using grooved rollers to produce iron bars quickly and economically) significantly increases iron production, and Cort becomes known as the father of the iron trade.

1784 · Invention of shrapnel. Henry Shrapnel (1761–1842), an English artillery expert, invents "spherical case" shot. This spherical projectile or round shell is filled with bullets and is set off by a timed fuse. As the shell moves through the air toward its target, it explodes and sends bullets flying in all directions. Later, the round shell is changed to a cylindrical shape, and by using high-explosive ammunition, the exploding shell itself achieves the same lethal effect. Eventually, the term "shrapnel" comes to be used to designate this shell that splinters.

1786 · Clutch helps regulate machinery. A clutch to regulate the machinery used in a flour mill is invented by Scottish engineer John Rennie (1761–1821). A clutch is a device that connects the power source to the shaft it is turning, effectively transmitting power. By disconnecting the clutch, a machine can be kept running without its turning power being transmitted. This important device provides a convenient means of starting and stopping a machine and proves to be important to all driving motors.

1786 · Affect of carbon on iron and steel is established. French chemist Claude-Louis Berthollet (1748–1822) and French mathematicians Gaspard Monge (1746–1818) and Alexandre Theophile Vandermonde (1735–1796) publish a paper, "Memoire sur le fer" (Memoir on iron), that establishes that the difference between iron and steel is due to carbon. They demonstrate that adding carbon to iron is what toughens and hardens it. Carbon steels are much stronger than iron, and it is later learned that these properties of steel can be tailored to various uses by adjusting how the steel is made and treated.

1792 ▪ Coal gas is used to light house. Scottish inventor William Murdock (1754–1839) illuminates part of his house with coal gas. Coal gas is the gas produced by distilling coal or heating it in the absence of air. Murdock is the first to realize that gas is a more convenient energy source than coal and that it can be piped and easily controlled. He goes on to develop methods for manufacturing, storing, and purifying coal gas. Gas lighting eventually transforms the way people spend their evenings and allows factories to operate for longer hours. In December 1806, the first gas mains laid in a public street connect Haymarket to St. James Street in London, England. On January 28, 1807, Frederick Albert Winsor (1763–1830), an English inventor, conducts the first successful demonstration of street lighting as he lights Pall Mall in London, England, using coal gas.

1794 ▪ Radial ball bearing is patented. Philip Vaughn of England receives a patent for a radial ball bearing to be used in conjunction with a carriage axle. His specifications are too precise for the machine tools of his time to make. Widespread use of ball bearings does not take place until the 1860s, when they are used by bicycle makers. Modern ball bearings are hardened steel balls that roll easily and translate a sliding action into a rolling action.

1795 ▪ Automated flour mill is designed. *The Young Millwright and Miller's Guide* is published by American inventor Oliver Evans (1755–1819). In the guide Evan's details his automation of a flour mill and inventions of the grain elevator, conveyor, drill, hopper boy, and descender. His mechanized flour mill becomes the first in the United States to be powered by steam.

1796 ▪ Hydraulic press is made practical. Joseph Bramah (1748–1814), an English engineer and inventor, builds a practical hydraulic press that operates by a high-pressure plunger pump. This powerful device is able to squeeze, cut, bend, and shape metal. In 1812 Bramah patents a hydraulic jack to raise heavy weights. A hydraulic system operates by the pressure or movement of a liquid and is an effective way of producing a large force. It consists of a pipe with fluid that connects two cylinders that contain pistons (plugs that fit tightly in a cylinder and can slide up and down). Moving one small piston pushes on the liquid, increasing the pressure on the large cylinder and producing a larger force. These are the first practical applications of hydraulic principles, opening a

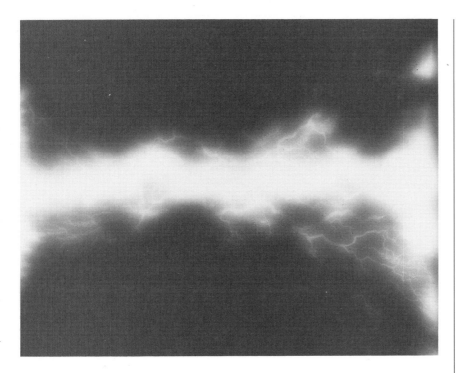

Electrical discharges
between two
metal objects.

major new source of power to the manufacturers and builders of the Industrial Revolution.

1799 ▪ Thermolamp and gas lighting. French chemist and engineer Philippe Lebon (1767–1804) patents a method of distilling gas from wood and uses it in a lighting fixture he calls a "thermolamp." Although the French government declines to finance his plans for a large-scale lighting system, Lebon is considered a pioneer of gas lighting. In 1801 Lebon uses his gas thermolamp to illuminate the Hôtel Seignelay in Paris. This is the first time an entire building is lit with gas.

March 20, 1800 ▪ Invention of voltaic pile. The voltaic pile or the first real battery is invented by Italian physicist Alessandro Giuseppe Antonio Anastasio Volta (1745–1827). He duplicates the "animal electricity" experiments of Italian anatomist Luigi Galvani (1737–1798), who found that when he hung a frog's leg by the nerve from a brass hook with the toe touching a silver plate, the leg kicked. Galvani understood that electricity caused this, but he argued wrongly that the electricity came from the muscles themselves. Volta does not use animals, but rather bowls of salt solution connected by strips of different metal dipping from one bowl to the next, with one end of the strip being copper and the other tin or zinc. This produces a steady flow of electrical current. He later streamlines this by stacking disks of metallic plates in a certain order, separating them by pieces of leather soaked in salt water, thus creating a "pile" or battery that produces a continuous and controllable electric current. He is later honored by having the electromotive force that moves the electric current named the "volt" after him. **(See also 1836)**

1802 ▪ High-pressure steam engine is patented. English engineer Richard Trevithick (1771–1833) patents and builds a direct-acting, portable steam engine that uses high-pressure steam. Using steam pressure above 145 pounds per square inch, he is able to use a smaller cylinder and still produce more power than old, low-pressure steam engines. With metallurgical (science and technology of metals) techniques greatly improved, Trevithick proves that small, high-pressure engines can be safely used to power machinery.

1805 ▪ Percussion lock for guns debuts. The first percussion lock for guns is created by Alexander John Forsyth (1769–1843), a Scottish inventor. This firing mechanism for guns is based on the detonation of an explosive when struck sharply and is the predecessor of the percussion cap. This method takes advantage of the explosive property of potassium chlorate and fulminate of mercury, both of which detonate when struck with a sharp blow. In 1814 Joshua Shaw (1777–1860), an English-American artist, makes the first percussion cap for a bullet. He fits a small copper cap containing a tiny charge of fulminate of mercury over a metal nipple. When the gun hammer hits the cap it explodes, sending a jet of flame down an open channel in the nipple, and firing the bullet. Percussion weapons have the advantage of speed and sureness of fire over the old flintlocks. They are also simpler, cheaper, and easier to maintain. Still, they do not replace flintlocks for another thirty years.

1821 ▪ Electric motor is invented. The first electric motor is invented by English physicist and chemist Michael Faraday (1791–1867). A year earlier Danish physicist Hans Christian Ørsted (1777–1851) discovered that an electric current can produce a magnetic field. Faraday then attempts to do the opposite and convert magnetism into electricity. He builds a device consisting of a hinged wire or needle, a magnet, and a chemical battery. When the current is turned on, a magnetic field is set up in the wire, and it begins to spin around the magnet. This demonstrates in a simple way the principle of an electric motor. In 1832 French engineer Hippolyte Pixii

(1808–1835) uses Faraday's discovery—called electromagnetic induction—to build the first practical generator. Pixii's hand-driven machine produces an alternating current (AC) and has stationary coils around which a field magnet revolves. This first generator produces alternating current that Pixii later is able to convert into direct current (DC).

1823 ▪ Development of elongated bullets. J. Norton first develops the elongated bullet, which is far superior aerodynamically to a round ball since it maintains its velocity in flight much better. The introduction of rifling (the spiral grooves cut into a rifle's barrel) makes this change from round lead balls to an elongated shape possible.

1827 ▪ Construction of modern water turbine. The first modern water turbine is built by French engineer and inventor Benoît Fourneyron (1802–1867). A turbine is a motor in which a set of blades rotate when struck by a moving stream of liquid or gas. Fourneyron's reaction turbine can produce about 6 horsepower and uses water directed through stationary guide vanes at the center into curved blades of an outer runner. In 1824 French mining engineer Claude Burdin (1778–1873) coined the term "turbine" to describe a power source that comes from the movement of a fluid or a gas. He took it from the Latin *turbo* for spinning top.

1828 ▪ Multiple fire-tube boiler improves steam engine. Marc Séguin (1786–1875), a French engineer, patents his multiple fire-tube boiler that proves to be a marked advance over the water-tube boiler used in traditional steam engines. Fire-tube boilers get their name because the hot gases circulate through tubes to heat the water surrounding the tubes. These boilers, though limited in maximum pressure and capacity, are very reliable. It is this efficient engine that English inventor George Stephenson (1781–1848) uses to power his "Rocket" locomotive in 1829.

1836 ▪ Daniell cell—new electrochemical battery. English chemist John Frederic Daniell (1790–1845) invents a new electrochemical, zinc-copper battery called the Daniell cell. This is a major improvement over the original Volta battery. The Volta battery created electricity when its salt solution broke up copper and zinc molecules (which also caused a thin film of hydrogen to form and decrease electrical output). By placing a barrier between the zinc and copper, Daniell stops the formation of hydrogen that impairs its function. His improvement makes this the first reliable source of electric current. **(See also March 20, 1800)**

1836 · Colt patents revolver. The revolver or repeating pistol is patented by American inventor Samuel Colt (1814–1862). He uses a pawl or ratchet mechanism to rotate the cylinder that holds the bullet, and the cylinder is then locked into place by cocking the hammer. His rapid-fire weapon does not become accepted until after 1846 when the United States realizes its value during the Mexican-American War (1846-48). Colt becomes the largest arms manufacturer in the world by 1855.

1836 · Breech-loading needle rifle is patented. German inventor Johann Nikolaus von Dreyse (1787–1867) patents the "needle" rifle with a bolt breech-loading mechanism. It is named needle because it has a long, sharp firing pin that pierces the charge at the base of the bullet. This gun is loaded through the rear of the barrel, a design that proves to be the preferred method of loading both large and small modern guns.

A modern revolver.

Front sight

Barrel

Rear sight

Hammer

Bullet

Cylinder

Frame

Trigger spring

Trigger

Trigger guard

Main spring

Frame

Grip

1839 ▪ Steam hammer is demonstrated. Scottish engineer James Nasmyth (1808–1890) demonstrates his steam hammer, a device that allows large materials to be forged (formed) with great accuracy. This huge yet extremely precise hammer can forge large iron parts needed by steamships and locomotives. This device proves to be a key element in England's Industrial Revolution.

1839 ▪ Creation of first fuel cell. The first fuel cell is created by English physicist William Robert Grove (1811–1896). A fuel cell is a type of battery that converts chemical energy into electrical energy (direct current). Grove develops the fuel cell when he discovers that he can produce electric power from the interaction of hydrogen and oxygen. This is a reversal of electrolysis, which uses an electric current to separate substances; the fuel cell instead combines hydrogen and oxygen to produce an electric current.

1849 ▪ The "Minié ball." French army captain Claude-étienne Minié (1804–1879) invents a bullet with a flat base and a pointed nose called the "Minié ball." Shaped much like modern bullets, it has great accuracy and range and can be loaded and fired quickly. The Minié system uses a hollow-base bullet made of soft lead that is smaller than the barrel, allowing it to easily slide down the barrel while loading. Highly accurate at 200 yards, these bullets are lethal to 1,000 yards, and effectively eliminate horse cavalry from battlefields.

1849 ▪ Corliss improves steam engine. American inventor George Henry Corliss (1817–1888) patents a more efficient and economical system of valves and governors to control steam and exhaust valves in steam engines. A valve is a device that allows a fluid or gas to flow in one direction only. A governor is an automatic device that controls the speed of a machine. Corliss gains fame by building a 700-ton, 1400–1600 horsepower steam engine that powers all the exhibits at the Centennial Exhibition at Philadelphia, Pennsylvania, in 1876. His engine runs continuously for six months. Although huge and powerful, his engines operate so smoothly that they can power textile mills without breaking any threads.

c. 1850 ▪ Kerosene is derived from coal and oil shale. Scottish chemist James Young (1811–1883) makes kerosene or coal oil, which he distills from coal and oil shale. Kerosene soon becomes the most popular fuel for oil lamps. The discovery of huge quantities of crude oil in America in 1859 will make all other sources of kerosene obsolete, and by the end of the century, kerosene is the chief product of American oil refineries. Because it belongs to the family of hydrocarbons called alkanes or paraffins, it is sometimes referred to as paraffin oil.

1850 · Hydraulic accumulator powers machinery.

The hydraulic accumulator or actuator that makes it possible for hydraulic machinery to be run some distance away from a direct water source is invented by English engineer William George Armstrong (1810–1900). A hydraulic system operates by the pressure or movement of a liquid and is an effective way of producing a large force. Armstrong's machine is basically a large water-filled cylinder with a piston (a plug that fits tightly in a cylinder and can slide up and down) that can raise water pressure within the cylinder and in supply pipes to 600 pounds per square inch. This allows machinery such as hoists, turntables, and dock gates to be operated in almost any situations.

1851 · Heat pump concept is described.

The concept of the heat pump is described by Scottish mathematician and physicist William Thomson, Lord Kelvin (1824–1907). He bases this concept on the principle that heat is given off when a gas condenses (changes into a liquid). Heat is absorbed by the expansion of a gas and given off at a higher temperature in a condenser. Although he does not build a heat pump, Kelvin is the first to describe the concept whereby a warm body can be made warmer and a cool body cooler. This concept remains untapped until twentieth century air conditioners and refrigerators make use of it.

1854 · Windmill tower revolutionizes wind power.

William Halliday of the United States revolutionizes the entire concept of wind power with his invention of a windmill tower. His tower is topped by a light wheel fitted with an automatic mechanism. This mechanism breaks the wheel's speed in high winds or when a tank of water is full. Easy to build, this type of windmill can generate enough electricity to power a small house and becomes commonplace in the settling of the American West.

1854 · Use of poisonous gas in warfare is proposed.

Lyon Playfair (1818–1898), an English chemist, proposes the use of poisonous gases in the Crimean War (the war between the Russians and the Ottoman Turks, 1854–56) but his suggestion is not followed. During World War I (1914–18), the Germans release chlorine gas in January 1915 against the Russians, but it has little effect. On April 22 of that year, the use of gas by the Germans proves to be the difference in a skirmish against the British and French.

Energy,
Power
Systems,
and
Weaponry

The wind power
captured by these
modern turbines at
Tehachapi Pass,
California, is a
sustainable source of
energy that does not
hurt the
environment.

When the Germans use the more deadly phosgene gas (carbonyl chloride that causes lung damage and death), the Allies respond in kind. The Germans escalate the use of poisonous gases with mustard gas (a powerful blistering agent) in 1917. By 1918 both sides use this new gas on a large scale. During World War II (1939–45), both sides produce but do not use poison gas. **(See also Chemistry: April 24, 1997)**

1856 · New converter makes steel manufacturing less expensive. English metallurgist Henry Bessemer (1813–1898) introduces his converter for the cheap manufacture of steel. Until this time steel was scarce because removing carbon from iron ore to make steel was a lengthy, complicated process. Bessemer's pneumatic conversion process uses a blast furnace that simply adds oxygen directly to the molten iron, raising the temperature and burning off the carbon. He accomplishes this without spending any additional money on fuel (by using ordinary cool air), and is eventually able to sell high-grade steel at one-tenth the going price, beginning an era of cheap steel. William Kelly (1811–1888), an American inventor, was actually the first to develop the pneumatic conversion process for making steel, discovering that blowing air through molten pig iron removed unwanted impurities, but did not patent the process immediately.

1857 · Smith and Wesson introduce their new revolver. Horace Smith (1808–1893) and Daniel Baird Wesson (1825–1906) of the United States introduce the first metallic cartridge revolver. Their new revolver has rim-fire copper cartridges (fired by a hammer striking a cap or primer at its base) that can be loaded quickly and easily from the rear of the weapon. It is not until the Smith-Wesson patent expires in 1872 that new revolvers appear. The first widely used semiautomatic pistol is designed by Hugo Borchardt of the United States in 1893.

1858 · Invention of compressed-air drill to bore through rocks. Germain Sommeiller (1815–1871), Italian-French engineer, invents a rock drill powered by compressed air. This device forces air into a closed container in order to build up pressure that is then released to power a drill. Sommeiller's pneumatic drill is used to tunnel under Mont Cenis between Switzerland and France and build the first major mountain tunnel.

August 27, 1859 · Drilling of first successful oil well. Retired American railroad conductor Edwin L. Drake (1819–1880) drills the first successful oil well in Titusville, Pennsylvania. Hired by the Seneca Oil Company, Drake develops the idea of driving iron pipe down into the hole to shore up its sides and keep water out. His success begins the world's oil industry. During November 1861, the first shipload of petroleum to cross the Atlantic is loaded at Philadelphia and embarks for London. This marks the beginning of regular traffic in full-cargo shipments of oil. Oil wells are drilled in Texas in 1866, and in 1900 the first offshore oil wells are drilled.

1859 · Development of the storage battery. French physicist Gaston Planté (1834–1889) invents the storage battery. Until his device, once a battery's chemical reaction had finished, the battery had to be discarded. Also called an accumulator, Planté's new battery system uses lead plates immersed in sulfuric acid and is completely rechargeable. To charge his battery, Planté uses a hand-driven generator. It is essentially the same battery used in today's automobiles. In 1867 French chemist Georges Leclanché (1839–1882) invents the dry cell battery. His new battery uses zinc and manganese, which react chemically within a container, and is a forerunner of today's portable batteries. In 1900 Thomas Alva Edison (1847–1931), American inventor, produces a nickel-iron battery. It has a long life and proves to be very durable. This battery can be overcharged, over-discharged, or even left idle with little negative effect.

1860 ▪ The repeating rifle. The repeating rifle is designed by B. Tyler Henry of the United States. His Henry rifle carries fifteen cartridges in a tube under the barrel and can mechanically feed them into the breech (at the rear of the barrel) to be fired, instead of needing the cartridges to be manually fed one at a time. His rifle is widely used in the American Civil War (1861–65) and his design forms the basis for the successful Winchester repeating rifle that becomes popular around 1870.

1862 ▪ Gatling invents machine gun. The first practical machine gun is invented by Richard Jordan Gatling (1818–1903), an American inventor. His Gatling gun fires 250 rounds per minute and consists of ten breech-loading (at the rear of the barrel) rifle barrels that are cranked by hand around a central axis. It makes its military debut at Butler's siege of Petersburg, Virginia, during the American Civil War (1861–65). The ten-barrel

Modern deep oil drilling rig near Bakersfield, California.

model, firing one thousand rounds per minute and covering a range of 2,400 yards, is a deciding factor in the battle of Santiago, Cuba, during the Spanish-American War of 1898. In 1884 Hiram Stevens Maxim (1840–1916), American-English inventor, demonstrates his single-barrel, belt-fed and water-cooled automatic gun. Capable of firing 666 rounds per minute, the automatic gun loads, fires, extracts, and ejects the cartridge all on the momentum of recoil. Operating off the energy from the erupting shell, it eventually renders the hand-cranked Gatling gun obsolete and is adopted by the armies of every major country.

1866 · Advent of modern torpedo. English engineer Robert White-head (1823–1905) invents the modern torpedo. His design is a spindle-shaped underwater missile driven by a compressed air engine. It can move at 6 knots for a few hundred yards while carrying an explosive charge in its head. It can also be made to stay at a set depth by a valve activated by water pressure and linked to horizontal rudders. In 1876 Whitehead improves this weapon by adding a servomotor (a small motor that supplements a larger one) to give it a truer course through the water, and in 1896 he adds a gyroscope (a wheel set on a free-moving axis that always indicates true north).

1867 · Dynamite is produced. Swedish inventor Alfred Nobel (1833–1896) produces the stable, solid explosive called dynamite. After exhaustive experimentation, he finds that the highly volatile liquid nitro-glycerine can be safely handled when absorbed by a porous clay called kieselguhr (pronounced key'-zel-gur). This special clay soaks up the nitro-glycerine without changing its chemical makeup, and the resulting dough-like substance can be made into hard cakes or sticks. Five times more powerful than gunpowder, dynamite revolutionizes the mining industry and soon finds many military applications. In 1875 Nobel introduces blasting gelatine. He mixes nitroglycerine and collodion (a low nitrogen form of gun-cotton) and finds that they form a jellylike mass that is water resistant and more powerful than dynamite. **(See also 1889: Cordite, a smokeless powder)**

1867 · Commercial generator for producing alternating current is built. Belgian engineer and inventor Zénobe Théophile Gramme (1826–1901) builds the first practical, commercial generator for producing alternating current (AC). A generator is a machine that converts movement (such as a turning blade) into electricity. Two years later, Gramme achieves the same thing with direct current (DC). With DC, the electric current

Thomas Alva Edison
in his laboratory.

flows in one direction only. With AC, the current changes direction and is easier to send over long distances. In 1873 while a Gramme dynamo is being shown at an exhibition in Vienna, Austria, it is accidentally discovered that the device is reversible and can therefore also be used as an electric motor. An electric motor is a machine that uses electricity to produce movement. With these first practical dynamos (generators), Gramme essentially establishes and founds the electrical industry.

1875 ▪ Introduction of petroleum jelly. Robert Augustus Chesebrough (1837–1933), American manufacturer, introduces Petrolatum, which becomes known by its product name of Vaseline. This smooth, semi-solid blend of mineral oil with waxes crystallized from petroleum becomes useful as a lubricant, carrier, and waterproofing agent in many products.

October 21, 1879 ▪ Edison invents incandescent light bulb. The first practical incandescent (glowing) light bulb is produced by American inventor Thomas Alva Edison (1847–1931). After spending fifty thousand dollars in one year's worth of experiments in search of some sort of wire that could be heated to incandescence (so it would glow and give off light but not be used up) by an electric current, Edison finally abandons metal altogether. He then discovers a material that will warm to white heat in a vacuum without melting, evaporating, or breaking. Using a simple filament of scorched cotton thread, his electric light burns for forty continuous hours and the age of the electric light is born. Before Edison, Joseph Wilson Swan (1828–1914), an English physicist and chemist, invented a primitive electric light using a filament of carbonized paper in a vacuum glass bulb in 1860. Lack of a good vacuum prevented it from working very well, and it was basically this design that Edison used. In 1881 Edison builds the first central electric power station at Pearl Street, New York. It has three 125-horsepower steam generators that supply electric current to 225 homes. Edison develops an entire system for generating and distributing electricity from a central source. Some regard this accomplishment as a greater achievement than his invention of the light bulb.

1882 ▪ First U.S. hydroelectric generating plant is built. The first hydroelectric generating plant in the United States is built at Appleton, Wisconsin. A hydroelectric power station uses a turbine driven by falling water from a dam. The turbine drives the generator (which produces electric current). The first dam built specifically to generate power for a hydroelectric plant is built in 1894 on the Willamette River site in Oregon where a plant already exists.

1884 ▪ Steam turbine and generator is patented by Parsons. English engineer Charles Algernon Parsons (1854–1931) patents and builds the first parallel-flow reaction steam turbine and high-speed, direct current (DC) generator. It operates on the turbine principle that energy can be derived from the movement of a fluid or gas past a set of blades. Parsons's steam turbine consists of a rotor (a rotating coil) in which several vaned wheels are attached to a shaft (like a propeller). Steam enters and expands, causing the shaft wheels to rotate. Other stationary blades force the steam against those that rotate, making use of as much energy as possible. The steam continues and encounters another set of turbine blades designed to work with the same steam at a slightly lower pressure. Parsons's new turbine achieves a speed of 18,000 revolutions per minute (rpm) compared to the previous maximum of 1,500 rpm. Turbines later become the most widely used method of providing electricity for large-scale processes.

1884 ▪ Electric alternator is created. Croatian-American electrical engineer Nikola Tesla (1856–1943) invents the electric alternator, an elec-

Thomas Alva Edison and His "Invention Factory"

During Thomas Alva Edison's lifetime (1847–1931), more than 1,300 patents were issued in his name, far more than have ever been credited to anyone else. As a young man with few resources, Edison did his inventing on his own, but once his inventions brought in enough money, he established a workplace for many people to carry out technological research. While the products created in his laboratories shaped American daily life, the labs themselves shaped the way industrial advances are made today.

In 1869, at the age of twenty-three, Edison opened an "invention factory" that began as a group of fifty consulting engineers working in Newark, New Jersey. Later, in 1876, the laboratory moved to larger quarters at Menlo Park, New Jersey. Menlo Park was the site of amazing productivity. There, among many other creations, the "Wizard of Menlo Park" invented the phonograph and the incandescent light bulb, and created the first electric light power station. In 1887, Edison built a huge new laboratory in West Orange, New Jersey. At peak production of this facility, he received an average of one patent every five days (including one for the kinetograph, his early form of the moving picture). Edison's "invention factory" is considered the forerunner of the modern industrial research laboratory.

tric generator that produces alternating current (AC). He is convinced that AC has many advantages over DC (direct current, which Edison supports), and he is eventually proven correct. With DC the electric current flows in one direction only. AC, in which the current changes in intensity and direction, is easier to send over long distances and makes machines perform better. In the following year, American electrical engineer William Stanley

(1858–1916) perfects the electric transformer, which can change ("transform") the voltage (power) and amperage (rate of current) of a supply of electricity. Transformers can convert high-voltage current into low-voltage, high-amperage current, which proves to be the form in which it can do its best work. Stanley's transformer works only with alternating-current.

c. 1885 ▪ Beginnings of solar cells. The first solar cells are made by Charles Fritts, an American inventor. This new power source employs the photoelectric effect (an electric current is produced when light or other radiation falls upon certain materials). Fritts's thin wafers, the size of a quarter, are made of the light-sensitive metal selenium. Although an electric current is generated when sunlight strikes the cells, his system is extremely inefficient with less than 1 percent of the light energy actually being converted into electrical energy. **(See also 1954)**

1889 ▪ Cordite, a smokeless powder. English chemist Frederick Augustus Abel (1827–1902) and Scottish chemist and physicist James Dewar (1842–1923) patent cordite, a smokeless powder derived from nitroglycerin and guncotton (nitrocellulose) to which some petroleum jelly is added. It is safe to handle in its jellylike state and can be shaped, dried, and cut into precisely divided sizes (or cords, from which it gets its name). It is used exclusively for firing shells since it is smokeless and allows a battle's progress to be seen better. It also allows armies to conceal their battle positions.

1889 ▪ First successful gas-operated machine gun. John Moses Browning (1855–1926), an American inventor, begins work on what becomes the first successful gas-operated machine gun. He discovers a way of using the expanding gases and recoil from exploding ammunition to eject, reload, and fire his weapon automatically. His rapid-fire weapon becomes an enormous success. In 1918 Browning perfects his .30 caliber, gas-operated Browning automatic rifle and it is adopted by the U.S. Army. Browning machine guns play a later role in World War II (1939–45) and the Korean War (1950–53).

1897 ▪ Diesel engine is built for commercial use. German inventor Rudolf Diesel (1858–1913) builds his first commercial Diesel engine. As an internal combustion engine, its fuel is burned inside the engine and its power comes from the expansion of the gases being burned. Diesel's high compression engine is four times as efficient as a steam engine, but unlike a regular internal combustion engine, it does not need a complex ignition system to ignite the fuel. Because it injects fuel (of almost any kind) into an engine whose piston (a plug that fits tightly in a cylinder and can slide up and down) compresses air as high as twenty-five times, this high compression causes the air to reach temperatures of nearly 1000° C, high enough to ignite fuel spontaneously. As a large, heavy engine, its early applications are primarily for stationary purposes. It eventually is improved and finds widespread application in the shipping and locomotive industries.

1901 ▪ Invention of the mercury vapor discharge lamp. Peter Cooper Hewitt (1861–1921), an American electrical engineer, invents the mercury vapor discharge lamp. Based on the knowledge that electricity—when passed through certain gases at very low pressures—discharges a glowing light, Hewitt builds the ancestor of the neon light and fluorescent lamp. In contrast to incandescent (glowing) light bulbs, discharge lamps deliver nearly all their energy in the form of light or ultraviolet rays (invisible to the human eye), rather than in producing useless amounts of heat. In 1934 the first practical fluorescent lamp is developed by a team of American scientists at a General Electric laboratory. Based on Hewitt's lamp, which it improves by reducing the operating voltage, this new light employs the principle that fluorescent chemicals called phosphors will convert ultraviolet light to light that is visible to the human eye.

1902 ▪ Building of the first military tank. The first military tank is built by F. R. Simms of England. This armored car is powered by an internal-combustion engine and carries three guns. An internal combustion engine burns fuel inside the engine and its power comes from the expansion of the gases being burned. In October 1914, E. D. Swinton of England suggests that tractor tracks be added to this armored vehicle for increased mobility, and the British army begins calling this new offensive vehicle a "tank." During World War I (1914–18), in September 1916 the British army first uses a tank in battle. It gets bogged down in the cratered battlefield but is used much more effectively the following year at the Battle of Cambrai in northern France.

1904 ▪ Attempting to harness geothermal power. The first efforts to harness geothermal power are made in Italy. Geothermal energy flows from the Earth's hot interior to its surface in certain places. Work begins this year to capture this energy and to generate power from the underground steam that pours from the "fumaroles" or natural crevices at Larderello in Tuscany, Italy. Wells are driven as deep as 2,000 feet and they produce superheated steam at great pressure. The steam is used to drive turbines, which then generate electricity. The following year a 25-kilowatt steam-driven generator is installed.

1910 ▪ Neon light makes first appearance. Georges Claude (1870–1960), French engineer and chemist, produces the first neon light when he discovers that a glass tube filled with neon gas glows with an eye-catching red color when it is charged with electricity. Neon lights will eventually replace ordinary incandescent (glowing) bulbs in advertising signs and neon signs soon decorate the exteriors of commercial buildings. Experiments with other gases allow a variety of different colors to be produced.

1915 ▪ First use of depth charges. Depth charge bombs are first used by the Allies against German submarines at this time during World War I (1914–18). The depth charges consist of canisters filled with explosives and fitted with a valve that is triggered by water pressure against a spring. Designed by the British Navy to protect their surface boats against German submarine attack, these timed bombs can be set to explode at a certain depth by adjusting the tension on their springs. They explode underwater and create damaging and sometimes lethal shock waves.

1918 ▪ Successful submachine gun is introduced. Louis Schmeisser of Germany invents the first successful submachine gun. It is a fully automatic shoulder weapon that can fire 400 rounds per minute. This automatic weapon proves that a shoulder weapon that fires pistol ammunition can be useful militarily. It has a barrel only 7.9 inches long. In 1920 American inventor John Taliaferro Thompson (1860–1940) develops a submachine gun that has a large drum magazine (a chamber to hold cartridges and feed them into the gun) and fires .45 caliber cartridges. Capable of firing 800 rounds per minute, it is first used in combat by the U.S. Marines in Nicaragua in 1925. Called the "Tommy gun," this easy-to-use automatic weapon becomes associated with the criminal gangland wars of the 1920s and 1930s.

c. 1942 ▪ Bazooka is developed. The U.S. military first introduces a shoulder-type rocket launcher called the bazooka. Developed for attacking tanks and fortified positions, it is a smooth-bore steel tube that is recoilless (giving no kickback) and delivers a powerful explosive. Weighing about 10 pounds, it is operated by two people. One positions it on his shoulder and the other loads the ammunition. It can hit a target up to several hundred yards with great accuracy.

July 16, 1945 · Successful test of atomic bomb. The first atomic bomb, made of plutonium, is successfully tested in a desert area near Alamogordo, New Mexico, by the United States. Plutonium is a radioactive, silver metal not found naturally as an ore, but is made from uranium in nuclear reactors. This successful detonation achieves the goal of the secret World War II Manhattan Project, a research team appointed to carry out the U.S. goal of building the first atomic bomb. On August 6, 1945, a plutonium bomb weighing 2,000 tons and with an explosive energy of 20,000 tons of TNT (trinitrotoluene) is dropped on Hiroshima, Japan, by the United States. After an equally destructive plutonium bomb is dropped on Nagasaki, Japan, three days later, Japan surrenders unconditionally, ending World War II (1939–45). On March 1, 1954, the United States successfully tests its first dropped thermonuclear bomb (a hydrogen bomb), which explodes at Eniwetok Atoll. Plutonium bombs work by nuclear fission or the splitting of nuclei to release energy. Splitting a great many nuclei in a fraction of a second causes a powerful explosion. Thermonuclear or hydrogen bombs (H-bombs) work by nuclear fusion or the combining of nuclei to release energy. A fusion reaction is what powers the Sun and as a weapon, it is much more destructive than a fission weapon. **(See also Physics: 1934, 1939, 1942)**

Atom bomb explosion.

August 11, 1947 · Peacetime nuclear reactor is constructed. Construction of the first peacetime nuclear reactor in the United States begins at Brookhaven, New York. A nuclear reactor produces energy by controlled nuclear fusion. As a large, shielded container for this reaction, it uses control rods and coolant to produce heat at an even rate. The heat creates steam that drives turbines that generate electricity. In 1952 the first experimental breeder reactor (EBR-1) is put into operation by the United

States at Arco, Idaho. A breeder reactor is a type of nuclear reactor that produces new fuel (converting uranium to plutonium) as it works. The heat this nuclear process creates is used to generate 1,400 kilowatts of heat and 170 kilowatts of electricity—the first significant amount of electricity produced in this manner. In 1954 the Soviet Union opens its first nuclear power plant, and in 1957 Great Britain does the same.

1954 ▪ Solar cell technology advances. Bell Telephone Laboratories researchers first develop the silicon photovoltaic cell that revolutionizes solar cell technology. Photovoltaic cells change sunlight into electricity. At first the cells achieve a conversion efficiency of 6 percent, which is later improved to 15 percent. In 1957 the first use of silicon solar cells as a power source is achieved as Bell Telephone uses them experimentally to power a telephone repeater station in rural Georgia. On March 17, 1958, the first practical application of silicon solar cells is achieved when a solar array is used to provide electricity for the radio transmitter on the American satellite, *Vanguard 1*. Solar cells have been used on almost every scientific satellite since.

1957 ▪ Intercontinental ballistic missile is developed. The Soviet Union develops an intercontinental ballistic missile (ICBM), and the United States responds, beginning the "arms race" in nuclear weaponry delivery systems. These long-range rockets or missiles prove relatively immune to electronic countermeasures since they use inertial guidance systems. The automatic navigational system uses feedback and carries instruments such as a gyroscope and a computer to keep it on course. The missiles evolve into potentially highly lethal mass-killing systems by the use of multiple, independently targeted warheads, so one missile can deliver scores of nuclear bombs that fly off to separate targets. None have ever been used in warfare. With the breakup of the Soviet Union in 1991, both Russia and the United States are attempting to eliminate or at least reduce the stockpiles of these weapons of mass destruction.

1960 ▪ Introduction of halogen lamp. The halogen lamp is first introduced. This incandescent (glowing) lamp filled with a halogen gas, such as iodine, produces a light much brighter than a regular light bulb because the gas regenerates the filament (heating it to a higher temperature) and makes it glow even brighter. A regular light bulb is filled with unreactive gas—such as nitrogen or argon—which prevents the glowing filament from burning out as it would in air, but does not increase its brightness.

1966 · Tidal power plant produces electricity. The largest electricity-producing power plant to use tidal power is built on the coast of France. Tidal power is a form of hydroelectricity (electricity from water power) that is produced by the ebb and flow of the tides. Barriers containing reversible turbines are built across an estuary or gulf where the tide is the widest. The Rance Tidal Works in the Gulf of St. Malo, Brittany, in France, has a 2,500 foot-long (750 meter) dam at the mouth of the Rance River, and its generators produce 240 megawatts of electric power.

April 1971 · Electrical power from magnetohydrodynamic generators. Magnetohydrodynamic (MHD) power generators begin operations in both the Soviet Union and in Germany. This new technology generates electrical power by passing a conducting fluid or gas through a strong magnetic field. Although it is expected to have a higher efficiency rate than traditional electric generators, an optimum design has not yet been deter-

Three Mile Island nuclear reactors in the background of a rural scene.

mined. MHD results in extremely high temperatures, and the stability of the entire operation is the still the main concern.

March 28, 1979 · Three Mile Island nuclear accident. The first major American nuclear accident occurs as a technician error at the Three Mile Island nuclear power plant in Pennsylvania results in a partial meltdown. A meltdown is a very serious situation in which the reactor core (where nuclear fission or nuclei splitting occurs) begins to melt. This happens if the cooling system does not prevent heat buildup. If uncontrolled, heat buildup would burn through the shield or explode, contaminating a wide area. Since this situation is a partial meltdown, some radioactivity escapes but no one is injured. The unit is permanently shut down.

1986 · Laser is used to produce fusion reaction. The first fusion reaction caused by a laser occurs for one-billionth of a second at the Lawrence Livermore Laboratory in the United States. A laser is a device that produces a beam of high-energy light or concentrated, coherent radiation. Fusion is the combining of nuclei to release energy—the nuclear process that powers the sun as well as a hydrogen bomb. As such, it results in an enormous production of energy. If fusion could be controlled and kept going, it would provide a safe and inexhaustible energy source. Currently, more energy goes into the process of causing fusion than is produced.

1988 · Establishment of the Draper Prize. The Draper Prize is first established by the National Academy of Engineering in the United States. Named in honor of American aeronautical engineer Charles Stark Draper (1901–1987), it bestows a prize of $375,000 on the winner and is considered the engineering equivalent of the Nobel Prize.

1991 · New light bulb uses electromagnetic induction. The Philips Company of the Netherlands develops a new light bulb that uses electromagnetic induction to excite a gas and produce light. Electromagnetic induction is the use of magnetism to produce electricity. Although used in motors, microphones, and engine ignition systems, this phenomenon has never been used for illumination. The breakthrough bulb is extremely energy efficient, having no parts to wear out, and will last for up to 60,000 hours.

1994 · Development of lithium battery with a water-based electrolyte. The first lithium battery with a water-based electrolyte is developed by Canadian physicist Jeff Dahn. An electrolyte is a substance (a liquid or a paste) in a battery that acts like a catalyst and helps the electrodes (metal rods or plates) react and create an electric current. Although lithium (a soft, light metal) used in a battery had proven powerful enough, it reacts violently and produces a gas when immersed in water. This entirely new battery, however, is designed to use a water-based electrolyte, thus making it not only environmentally nontoxic but safe and inexpensive. Although only a prototype, it can potentially be the battery to power the electric cars of tomorrow. Electric vehicles currently lack a battery that is powerful, safe, and cheap.

1996 · Opening of 100-megawatt solar power plant. The first 100-megawatt solar power plant opens in the Nevada desert. This joint venture between the American corporations Enron and Amoco plans to spend $150 million on a solar power plant that will use the sun's energy to power a city with a population of one hundred thousand. The corporations plan to initially sell energy for 5.5 cents a kilowatt-hour, about 3 cents cheaper on average than electricity generated by oil, coal, or gas. The technology used is fairly traditional and uses a conventional thin-film, silicon-based photovoltaic cell able to transform about 8 percent of the sunlight that reaches it into electricity. The low price will be maintained by tax exemptions and guaranteed governmental purchases.

Mathematics

c. 30,000 B.C. ▪ Early evidence of a tally system. The earliest evidence of Stone Age man's ability to devise a tally system is the notched shinbone of a young wolf dating to this time period. The tally system (by which a count, score, or record of something is kept) is the earliest and most direct way of visibly expressing the idea of numbers, for it matches the things being counted with some easily used set of objects such as fingers, stones, or marks on a stick (one mark on a stick equals one thing being counted). This 7-inch long bone found in 1937 in Czechoslovakia has fifty-five deeply cut notches, more or less equal in length, arranged in groups of five.

c. 8000 B.C. ▪ Clay tokens are used to count. Clay tokens are first used in Mesopotamia to record numbers of animals and plants. The shape of these tokens is used to represent a specific thing or amount. For example, a cylinder shape stands for an animal, while cones and spheres refer to certain quantities of grain. Each token functions on a one-to-one basis and represents a single thing. By 6000 B.C., clay tokens have spread throughout the Middle East and are eventually replaced by tokens with more elaborate markings. Around 4000 B.C., even more complex clay tokens appear with a wider variety of shapes and markings. These are believed to reflect the increasingly complex structure of Sumerian (southern Babylonian) society with its increased number of finished goods. Some speculate that it may also be an indication of the first system of enforced taxation.

c. 3500 B.C. ▪ Egyptian number system is fully developed. The first fully developed number system (a method of writing numbers) is used in Egypt. This system allows counting to continue indefinitely with only the occasional introduction of a new symbol. As a system with a base of ten, it uses special pictographs or symbols for each new power of ten up to ten million. It is thought that they have ten as the base in their counting because they can count to ten on their hands. The emergence of Egyptian government and administration could not have taken place without such a system of numbers.

c. 2400 B.C. ▪ Positional notation is used by the Sumerians. Positional notation first comes into use in Mesopotamia by the Sumerians (southern Babylonians), the only pre-Grecian people to make even a partial use of such a number system. Positional notation is based on the notion of place value, in which the value of a digit or symbol depends on the position it occupies in the numerical group. The great advantage of this system (that we still use today) is that it does not require a great many symbols to express numbers, no matter how big or small. An example of this is the number 515. Starting from left to right, the first 5 is in what we recognize as the hundred position, and thus it stands not for 5 of something but for 500. The 1 is in the ten position, and the second 5 is in the one or single-unit position. The Sumerian system has a base of sixty and uses cuneiform writing (a system that uses wedge-shaped symbols for its alphabet). **(See also 773)**

c. 1700 B.C. ▪ Oldest existing mathematical document. The oldest mathematical document in existence is an Egyptian papyrus written by a scribe named Ahmose or Ahmes. Dated to this period, it becomes the main source of our knowledge of Egyptian mathematics (along with another papyrus, the Golenischev or Moscow papyrus, dated slightly after this time). As a practical handbook telling how to solve everyday problems, it informs us how the Egyptians counted, reckoned, and measured. It contains eighty-five problems and shows the use of fractions, the solution of simple equations, some geometry, how to measure area and volume. No generalizations or rules for solving a particular type of problem are given, however. It is also called the Rhind papyrus after the Scottish collector Alexander Henry Rhind, who purchased it at a Nile resort.

876 B.C. ▪ Symbol is used to represent zero. The first-known reference to the use of a symbol for zero is made in India. An unknown Indian mathematician suggests that an untouched abacus level be given a special symbol meaning zero. Until this innovation, a gap or blank space was often used in positional notation systems, but it was not always used and confusion sometimes resulted.

585 B.C. ▪ First treatment of geometry as an abstract study. The first to treat geometry in an abstract way is Greek philosopher Thales of Miletus (c. 625–c. 547 B.C.). Borrowing Egyptian geometry, he converts it into an abstract (theoretical) study by stating that it deals with imaginary lines of zero thickness and perfect straightness. He also is the first to prove a mathematical statement using a regular series of arguments, and he insists on the now-obvious notion that things must be proved to be true. His method is to state what is known and then to proceed in a step-by-step manner to reach the desired proof. In this he can be said to be the inventor of deductive mathematics. Deduction is the kind of reasoning we use everyday to show that a conclusion follows from its premises or previous statements.

c. 550 B.C. ▪ Mathematical ratios of musical intervals are discovered. The first to discover the mathematical ratios of the musical intervals is Greek philosopher Pythagoras (c. 580–500 B.C.). Noticing that shorter strings produce higher notes, he finds that the relationship of pitch can be simply correlated with length. If one string is twice as long, it emits a sound an octave lower. If the length ratio is three to two, the musical interval is called a fifth; if it is four to three, the interval produced is called a fourth. Pythagoras also posits that numbers and the proportions they contain (which he calls harmonies) are the first principle of nature. **(See also c. 500 B.C.)**

c. 500 B.C. ▪ Theory on the significance of numbers and their relationships. Greek philosopher Pythagoras (c. 580–500 B.C.) formulates the idea that everything in the universe depends on numbers and their relationships. Several mathematical principles and discoveries are attributed to him and his followers. One of these is the Pythagorean theorem, in which Pythagoras worked out by strict mathematical deduction (proof) that the square of the length of the hypotenuse (the longest side) of a right triangle is equal to the sum of the squares of the lengths of its sides. Pythagoras also studies sound and finds that the relationship of pitch (high or low sound) is directly related to the string length of a musical instrument. The Pythagoreans believe that "all is number;" they viewed the world as a perfect harmony of numerical structures and sought to achieve balance by understanding this numerical basis of all things. This approach deeply influences the development of classical Greek philosophy and medieval European thought.

c. 500 B.C. · Appearance of Chinese rod numeral system. Chinese rod numerals first appear. This system uses eighteen separate symbols made up of variations of vertical and horizontal lines to represent the digits one through nine and the first nine multiples of ten. Using this stick-figurelike system, the Chinese can represent numbers as large as desired or needed. Throughout early Chinese history, the main purpose of mathematics is to maintain the calendar correctly. Since this is a right granted only by the emperor, few outside his select circle of advisers know or can practice any mathematics.

c. 440 B.C. · First-known geometry textbook. The first-known textbook on geometry, *Elements*, is written by Hippocrates of Chios, a Greek geometer. He arranges the known propositions of geometry in a scientific fashion, and this work may have served as a model for Greek mathematician Euclid's work, also named *Elements*. A proposition is a statement that can be found either "true" or "false." Hippocrates's book is known through the writings of others, however, since no trace of it remains. He is also believed to be the first to support himself by openly accepting payment for teaching mathematics. Hippocrates of Chios should be distinguished from his more famous contemporary, Greek physician Hippocrates of Cos (c. 460–c. 377 B.C.).

389 B.C. · Founding of first university. The first university is founded at Academaeus in Athens, Greece, by Greek philosopher Plato (c. 428–c. 347 B.C.), who teaches that geometry is a necessary preparation for the study of philosophy. Although not an original mathematical thinker, one of Plato's greatest contributions is the refinement of the analytic method or analysis as a method of proof. This logical technique begins with what is given and then proceeds step-by-step to what is proved. Plato also suggests that one can reverse the process and begin with the proposition that is to be proved and from it deduce a conclusion that holds. Plato is perhaps most important to the history of mathematics for his role as an inspiration to others and his extreme emphasis on the importance of mathematics. The motto above the door of his academy reads: "Let no one ignorant of geometry enter here."

c. 250 B.C. · Calculation of pi. Greek mathematician and engineer Archimedes (c. 287–212 B.C.) calculates the most accurate arithmetical value for pi (pronounced *pie*) to date. Pi is the ratio of a circle's circumference (the distance completely around it) to its diameter (the distance across its middle). Archimedes uses this value to figure the areas and volumes of curved surfaces and circular forms. Besides his many contributions to pure mathematics, he is best known for applying mathematics to hydrostatics (the behavior of fluids) and to mechanics (the study of the effects of forces upon objects). In addition to the major status he holds in physics, he is considered the greatest mathematical genius of antiquity.

c. A.D. 150 · Minutes and seconds make appearance. The first use of the terms "minutes" and "seconds" is made by Greek astronomer Claudius Ptolemy (c. 100–c. 170), also known as Claudius Ptolemaeus. He subdivides each degree in a circle into sixty *partes minutiae primae* (for minutes) and each of these again into sixty *partes minutiae secundae* (for seconds). Similar to the division of a clock, one minute equals one-sixtieth of a degree, and one second equals one-sixtieth of a minute. This allows finer and more precise measurements. Claudius Ptolemy also begins using the Greek letter *omicron* to designate a blank in numbers (since *o* is the first letter of this Greek word for "empty or nothing"), but it is not used in the manner of today's zero.

Archimedes is considered the greatest mathematical genius of ancient times.

c. 250 · Earliest existing study of algebra. Greek mathematician Diophantus (c. 210–c. 290) writes his *Arithmetica* (Arithmetic), which includes the earliest written study of algebra that still exists. Diophantus is also the first Greek to write a significant work on algebra, solving problems using his own symbols and using what would now be called algebraic equations. (Algebra solves problems in arithmetic by using letters or symbols to stand for quantities.) In addition, he is also the first Greek to treat fractions as numbers and is credited with introducing the symbol for minus ($-$).

773 · Rediscovery of positional notation. Positional notation is rediscovered by the Arabs when al-Mansūr (709–775), second caliph of the Abbāsid dynasty, commissions a translation of a written Hindu astronomical study. In translating this document, it is learned that the position of a

Hypatia of Alexandria and Maria Gaetana Agnesi: Pioneering Women in Mathematics

Greek mathematician Hypatia of Alexandria (c. 370–415) was the only notable woman scholar of ancient times and the first woman mentioned in the history of mathematics. As the head of the Neoplatonist school of philosophy at Alexandria and a devotee of pagan learning, her eloquence, beauty, modesty, and remarkable intellectual gifts attracted a large number of pupils. Her death by stoning and slashing by a fanatical Christian mob led to the departure of many scholars from Alexandria and marked the beginning of Alexandria's decline as a major center of ancient learning. The first woman to occupy a chair of mathematics on a university faculty is Italian mathematician and philosopher Maria Gaetana Agnesi (1718–1799), in 1750. The daughter of a mathematician, she is a child prodigy who masters Latin, Greek, and Hebrew at an early age and writes a published defense of higher education for women when she is only nine years old. An expert in **calculus** (using algebraic symbols to calculate changing quantities), she is recognized by Pope Benedict XIV (1675–1758) and appointed to the chair of mathematics and natural philosophy at the University of Bologna.

digit in a column can affect its value. Using a zero to indicate an empty column is also learned. These numerals and positional notation eventually come to the West as "Arabic numerals" (the number symbols such as 1, 2, 3, 4 that we use today) and are used in the early ninth century by Arab mathematician al-Khwārizmī (c. 780–c. 850). Al-Khwārizmī produces the first astronomical tables in Arabic. **(See also c. 2400 B.C.)**

c. 850 ▪ Source of Arabic numerals and algebra. The writings of Arabian mathematician al-Khwārizmī (c. 780–c. 850) become the source for what is later called the "Arabic" number system as well as for the name "algebra." Al-Khwārizmī offers the first really detailed information on the Hindu numerical system (the number symbols such as 1, 2, 3, 4 that we use today), and when his work is later translated into Latin, the system comes to be called Arabic numerals instead of Hindu. Another of al-Khwārizmī's books whose title contains the Arabic word *al jabr* meaning transposition, becomes the source for the modern term "algebra." **(See also 1202)**

870 · Greek mathematical works are translated into Arabic.

Arabian mathematician Thābit ibn Qurrah (c. 836–901) founds a school of translators and translates most of the major Greek mathematical works. It is mainly because of his work in translating these Greek works into Arabic that the West eventually comes to know so many of them. Had it not been for his efforts, the body of Greek mathematical works available today would be much smaller. He was also an original, first-rate mathematician in his own right.

Euclid, Greek mathematician whose work from 300 B.C. introduced geometry to Europe.

c. 980 · Rebirth of learning in Europe.

French scholar Gerbert (c. 945–1003) helps initiate the rebirth of learning—especially mathematics—in Europe, after a long period in the early Middle Ages when European culture had become fairly primitive, without structured government or learning. As one of the first Christians to study in the Moslem schools of Spain, he reintroduces the abacus to the West and uses Arabic numerals (the number symbols such as 1,2,3,4 that we use today), although not a zero. Gerbert is not only a profound scholar but in 999 he is elected pope, taking the name Sylvester II.

1120 · Euclid's *Elements* is translated into Latin.

Adelard of Bath (c. 1090–c. 1150), an English scholar, makes the first Latin translation of Greek mathematician Euclid's *Elements* from an Arabic version. Euclid lived and taught geometry in Alexandria in about 300 B.C. When Adelard introduces Euclid's work to Europe, it serves as the major geometry textbook in the West. Adelard also introduces Arab trigonometry (the branch of mathematics that studies triangles) to the West and uses Arabic numerals (the number symbols such as 1, 2, 3, 4 that we use today).

1202 · Use of Arabic numerals is promoted in the West. The first great Western mathematician to advocate the adoption of "Arabic notation" or Arabic numerals (the number symbols such as 1, 2, 3, 4 that we use today) is Italian mathematician, Leonardo Fibonacci (c. 1170–c. 1240), also called Leonardo da Pisa. Since Fibonacci's father is engaged in business in northern Africa, the son studies under a Muslim teacher and travels in Egypt, Syria, and Greece. He becomes very familiar with Hindu-Arabic numerals. In *Liber abaci* (Book of the abacus), his book on algebraic methods, he explains the use and advantages of Arabic numerals over Roman numerals and makes clear the values of positional notation using a base of ten. He also describes the sign for zero (0). Called *zephirum* in Arabic, this word and its variations account for our present words "cipher" and "zero."

1435 · Account of uses of perspective is published. The first formal account of the uses of perspective (drawing a picture that has distance and depth in it) is given by Italian artist Leon Battista Alberti (1404–1472), in his *Della pittura* (On painting). In this written study on how to graphically give the illusion of three-dimensional space on a flat surface, Alberti mentions his debt to Italian architect Filippo Brunelleschi (1377–1446), who around 1410 discovered the mathematical laws of perspective. Alberti's study is a forerunner of what is today called "projective geometry."

1489 · Origins of the "+" and "-" symbols. Johannes Widman (c. 1462–c. 1500), a German mathematician, publishes a work on arithmetic which is the first printed book to contain the "+" and "-" symbols. They are not used as symbols of operation (to tell the user to add or subtract) but merely to indicate excess and deficiency. Since Widman's book is business-oriented, he uses the symbols to indicate a surplus or lack of warehouse supplies.

1492 · Long division is demonstrated. The first printed example of the modern process of long division is demonstrated by Filippo Calandri of Italy in his *Aritmetica* (Arithmetic). It also contains the first illustrated mathematical problems published in Italy. The first to use the symbol for division ($\div$) is Swiss mathematician and astronomer Johann Heinrich Rahn (1622–1676) in his 1659 work on algebra. This symbol is introduced to England in a 1668 translation of Rahn's work. In 1631 the cross multiplication sign ($\times$) is first used by English mathematician William Oughtred (1575–1660) in his book *Clavis Mathematicae* (The key to mathematics).

Oughtred puts particular emphasis on the use of mathematical symbols and uses more than 150 of them, but this is the only one that really takes hold.

1557 · Publication of first algebra book in English. The first English study of algebra is written by English mathematician Robert Recorde (c. 1510–1558). In his book, *The Whetstone of Witte*, he uses the modern symbol for equality (=) for the first time. He states that he selected this symbol because "no two things could be more equal than two parallel lines."

1585 · Practical use of decimal fractions is demonstrated. The first comprehensive system of decimal fractions and their systematic, practical applications is published by Belgian-Dutch mathematician and engineer Simon Stevin (1548–c. 1620) in his *La Thiende* (The tenth). A decimal fraction is another way of expressing a number that is less than one (.1 instead of the fraction 1/10). While in no way the inventor of decimal fractions, Stevin is certainly the first systematic user of them, and it becomes his goal to explain their base-ten advantages so they will be more popularly adopted. It is his wish to teach everyone "how to perform with an ease, unheard of, all computations necessary between men by integers without fractions."

1591 · Introduction of systematic algebraic notation. The first systematic algebraic notation is introduced by Franciscus Vieta (1540–1603), a French mathematician also known as François Viète. Algebra solves problems in arithmetic by using letters or symbols to stand for quantities, and Vieta's book, *Isagoge in artem analyticum* (Introduction to the analytic art), founds modern algebra. Vieta introduces the practice of using letters as symbols (vowels to represent unknown quantities and consonants to represent known ones), and thereby contributes to the development of symbolic algebra. His book is the first that would be recognized by a modern-day student as a book on algebra. Vieta himself does not use the term algebra but prefers the term "analysis," and as a result, analysis comes to mean the use of algebraic methods to solve problems.

1594 · Creation of logarithms. Scottish mathematician John Napier (1550–1617) first conceives of the notion of obtaining exponential expressions for various numbers, and begins work on the complicated formulas for what he eventually calls "logarithms." Napier uses the distinction between arithmetic and geometric progression, and it occurs to him that a number can be expressed in exponential form. That is, 4 can be written as 2 to the second power (2^2, or 2 times 2), and 8 can be 2 to the third power (2^3, or 2 times 2 times 2). Written in this manner, multiplication is reduced to addition or subtraction of only the exponents. Napier works for the next twenty years to create tables for the exponential expression of various numbers. **(See also 1614)**

John Napier, Scottish mathematican and discoverer of logarithms.

c. 1600 · Mathematician surveys New World.

The first noted mathematician to set foot in the New World is Thomas Harriot (1560–1621), an English mathematician and astronomer. He is sent as a surveyor by his patron, Walter Raleigh (1554–1618), to the colony in Virginia in 1585. After returning to England, Harriot introduces the mathematical symbols for "greater than" (>) and "less than" (<). It is his adoption and regular use of English mathematician Robert Recorde's (c. 1510–1558) equal sign (=) that leads to its ultimate acceptance.

1614 · Publication of logarithm tables.

The first tables of logarithms are published by Scottish mathematician John Napier (1550–1617), in his *Mirifici Logarithmorum Canonis Descriptio* (Description of the marvelous rule of logarithms). As the originator (see 1594) of the concept of logarithms as a mathematical device to aid in calculations, Napier initially calls them "artificial numbers," but later coins the term "logarithm," meaning "number of the ratio." His tables, which simplify routine calculations and reduce multiplication to simple addition or subtraction, quickly become a powerful tool in computations, especially so for astronomy. Most agree with the famous saying that the invention of logarithms, "by shortening the labors, doubled the life of the astronomer." Altogether, logarithms are a revolutionary tool for mathematicians.

1637 · Descartes publishes study of geometry.

French mathematician and philosopher Rene Descartes (1596–1650) publishes his *Discours de la méthode* (Discourse on the method), which contains a 106-page essay titled "La Geometrie" (Geometry). In this essay, he founds analytic geometry by combining algebra and geometry and showing how geometric forms may be systematically studied using algebra. His new method can solve problems much more easily than either one could separately. This application of algebra to geometry paves the way for the eventual development in 1669 of calculus by English scientist and mathematician Isaac Newton (1642–1727). Among Descartes's other mathematical contributions, he is the first to use the letters near the beginning of the alphabet for constants and those near the end for variables. It is because of Descartes that we use x's and y's in today's algebra. He also introduces the use of a symbol for the square root sign ($\sqrt{}$).

1656 ▪ First use of infinity symbol (∞).
The first to use ∞ as the symbol for infinity is John Wallis (1616–1703), an English mathematician. Considered one of the first to write a serious history of mathematics, Wallis is one of the most influential mathematicians of his time, and his work is a precursor to calculus.

1657 ▪ Study of probability.
The first formal study on the mathematical treatment of probability is written by Dutch physicist and astronomer Christiaan Huygens (1629–1695). Probability is the degree of chance that something might happen. Huygens's short work, *De ratiociniis in ludo aleae* (On reasoning in games of dice), introduces the important concept of "mathematical expectation," or as he calls it, "the value (price) of the chance" to win a game. The first full-length treatment of the theory of probability is the posthumously published *Ars conjectandi* (The art of conjecturing) by the Swiss mathematician Jakob Bernoulli (1654–1705) in 1713. **(See also 1921 and 1944)**

Rene Descartes, founder of analytic geometry.

1662 ▪ Applying mathematics to vital statistics.
The first to apply mathematics to vital statistics (statistics relating to births, deaths, marriages, health, and disease) is John Graunt (1620–1674), an English statistician, in his *Natural and Political Observations ... Made Upon the Bills of Mortality*. He obtains his information from the weekly and yearly statistics published in the Bills of Mortality, which totals the number of burials and other related information in several London parishes. Reducing fifty-seven years of statistics (1604–1661) to a series of tables, he notes that more male

babies are born than female, and that women live longer than men. Graunt also concludes that thirty-six out of every one hundred people die by the age of six and that hardly anyone lives to be seventy-five. As the first to establish life expectancy and to publish a table of demographic (population) data, he is considered the founder of vital statistics. In 1693 English astronomer Edmond Halley (1656–1742) compiles the first set of detailed mortality tables of the sort currently used in the insurance business, making possible the statistical study of life and death.

1669 ▪ Newton writes about calculus. The first systematic account of the discovery of calculus is contained in a paper written this year by English scientist and mathematician Isaac Newton (1642–1727), but not published. Calculus is the use of algebraic symbols to calculate changing quantities. By Newton's time, mathematicians were attempting to solve increasingly complex algebraic problems involving changing quantities of motion, mass, and energy with little success. Newton's calculus gives them a new tool capable of revealing simple patterns in complex and subtle natural phenomena. Calculus proves to be an indispensable scientific tool without which it would have been impossible to understand the behavior of gravity, the motion of the planets, or such forces as light, electricity, and magnetism. In 1684 German mathematician and philosopher Gottfried Wilhelm Leibniz (1646–1716) publishes an account of his own discovery of calculus. He discovers it independently later than Newton's discovery, but Newton does not publish his own account until after Leibniz.

1706 ▪ The symbol for pi is first used. The first use of the sixteenth letter of the Greek alphabet π (pi) as the symbol for the ratio of a circle's circumference (the distance completely around it) to its diameter (the distance across its middle) is made by English mathematician William Jones in his *Synopsis palmariorum matheseos* (A new introduction to the mathematics). In this book for beginners, Jones gives the circumference-to-diameter ratio to one hundred decimal places, all correct. It is not until the famous Swiss mathematician Leonhard Euler (1707–1783) uses this symbol in 1737 that it becomes generally adopted. It is thought that this letter is chosen because it is the first letter of the Greek word for perimeter, *perimetros*. **(See also 250 b.c.)**

1719 ▪ Arithmetic comes to the colonies. The first arithmetic printed in the American colonies is James Hodder's *Arithmetick; or that Necessary Art Made Easy* published in Boston. It was originally published in London in 1661. The first arithmetic written by someone born in America is the *Arithmetick* by Isaac Greenwood (1701–1745), published in 1729 in Boston.

1765 · Proving the number for pi is irrational. The first to prove that the number for pi (π) is irrational is German mathematician Johann Heinrich Lambert (1728–1777). This means that it is not expressible as an integer (whole number) nor as the quotient of two integers (the product of dividing two numbers). Pi is the symbol for the ratio of a circle's circumference (the distance completely around it) to its diameter (the distance across its middle).

1799 · Projective geometry. Gaspard Monge (1746–1818), a French mathematician, publishes his *Géométrie descriptive* (Descriptive geometry). This work revolutionizes engineering design. A skilled draftsman at only sixteen, Monge develops his own method of applying geometry to construction problems. He displays his skills and new method by working out the proper locations of gun placements for a proposed fort. Usually, such an operation could be performed only by a lengthy, time-consuming process. Monge's new geometrical method works so well and so quickly, that it is classified a military secret until 1795. In 1822 French mathematician Jean-Victor Poncelet (1788–1867) publishes his *Traité des propriétés projectives des figures* (Treatise on the projective properties of figures) and becomes the first mathematician of stature to argue for the development of projective geometry as a separate branch of mathematics.

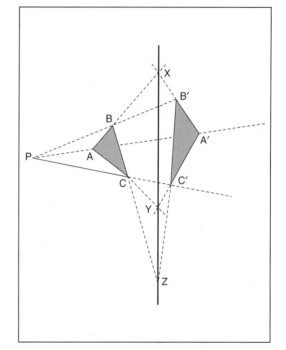

With projective geometry, pictured here, the principles of geometry can be applied to construction problems.

1801 · Gauss publishes classic work on mathematics. German mathematician Johann Karl Friedrich Gauss (1777–1855) publishes his *Disquisitiones arithmeticae* (Arithmetical investigations), which is one of the great classics of mathematical literature. In this major work, Gauss brings together algebraic, arithmetic, and geometric ideas and makes original contributions to nearly all areas of mathematics. This difficult work is considered to be one of the most brilliant achievements in the history of mathematics, and Gauss is quickly recognized as the greatest mathematician of his time. Eventually, history places him alongside Greek mathematician and engineer Archimedes (c. 287–212 B.C.) and English scientist and mathematician Isaac Newton (1642–1727), as the greatest mathematicians of all time.

February 1829 · Lobachevsky's discovery of non-Euclidean geometry. Non-Euclidean geometry is discovered by Russian mathematician Nikolay Ivanovich Lobachevsky (1792–1856). This system includes the seemingly impossible concept that any number of lines can be drawn parallel to a given line through a given point. Euclid's well-known parallel axiom stated that through any given point, one and only one line can be drawn, infinitely and in both directions, that is parallel to a given straight line. Lobachevsky finds that by denying this axiom, the results show no contradictions but rather are as self-consistent as Euclid's. Lobachevsky's conclusion that there can be other geometries as valid as Euclid's goes against two thousand years of mathematical thinking and leads to the modern notion that pure mathematics need not be true or false in the same sense as physics, but need only be self-consistent. At about this same time, Hungarian mathematician János Bolyai (1802–1860) is making the same, independent discovery as Lobachevsky. **(See also 1832)**

May 1829 · Creation of group theory in algebra. Group theory or the study of groups in algebra is created by Évariste Galois (1811–1832), a French mathematician. Despite repeated attempts to get his short paper on his discovery published, he is unable to do so. He then becomes involved in radical French politics and is killed in a duel. His papers are finally published with annotations in 1846 by French mathematician Joseph Liouville (1809–1882). Galois's genius is eventually recognized, and his structural and unifying concepts are remembered by the use of "Galois group," "Galois field," and "Galois theory"—all of which become an integral and accepted part of mathematics.

1832 · Bolyai's discovery of non-Euclidean geometry. Publication of the independent discovery of non-Euclidean geometry is made by Hungarian mathematician János Bolyai (1802–1860). This discovery of a self-consistent mathematical system that includes the concept that an indefinite number of lines can be drawn in a plane parallel to a given line through a given point, may have been made by Bolyai as early as 1823. Priority, however, goes to Russian mathematician Nikolay Ivanovich Lobachevsky (1792–1856), who published the theory first in 1829. Bolyai publishes his discovery this year in a twenty-six-page appendix to his father's semiphilosophical book on elementary mathematics. Bolyai's work is totally independent of Lobachevsky's, and when Bolyai finally sees the Russian's work, he thinks it has been copied from his own. **(See also February 1829)**

1854 ▪ Founding of symbolic logic. Symbolic logic is founded by English mathematician and logician George Boole (1815–1864). In his highly significant book, *An Investigation of the Laws of Thought*, Boole establishes what is now called symbolic logic by devising a system that applies algebra to logic (thus converting logic into mathematical symbols). He selects logical axioms (self-evident principles) and then chooses symbols and operations similar to algebraic notation (in which letters represent things) to express those logical forms and to perform operations. Boole's algebra of logic, or Boolean algebra, eventually proves basic to the design of computers.

1899 ▪ Geometry gets set of axioms. The first book to contain a really satisfactory set of axioms (self-evident principles) for geometry is *Grundlagen der Geometrie* (Foundations of geometry) written by German mathematician David Hilbert (1862–1943). Since Euclid's geometry is not rigorous in that it simply assumes many things to be so or to be obvious, Hilbert sets out to give it a logical foundation and to make it self-consistent. In doing this, he defines it in terms that do not require a human interpretation to give it form, and thus shifts the foundation of geometry from intuition to logic. His book also founds the formalist school whose thesis is that mathematics is concerned with formal symbolic systems.

1907 ▪ Introduction of four-dimensional, space-time form of geometry. A four-dimensional, space-time form of geometry is first introduced by Russian-German mathematician Hermann Minkowski (1864–1909) who publishes his *Raum und Zeit* (Space and time) this year. In this work he demonstrates that German-Swiss-American physicist Albert Einstein's (1879–1955) new special relativity theory makes it necessary to take time into account as a kind of fourth dimension (treated mathematically somewhat differently from the three spatial dimensions of length, breadth, and height). Minkowski argues that neither space nor time exists separately, and since everything moves in time as well as space, the universe consists of a fused "space-time continuum." His work provides Einstein with the mathematical basis for his later general theory of relativity.

1921 ▪ Theory of games is developed. The first to define games of strategy and to develop a game theory is French mathematician Félix-Édouard-émile Borel (1871–1956). Game theory is a branch of mathematics concerned mainly with probability (the degree of chance that something might happen). Borel initiates the modern mathematical theory of games by closely analyzing several familiar games. **(See also 1944)**

1931 · Presentation of Gödel's theorem. Gödel's theorem is first propounded by Austrian-American mathematician Kurt Gödel (1906–1978). This year he submits a paper whose "incompleteness theorem" startles the mathematical world. Also called Gödel's proof, it states that all formal systems (based on axioms or self-evident principles) result in inconsistent mathematical statements that cannot be decided upon by using the rules that govern that particular formal system. In other words, proving something in a mathematical system by basing the proof on that system's own preexisting rules or conditions is something of a setup, and real proof should come from somewhere outside that system. This means that one has to go "outside" those formal rules to resolve certain problems of any axiom-based mathematics. Gödel's discovery has great impact by showing that the search for absolute certainty in mathematics cannot and does not exist.

The probability of rolling snake eyes (two ones) with a pair of dice is 1 in 36.

1944 · Game theory—new mathematics branch. A new branch of mathematics called "game theory" is founded by Hungarian-American mathematician John von Neumann (1903–1957). He argues that mathematics that was developed for physical science is inadequate for economics, which involves human action based on choice and chance. He proposes a different mathematical approach more suitable for the social sciences and provides an analysis of strategies that take into account the interdependent choices of two or more "players." Game theory involves probability (the degree of chance that something might happen) and is best used for complex decision-making processes. **(See also 1921)**

c. 1960 · Introduction of new math in American schools. "New math" is first introduced into the curriculum of American public schools. In comparison with traditional mathematics instruction, this new method

Solving Fermat's Last Theorem

In 1626 French lawyer and number theorist Pierre Fermat scrawled a general math equation in the margin of a book along with a bold statement declaring that the equation $X^2 + Y^2 = Z^2$ can never be true when the exponent is greater than two. He provided no proof of this theorem. The theorem concerns an equation similar to the famous Pythagorean theorem that states that the square of the longest side of a triangle equals the sum of the squares of the other two sides ($a^2 + b^2 = c^2$). For example, 3 squared (9) plus 4 squared (16) equals 5 squared (25). Fermat's theorem states that although the numbers to be squared can change, if the exponent is any other number than 2, the equation will not be true.

In 1954 Japanese mathematician Yutaka Taniyama offered a solution to Fermat's theorem, making use of elliptical curves. His proposal was called the Taniyama conjecture. In the 1980s a German mathematician, Gerhard Frey, suggested that an elliptical curve can be used to represent all the solutions to Fermat's equation. In 1986 American Kenneth Ribet proved Frey's idea. Princeton math professor Andrew J. Wiles studied the problem for several years and in 1993 announced that he had proven the Taniyama conjecture. He added that this meant that Fermat's Last Theorem was also proven true. His work is undergoing review by other mathematicians—if upheld, a centuries-old problem will be considered solved.

places greater emphasis on mastering mathematical concepts and theories, and less on practicing computation skills.

1961 · Discovery of chaotic behavior in mathematical system.

American meteorologist Edward Norton Lorenz (1917–) discovers the first mathematical system containing chaotic behavior. Chaos is a branch of science that studies very complex systems whose behavior seems random and unpredictable. Working on large-scale atmospheric circulation and statistical approaches to weather prediction, Lorenz finds chaotic behavior in a computer model of how the atmosphere behaves. This work gets the attention of others and leads eventually to an entirely new branch of mathematics, chaotic dynamics. The mathematical equations used in this field are inherently nonlinear, or so complex that they cannot be computed, predicted, or sometimes even defined. **(See also 1975)**

1974 ▪ Computer calculates pi to one million places. The value of pi is calculated to one million places for the first time by a CDC 7600 computer. Pi (π) is the symbol for the ratio of a circle's circumference (the distance completely around it) to its diameter (the distance across its middle).

1975 ▪ Fractals make first appearance. Fractals are first suggested by Polish mathematician Benoit Mandelbrot (1924–) in his book *Les Objets fractals* (Fractal objects). Based on his conversations with geologists, meteorologists, and cartographers, he develops fractal mathematics. This subject deals with geometric shapes that are self-similar or identical and have a similar appearance at any level of magnification. A new field of mathematics, it is based on the study of the irregularities in nature. It becomes useful in the field of statistical physics by helping to analyze complex, random-seeming events. There are strong links between the dimensionality of fractal shapes (the same shape keeps reappearing no matter how closely it is examined) and chaotic motions that contribute later to a new branch of physics called chaos theory. **(See also 1961)**

1976 ▪ Four-color conjecture is resolved. Kenneth I. Appel (1932–), an American mathematician, and Wolfgang Haken, a German-American mathematician, resolve the century-old Four-Color Conjecture first posed in the 1852 by English mathematician Francis Guthrie. This conjecture poses the question: can every map drawn on a plane be colored with four colors so that adjacent (bordering) regions receive different colors? Using a new combination of computer methods and theoretical reasoning, Appel and Haken prove for the first time that the four-color conjecture is true. Their proof requires over two thousand hours of computer time and contains several hundred pages of complex detail.

June 1993 ▪ Proving Fermat's last theorem. Proof of Fermat's last theorem is first obtained by English-American mathematician Andrew John Wiles (1953–). Wiles produces a two hundred-page paper that is the result of his seven-year attack on this 325-year-old algebraic problem that had been declared unsolvable by generations of mathematicians. Wiles dreamed of solving Fermat's last theorem since he encountered it in a book when he was ten.

Medicine

c. 2900 B.C. ▪ Invention of the principles of yin and yang. Chinese Emperor Fu-Hsi (the first of China's mythical emperors) invents the principles of yin and yang that become the basis of ancient Chinese medicine. These two opposite but complementary forces or principles are believed to be part of all aspects of life. In the area of medicine, it is believed that health is found in the perfect equilibrium between these two principles that continually ebb and flow.

c. 2700 B.C. ▪ Acupuncture is invented. Acupuncture is invented by the Chinese Emperor Shen-Nung (the second of China's mythical emperors) who also writes the *Pen-Tsao Kang Mu* (Great pharmacopeia), considered the first medical herbal text. Acupuncture involves the insertion of metal needles into the skin and tissues. This ancient medical technique for relieving pain and restoring health is practiced in many parts of the world today. The ancient Chinese believed that the needles penetrated one or more of the twelve canals in the body called *chin*, which are channels for the body's vital principles. Acupuncture is supposed to stimulate or slow these principles and therefore put the body back into balance.

c. 500 B.C. ▪ First dissection of the human body. The first recorded dissection of the human body for research purposes is conducted by Greek physician Alcmaeon. Around 300 B.C., Herophilus (c. 335–c. 280 B.C.), a Greek anatomist often called the father of scientific anatomy (structure), is the first to study systematically the anatomy of the brain and spinal cord and differentiates between nerves and blood vessels. To him we owe the clear statement that the brain is the central organ of the nervous system and the site of intelligence.

A bust of Galen, Greek physician and founder of experimental physiology.

c. 400 B.C. ▪ Hippocrates becomes known as the "father of medicine". Greek physician Hippocrates (c. 460–c. 370 B.C.) establishes medicine as a science based on reason, observation, and a code of conduct and becomes known as the "father of medicine." He teaches that the physician should interfere as little as possible with the natural healing process. He also provides the first detailed description of tuberculosis (also called phthisis, from the Greek meaning to decay and waste away), a communicable disease.

c. A.D. 75 ▪ First book of medical drugs. Dioscorides (c. 40–c. 90 B.C.), a Greek physician, writes the first systematic pharmacopoeia (book of medical drugs). His *De materia medica* (On medicinal substances) provides accurate botanical and pharmacological information. As a physician to the Roman legions, he is able to collect plants from a wide area of the ancient world. His herbal writings name and describe each plant, telling where it comes from, any special features it might have, and discusses the maladies or symptoms for which it is useful. His work is preserved by the Arabs, and when translated into Latin and printed in 1478 in the West, becomes a standard botanical reference.

169 ▪ Importance of the pulse in diagnosis. One of the first to understand the value of the pulse as a diagnostic technique is Galen (129–c. 199), Greek physician to the Roman emperor Marcus Aurelius (121–180). Galen founds experimental physiology (the study of processes or how things work), and much of his knowledge is gained from dissecting Barbary apes. His writings are medical gospel for more than fourteen centuries and his reputation is rivaled only by that of Greek physician Hippocrates (c. 460–c. 370 B.C.). **(See also c. 400 B.C.)**

c. 400 · First hospital in Western Europe. Fabiola (St. Fabiola), a Christian noblewoman, founds the first *nosocomium* or hospital in Western Europe. After establishing this hospital in Rome, she founds a hospice for pilgrims in Porto, Italy. About this time, Christianity was becoming more popular, and its practitioners placed great emphasis on helping the sick, eventually making it an ethical and religious duty upon the individual and the community.

430 · Earliest recorded European plague. The earliest recorded plague in Europe is an epidemic that breaks out in Athens, Greece. For the next thousand years, plagues come and go, and it is not until 1374 that the Republic of Ragusa (on the eastern shore of the Adriatic Sea) places the first quarantine on crews of ships thought to be infected. The authorities detain a suspected ship's crew for one month before allowing them to enter the city. Called a *trentina* for its thirty days' worth of detention, it

An illustration of a doctor treating a plague victim.

eventually becomes stretched to the more common forty days. This leads to the now-familiar name based on *quaranta giorna* or *quarantina*. Unable to cure the afflicted or affect the course of this fast-spreading epidemic, the authorities considered prevention their only weapon.

896 ▪ Measles and small pox are studied. Rhazes (c. 865–c. 930), a

Persian physician and alchemist (chemist), distinguishes between the specific characteristics of measles and smallpox and gives the first accurate description of both. He is also believed to be the first to classify all substances into the great classification of animal, vegetable, and mineral. This simple but powerful classifying device was accepted and continues to today.

1010 ▪ First independent medical school —School of Salerno. The School of Salerno flourishes in Italy. Begun around the start of the ninth century as the first independent medical school, it reaches its greatest influence at this time and preserves its fame to the end of the fourteenth century. This medical school in southern Italy grants the first medical diplomas and becomes a place to which students from Europe, Asia, and northern Africa flock. The founding of this school indicates a break with the confused medicine of medieval times in that it studies diseases in a straightforward, common-sense manner and uses rational therapy.

A woodcut of Italian anatomist Mondina de'Luzzi directing a dissection.

1302 ▪ First recorded autopsy. The first formally recorded postmortem or judicial autopsy is performed in Bologna, Italy, by Italian physician Bartolomeo da Varignana. This postmortem is ordered by the court to decide a case of suspected poisoning. Dissection of a human corpse was a sensitive subject at this time, and official authorization was usually required before an autopsy could be performed for teaching purposes or to discover the exact cause of a suspicious death.

1507 ▪ Benivieni founds pathological anatomy. Italian physician Antonio Benivieni (c. 1440–1502) founds pathological anatomy with the posthumous (occurring after death) publication of his book that explains how the dissection of cadavers (dead bodies) can be used to study the internal causes of disease and to determine the cause of death. In 1556 Guillaume Rondelet (1507–1566), a French naturalist and physician, builds the first anatomy amphitheater in Montpelier, France. This facility allows the observing students to surround the dissecting instructor and view the dissection from above.

1543 ▪ First accurate book on human anatomy. Belgian anatomist Andreas Vesalius (1514–1564) publishes his *De humani corporis fabrica* (On the structure of the human body), the first accurate book on human anatomy. Its illustrations are of the highest level of both realism and art, and the result is a true masterpiece that ranks as one of the greatest medical works ever written. His work was a landmark work since it broke totally with the past and discarded the traditions based on the writings of the Greek physician Galen (129–c. 199; see 169). Because of this, Vesalius met with resistance most of his life.

1558 ▪ First experiments with living animals. Italian anatomist Matteo Realdo Colombo (1516–1559) is the first to use living animals (dogs) in laboratory experiments (especially to study the function of the heart and lungs). With this, he demonstrates that blood passes from the lung into the pulmonary vein. This is known as the lesser or pulmonary circulation.

1597 ▪ Early plastic surgery. Gaspare Tagliacozzi (1545–1599), an Italian surgeon, performs rhinoplasty or plastic surgery of the nose. Although rhinoplasty was known to the ancient Hindus, Tagliacozzi practices this surgery based on solid anatomical knowledge and writes the first book about it. He also performed other surgical repairs of the face.

c. 1600 ▪ First practical obstetrical forceps. The invention of the first practical obstetrical (associated with childbirth) forceps occurs sometime during this period and is credited to a member of the Chamberlen family. This tool, which consists of two metal blades joined together at the handle like tongs, is used to deliver a baby in difficult births. It is known to have been suggested by Pierre Franco of France in 1561, and it is believed that William Chamberlen (c. 1540–1596) took the secret of its design with him when he fled to England from France in 1576. Both of his sons were named Peter, and one of them (1572–1626) is most often credited with the invention. This family of doctors kept the forceps a closely guarded secret for more than a century.

1628 · Harvey accurately describes human circulatory system.

The first accurate description of the human circulatory system is offered by English physician William Harvey (1578–1657) in his landmark work, *Exercitatio Anatomica de Motu Cordis et Sanguinis Animalibus* (Anatomical exercise on the motion of the heart and the blood in animals). While a medical student in Italy, Harvey had learned that arteries and veins have one-way valves, and he puts this knowledge to use to demonstrate conclusively that blood does not go back and forth as the ancients thought but rather circulates in a one-way system. Harvey also viewed the heart as a pump that was the motive force behind the blood's circulation.

1628 · Blood transfusion is described.

The first printed description of blood transfusion is published by Italian physician Giovanni Colle (1558–1630). Although earlier writers made vague references to blood transfusions, its history really begins after English physician William Harvey's (1578–1657) discovery that blood circulates around the body in a closed system. Later transfusions from animal to man are seldom successful, and transfusions are eventually banned for a time by the authorities. **(See also February 1665)**

1642 · Treatment of malaria with cinchona bark.

The first study on the use of cinchona bark (quinine powder) for treating malaria (an infectious disease) is written by Spanish physician Pedro Barba (1608–1671). This processed bark was brought to Europe from Peru in 1632 by Jesuit priests, and the use of the antimalaria drug had a revolutionary effect on old-style medicine. The treatment of malaria with quinine marks the first successful use of a chemical compound in combating an infectious disease. In 1820 Pierre-Joseph Pelletier (1788–1842) and Joseph-Bienaimé Caventou (1795–1877), both French chemists, first isolate quinine, the active substance in cinchona bark. It is not until 1944, however, that complete laboratory synthesis of quinine is achieved.

1648 · First European textbook on physiology.

French philosopher and mathematician René Descartes (1596–1650) writes the first European textbook on physiology (the study of living processes). He considers the body to be a machine and, reducing all physiology to physics, he treats movement, respiration, and digestion as mechanical processes. Every organ has a mechanical counterpart: bone and muscle actions are explained by levers; teeth are similar to scissors; the chest is like a bellows; and the stomach is like a flask.

February 1665 ▪ Blood transfusions from one animal to another. The first direct transfusion of blood from one animal to another is accomplished by English physician Richard Lower (1631–1691), who experiments with dogs. Two years later he transfuses the blood of a lamb into a man. These experiments are eventually banned. In 1666 Jean-Baptiste Denis (1643– 1704), physician to French King Louis XIV (1638–1715), is the first to lose a patient following a blood transfusion. After transfusing the blood from a lamb into a human subject, Denis finds that his patient improves temporarily but then dies. Denis is later arrested and the French Chamber of Deputies soon bans such transfusions.

March 21, 1668 ▪ First successful intravenous injection on a human. The first successful intravenous injection on a human is made by the German physician Johann Daniel Major (1634–1693). At nearly the same time, another German doctor, Johann Sigmund Elsholtz (1623–1688), has the same success. In 1656 English architect and scientist Christopher Wren (1632–1723) injected opium, wine, ale, and other substances into the veins

The first illustration of an amputation.

of a dog. The significance of this experiment is not the substance injected but the fact that Wren was able to devise a method of tapping a vein and pumping a liquid into it.

1674 ▪ Invention of the tourniquet. A tourniquet to stop hemorrhages (heavy losses of blood from a wound) is invented by the French surgeon Morel at the siege of Besançon, France. This early version of the word is originally applied to the handle or stick that is turned to tighten a bandage that in turn applies pressure over a large artery to stop blood flow. Morel also calls it a "garrote" or strangler. In 1718 the screw tourniquet is invented by French surgeon Jean-Louis Petit (1674–1750). Until this device, there was no method during major amputations of controlling the bleeding. Petit's screw tourniquet is fixed to the lower abdomen and puts direct pressure on the main artery, controlling massive bleeding and making amputations on the battlefield practical.

1700 · First systematic treatment of occupational diseases. Italian physician Bernardino Ramazzini (1633–1714) publishes the first systematic treatment of occupational diseases. His book, *De morbis artificum diatriba* (On the diseases of tradesmen), opens up an entirely new department of modern medicine. Ramazzini's treatment includes ailments and hazards that plagued writers, doctors, hunters, and farmers as well as miners, potters, painters, and stone cutters. Further, he distinguished between the hazards of their particular environment (such as coal dust to miners) and the hazards of physical participation (such as writer's cramp or the round shoulders of the cobbler). Ramazzini also recognized the toxic effects of certain activities, noting the damage incurred to goldsmiths and physicians by their exposure to mercury and to potters and painters by lead. He advised that a physician should always ask his patient before doing anything else, "What is your work?"

1726 · Blood pressure is quantitatively estimated. The first quantitative estimate of blood pressure is made by English botanist and chemist Stephen Hales (1677–1761). Having studied the hydrostatics (the pressure and equilibrium of liquids) of sap movement in plants, Hales turns to the animal world and inserts a glass tube in the femoral (thigh) artery of a horse. This is the first manometer (an instrument for measuring the pressure of a gas or liquid). Also called a tonometer, this device allows Hales to make quantitative estimates of blood pressure, the capacity of the heart, and the speed of the circulating blood.

1753 · Research on the disease scurvy. James Lind (1716–1794), a Scottish physician, publishes his *Treatise of the Scurvy*, in which he details his experiments with twelve sailors suffering from the disease scurvy. He puts them all on the same basic diet but then gives each one a separate, controlled item to consume. After six days, only the man who ate oranges and limes was well enough to return to work. Scurvy, a vitamin-deficiency disease, had killed more sailors on long voyages than did battle with the enemy, but was finally eliminated in the British Navy some years after Lind's book. The Navy's practice of giving lime juice to their crews resulted in British sailors being called "limeys."

1761 ▪ Percussion method for diagnosing diseases of the chest. Austrian physician Leopold Auenbrugger von Auenbrugg (1722–1809) first describes his percussion method, which becomes a major contribution to the diagnosis and prognosis of diseases of the chest. Ever since, doctors use his thumping-on-the-chest method to diagnose the condition of a patient's chest.

1771 ▪ John Hunter advances the field of dental anatomy. English surgeon John Hunter (1728–1793) publishes his important work on dental anatomy and disease, *Natural History of the Human Teeth,* in which he first uses the terms "cuspid," "bicuspid," and "incisor." "Cuspid" or canine tooth, comes from the Latin *cuspis,* meaning a point. Teeth with two cusps are naturally called bicuspids. "Incisor" comes from the Latin *incidere,* to cut into, and this tooth is the cutting tooth in front of the canine teeth.

1793 ▪ Beginnings of psychiatry. The founder of psychiatry, French physician Philippe Pinel (1745–1826), is placed in charge of the Bicetre insane asylum in Paris, France, and pioneers the humane treatment of its inmates. He frees them from being chained and initiates systematic study of their maladies. He dismisses the popular belief that mental illness derives from demonic possession, and is the first to maintain well-documented case histories of mental ailments. In 1812 Benjamin Rush (1745–1813), an American physician, publishes his *Medical Inquiries and Observations Upon the Diseases of the Mind,* which is the first American treatise on psychiatry.

May 14, 1796 ▪ First smallpox vaccination. The first vaccination against smallpox is successfully carried out by English physician Edward Jenner (1749–1823). He inoculates a boy, James Phipps, with cowpox to protect him from the more severe disease smallpox. Jenner knew that people who worked with cows had no fear of catching smallpox if they had contracted cowpox earlier. Jenner tests this by giving the Phipps boy a case of the cowpox, which indeed proves to protect him against smallpox for the rest of his life. When the British royal family allows itself to be vaccinated, the entire population accepts it. Although Jenner has no idea why vaccination works, his efforts lay the groundwork for the first defeat of a major disease.

February 28, 1818 ▪ Invention of the stethoscope. René-Théophile-Hyacinthe Laënnec (1781–1826), a French physician, announces his invention of the stethoscope and develops the method of diagnosis by auscultation (listening to sounds within the body). Until Laennec, physicians would place their ear directly on a patient's chest to listen to the heart and lungs. Laënnec found this old method to be not only ineffective but "inconvenient and indelicate," so he rolled several pieces of paper into a tube and placed one end on a patient's chest with his ear at the other. Called "mediate auscultation," this method let him hear a heartbeat with greater clarity and distinction. Although initially resisted by the medical community, Laënnec's invention eventually revolutionizes diagnostic medicine.

June 6, 1822 · Human digestion is studied. The first accurate account of human digestion begins when a young French-Canadian named Alexis St. Martin is accidentally shot in the chest and upper abdomen. Treated by an American surgeon, William Beaumont (1785–1853), St. Mar-

Edward Jenner administers the first vaccination.

tin survives but has his stomach heal by attaching itself to the chest wall, resulting in a fistula or an abnormal, permanent opening or channel. This allows Beaumont actually to see into a working stomach and he takes advantage of this unique opportunity to study digestion firsthand. In 1833 Beaumont publishes his *Experiments and Observations on the Gastric Juice and the Physiology of Digestion*, which is based on more than two hundred experiments he conducts with St. Martin. By analyzing gastric (stomach) juices and suspending foods into the stomach via silk threads, he concludes that the stomach acts upon food chemically and that the basic ingredient of gastric juice is hydrochloric acid.

1825 ▪ First successful tracheotomy. Pierre-Fidèle Bretonneau (1778–1862), a French physician, performs the first successful tracheotomy for croup. This emergency cut made into the larynx allows a child whose windpipe has swollen shut to breathe. Bretonneau had previously performed this procedure successfully on animals, and he inserts a small, silver tube in a child's throat to save his life. Tracheotomy becomes a standard life-saving procedure for patients in severe respiratory distress, and is used today.

1826 ▪ First detailed study of diphtheria. Diphtheria, a serious bacterial disease of the respiratory system and a major killer of children, is first named by French physician Pierre-Fidèle Bretonneau (1778–1862). As the first to study closely its symptoms, Bretonneau names it by using the Greek word for parchment to describe the yellow-gray mucous membranes that form in the throat of the infected. The disease produces toxins that are carried throughout the body, and it ravages the very young in Europe and the United States.

1832 ▪ Codeine is discovered. Codeine is discovered by French chemist Pierre-Jean Robiquet (1780–1840). The isolation of morphine from opium in 1805 showed the way to obtain new drugs from the older, crude drugs. Codeine is an alkaloid (a naturally occurring constituent) also present in opium, and Robiquet's discovery shows it to be a derivative of morphine. It is used initially as a sedative and for reducing irritation of the respiratory passages, and goes into production this same year. Today it is often used in combination with aspirin or acetaminophen to relieve pain and as a cough suppressant. It is addictive but not as addictive as morphine.

March 30, 1842 ▪ First surgical use of anesthesia. The first recorded use of anesthesia in surgery is accomplished by American physician Crawford Long (1815–1878). After experimenting on himself earlier this year, Long removes a tumor from the neck of a patient who is rendered unconscious by ether. Long conducts at least eight other such operations with ether during the next few years but does not publish any account of it until 1849. By then, others had already received credit for being the first. **(See also October 16, 1846)**

1844 · Nitrous oxide makes debut as anesthetic in dentistry.

American dentist Horace Wells (1815–1848) is the first to use nitrous oxide as an anesthetic in dentistry. Wells shared a dental practice with William Thomas Green Morton (1819–1868), both of whom became familiar with the pain-killing properties of nitrous oxide, also called "laughing gas." Later, after Morton's successful demonstration of ether anesthesia during surgery in October 1846, Wells became bitter and began to self-experiment with several other chemicals. Eventually he became unstable, was jailed for throwing acid, and eventually killed himself in jail (at the same time that the Paris Medical Society was hailing him as the discoverer of anesthetic gases). **(See also October 16, 1846)**

October 16, 1846 · Anesthesia becomes essential in surgery.

Ether is used as an anesthetic in a surgical operation in Boston. American dentist William Thomas Green Morton (1819–1868) persuades renowned American surgeon John Collins Warren (1778–1856) to give the new drug a trial procedure, and Warren successfully removes a small tumor from the jaw of an anesthetized patient at Massachusetts General Hospital. The success of this painless operation makes anesthesia essential to the operating room. No longer would surgeons have to contend with a squirming, shrieking patient nor would a patient have to undergo the torture of being cut open while awake. **(See also 1844)**

November 4, 1847 · Chloroform anesthesia in childbirth is introduced.

James Young Simpson (1811–1870), a Scottish obstetrician, introduces the use of chloroform anesthesia in both labor and delivery. Despite this success, many patients and physicians refuse to believe that a woman should be relieved of the pains of childbirth, and Simpson wages a vigorous campaign to persuade them otherwise. The use of chloroform in delivery by English Queen Victoria (1819–1901) in 1853 signaled to the world that anesthesia, and especially chloroform, was acceptable and safe during childbirth.

1847 · Method to prevent childbed fever is introduced. The first method to prevent childbed fever is introduced by Hungarian physician Ignaz Phillipp Semmelweis (1818–1865). He is intrigued by the obvious fact that women who have their babies at home seldom contract puerperal sepsis or childbed fever, while those who deliver in a hospital attended by a physician were at very high risk and often died despite a normal birth.

Semmelweis then witnesses the death of a colleague who contracts blood poisoning from a minor scalpel wound he receives during an autopsy, and theorizes that doctors who go directly to their patients after examining dead bodies are responsible for transferring infectious matter from one patient to another. He then establishes procedures in his ward requiring all patients, students, and professors of obstetrics (the branch of medicine dealing with pregnancy and childbirth) to thoroughly wash their hands and disinfect them with a chlorinated lime solution. The death rate in his wards drops dramatically.

1849 · First American woman to receive a medical degree. The first woman to receive a medical degree in the United States is Elizabeth Blackwell (1821–1910). She graduates with highest honors this year from Geneva

Elizabeth Blackwell, the first woman in the United States to receive a medical degree.

Medical College (now a part of Syracuse University) in New York. Although she becomes the first female medical doctor in America, she encounters the same prejudice after graduation that she experienced while applying to medical school (having applied to twenty-nine schools before being accepted). In May 1849 she attends La Maternité in Paris, France, but is allowed to study only as a midwife and not as a doctor. While there, she contracts ophthalmia from a sick baby and loses her left eye. After studying in London, England, she returns to New York but is ostracized by the male medical profession and is unable to obtain a hospital position. In 1853 she opens a dispensary in a New York slum and eventually establishes a hospital of her own. The New York Infirmary for Women and Children initially begins training nurses and eventually becomes a three-year medical college in 1864. In 1869 Blackwell returns to London and founds the London School for Women.

1849 · Theories about cholera are offered. John Snow (1813–1858), an English physician, first states the theory that cholera is a water-borne disease and that it is usually contracted by drinking contaminated water. Cholera is an often fatal disease characterized by massive diarrhea, vomiting, and rapid and severe depletion of body fluids and salts. Snow's concept of the spread of cholera remains valid, although the disease's invisible agents are not identified for decades.

1851 · Ophthalmoscope revolutionizes eye treatment. Hermann von Helmholtz (1821–1894), a German physiologist and physicist, perfects the first ophthalmoscope. This new instrument, which allows the physician to see into the eye and examine the retina for disease, transforms ophthalmology into an exact science of the eye. His invention works by using a series of glass plates that serve as mirrors or reflectors to shine a beam of light into the eye, and the operator peers through a magnifying lens attached to the mirror. **(See also 1855: Iridectomy is introduced)**

1853 · Hypodermic syringe is invented. French physician Charles Gabriel Pravaz (1791–1853) publishes his description of a hypodermic syringe. This will open up an entirely new field for the administration of drugs. The key to the effectiveness of his invention is a hollow needle, which is then connected to a syringe and inserted under or into the skin.

March 1854 · Nightingale founds modern nursing. The modern nursing practice is founded by the work of English nurse Florence Nightingale (1820–1910), who organizes care for the sick and wounded during the Crimean War. (The Crimean War [1854–56] was fought in the Crimean Peninsula of the Black Sea with Britain and France on one side and Russia on the other.) In 1860, through dedication and hard work, Nightingale goes on to create a female nursing service and a nursing school at St. Thomas's Hospital in London, England. Her compassion and common-sense approach to nursing sets new standards and helps create a new era in the history of caring for the sick and wounded of wartime.

1855 · Invention of first modern laryngoscope. The first modern laryngoscope is invented by the Spanish singing teacher Manuel Patricio Rodríguez García (1805–1906), who devises this new instrument to examine the throats of his students. García begins by studying his own larynx with a dental mirror, and after much research, builds his new instrument. The device becomes a permanent part of laryngology (the branch of medicine that deals with the larynx, which is the upper part of the trachea that contains the vocal cords) within three years. Because of this instrument the medical specialty of laryngology is born.

1855 ▪ Iridectomy is introduced. Albrecht von Graefe (1828–1870), a German surgeon, introduces the operation of iridectomy (surgical removal of part of the iris) in the treatment of the eye diseases iritis, iridochoroiditis, and glaucoma. As the creator of modern surgery on the eye and one of the greatest of all eye surgeons, Graefe's eye clinic becomes world famous and his students include nearly all the best ophthalmologists of the nineteenth century. As the founder of modern ophthalmology, Graefe also develops a surgical treatment for cataract (a clouding of the lens of the eye) by extraction of the lens. He becomes the first to use the ophthalmoscope invented by German physiologist and physicist Hermann von Helmholtz (1821–1894). **(See also 1851)**

1858 ▪ Psychology as an experimental science. The first serious, written treatment of psychology (the study of the mind) as an experimental science is begun by German psychologist Wilhelm Max Wundt (1832–1920), who publishes *Beiträge zur Theorie der Sinneswahrnehmung* (Contributions to the theory of sense perception). In 1862 he teaches the first university course ever given in scientific or experimental psychology, and in 1879 he founds the first institute of psychology (at the University of Leipzig) and establishes a laboratory devoted entirely to experimental psychology.

1859 ▪ Cocaine is prepared for first time. Albert Niemann (1806–1877) of Germany first prepares cocaine by isolating the active principle of *Erythroxylon coca* known since ancient times as the "divine plant of the Incas." Peruvian natives had for centuries chewed on the leaves of this plant for its stimulating and exhilarating effects. After studying the white powder and noting its numbing effect on his tongue, he names it cocaine. For several decades, cocaine is used by the medical community as a pain reliever and a stimulant, and its addictive properties go unrecognized or unmentioned. Today it is used only occasionally for certain types of procedures, with the bulk of it being made and purchased illegally.

1860 ▪ Polio is described by Heine. Jakob von Heine (1800–1879), a German orthopedist, first describes "infantile spinal paralysis" which becomes known as poliomyelitis (polio for short). For many years it is known as "Heine-Medin's disease" after Heine and the Swedish pediatri-

The Development of
Schools of Psychology, 1805–1910

Sigmund Freud.

The Western scientific discipline of psychology is less than 150 years old and began in Germany in the mid-nineteenth century when scientists began to measure and analyze perception and sensation. Many schools of psychology then arose with different leanings as to what is involved in a scientific study of the human mind. Three of these schools are defined below.

Structuralism Founded in 1879 by German physiologist Wilhelm Wundt. The stucturalist school separated human thought into its most simple processes—perception, sensation, emotion, and association—and studied these systematically.

Behaviorism Founded in 1913 by American psychologist John B. Watson. Behaviorists believe that all behavior can be explained as response to stimuli in the environment and that the environment shapes behavior in a manner that works like reward and punishment. Behaviorists believe that observable, measurable behavior should be the focus of psychological study.

Pyschoanalysis Founded in the late nineteenth century by Austrian physician Sigmund Freud. Both a theory of personality and a treatment for psychologically ill patients, psychoanalysis works on the theory that the unconscious mind is one of the prime motivators of behavior—that behavior is determined by thoughts, wishes, and memories of which we are unaware. Psycholanalytic treatment often consists of bringing what is in the unconscious into awareness.

cian Oskar Medin (1847–1927), who describes it many years later. Polio is an acute infectious viral disease characterized by mild to severe paralysis of voluntary muscles. In 1894 the first major polio epidemic in the United States breaks out. In 1916 twenty-seven thousand Americans develop polio, nearly seven thousand of whom die. **(See also 1954: Polio vaccine is developed)**

1861 ▪ First localization of a brain function. The first localization of a brain function is achieved by French surgeon and anthropologist Pierre-Paul Broca (1824–1880). Through autopsies he demonstrates that damage to a certain spot on the cerebrum of the brain (the third convolution of the left frontal lobe) is associated with the loss of the ability to speak, called aphasia. This is the first clear-cut demonstration of a connection between a specific ability and a specific cerebral point of control.

1863 ▪ Discovery of barbituric acid. Barbituric acid is discovered by German chemist Johann Friedrich Wilhelm Adolf von Baeyer (1835–1917). In his extensive investigations of the derivatives of uric acid, he finds what turns out to be the parent of all the barbiturate drugs (sedatives and hypnotics). It is believed that Baeyer names this compound after a friend named Barbara.

April 9, 1864 ▪ Pasteur's proof of the germ theory. Before a meeting at the Sorbonne in Paris, France, French chemist Louis Pasteur (1822–1895) announces his proof of the germ theory. Having demonstrated earlier that lactic acid fermentation is due to a living organism, Pasteur turned to the study of how microscopic life arises. Many of his famous colleagues supported the traditional view of spontaneous generation that posited that living organisms (microbes or germs) could originate from nonliving matter. In 1860 Pasteur devised an experiment that would prove his theory that dust in the air included spores of living organisms, and that it was these that multiplied when they settled on a proper medium. He boiled meat extract and left it exposed to the air in a long, narrow neck flask that bent down and then up. This allowed air into the flask, but dust particles would settle at the bottom curve of the neck and not get in. When the meat did not decay and no organisms developed, Pasteur had proven the truth of the germ theory and disproved spontaneous generation once and for all.

August 12, 1865 ▪ Lister combats infection using an antiseptic procedure. The first antiseptic procedure to combat infection is used by

English surgeon Joseph Lister (1827–1912). After years of study and investigation, Lister concludes that infection is caused by something outside a wound that gets in it. This is contrary to the then-held belief that the pus that formed in wounds was a necessary part of the healing process. After learning of Pasteur's discovery that microorganisms cause the death of body tissues, he decides to find a way to kill bacteria in wounds as well as to keep it out. Lister then experiments with carbolic acid (phenol), which he eventually dilutes, and on this date he uses a spray of carbolic acid during surgery on a compound fracture to prevent infection. Two years later he publishes his paper telling of his success, and lays the groundwork for antisepsis—the critical procedure that prevents the growth and multiplication of bacteria.

1868 ▪ Relationship of temperature to disease. German physician Carl Reinhold August Wunderlich (1815–1877) publishes his major work on the relation of animal heat or fever to disease. He is the first to recognize that fever is not itself a disease but is rather a symptom. He insists on accurate records of a patient's fever, and his writing forms the basis of modern clinical thermometry (the measurement of patients' temperatures). Wunderlich was led to make careful observations of temperature in relation to disease by physicists' mathematical studies of heat.

1876 ▪ Anthrax is studied. Anthrax, a baffling disease deadly to animals and people since Biblical times, is first understood by German bacteriologist Robert Koch (1843–1910). By comparing the blood of animals dead from anthrax with that of healthy animals, he finds distinguishing rod-shaped bodies present only in the infected blood. He then discovers how to cultivate the anthrax bacteria outside the animal's body and consequently is able to study it at length and follow its entire life cycle. He finds that it forms spores that are resistant to outside influences, even heat or cold, and can remain suspended for a long period. Once the mystery of anthrax is solved by Koch, it becomes only a matter of time until the great French chemist Louis Pasteur (1822–1895) discovers a vaccine to defeat it.

1876 ▪ First practical blood-pressure measuring device. The first practical device to measure blood pressure is invented by Czech physician Samuel Siegfried Carl von Basch (1837–1905). It is also the first sphygmomanometer to determine blood pressure without cutting into an artery. The instrument consists of a small capsule, the bottom of which is formed by a rubber diaphragm. The cavity of the capsule is connected to a manometer (pressure gauge) by a rubber tube. To use it, Basch presses the diaphragm on the artery until the pulse stops, and the reading on the manometer at this point indicates arterial pressure. There is a very wide margin of error, however. It is replaced eventually by a much improved and more accurate device. **(See also 1896)**

1877 · Aerobic and anaerobic bacteria are first distinguished. French chemist Louis Pasteur (1822–1895) first distinguishes between aerobic and anaerobic bacteria and introduces the concepts of aerobism and anaerobism to science. An aerobe is an organism (such as certain yeasts) able to live and reproduce only in the presence of oxygen. Organisms that can live without oxygen are called anaerobic. This discovery comes from Pasteur's study of the nature of fermentation, specifically of beer and lactic acid. He finds that lactic-acid bacilli and butyric-acid bacilli not only can live without oxygen but flourish in an atmosphere of carbon dioxide.

1878 · Cause of traumatic infectious disease. German bacteriologist Robert Koch (1843–1910) publishes his landmark findings on the etiology or cause of traumatic infectious disease. It is these findings that establish the rules for properly identifying the causative agent of a disease. Koch states that the microorganism must be located in a diseased animal, and that after the microorganism is cultured or grown, it must then be capable of causing disease in a healthy animal. Finally, the newly infected animal must yield the same bacteria as those found in the original animal. Using his rules and techniques, he goes on to isolate the specific bacteria of a number of diseases, the most famous being tuberculosis.

1880 · Cause of malaria is discovered. The cause of malaria is discovered by French physician and bacteriologist Charles-Louis-Alphonse Laveran (1845–1922). He finds that it is not a bacterium as thought, but a parasitic protozoan that infects human blood. This is the first case in which a protozoan, or a one-celled animal, is shown to be the cause of a disease.

1881 · Modern era of surgery begins. The modern era of surgery begins as Austrian surgeon Christian Albert Theodor Billroth (1829–1894) removes a cancerous pylorus (the opening from the stomach into the intestine). He then successfully links the stomach directly to the duodenum at the upper end of the small intestine. Billroth achieves an operation that had been heretofore regarded as unthinkable, and intestinal surgery will soon become commonplace.

1881 · American Red Cross is founded. Clara Barton (1821–1912) of the United States first organizes the American Red Cross in Washington, D.C. (The Red Cross is an international humanitarian agency that provides medical and other relief for victims of war and other disasters.) Known as the "angel of the battlefield" for her service during the American Civil War (1861-65) and the Franco-Prussian War (1870-71), she brings the International Red Cross to the United States.

1881 · Steam sterilization is introduced. Steam sterilization is first introduced by the German physician Merke, who discovers the killing effect of steam on pathogenic microorganisms (disease-causing germs). His discovery is immediately taken up by the German bacteriologist Robert Koch (1843–1910), and soon becomes a standard method of assuring the cleanliness of medical instruments and proper laboratory techniques.

1882 · Bacteria that causes TB is first isolated. The tiny tubercle bacterium that causes tuberculosis (TB), *Mycobacterium tuberculosis*, is first isolated by German bacteriologist Robert Koch (1843–1910). Until this discovery, there was no certainty as to how or whether TB actually spread or if it was hereditary. Koch was able to identify the difficult-to-find bacterium by using methylene blue dye (the bacterium would not respond when stained by any standard dyes). Once he identified the bacterium, Koch was able to prove that TB was indeed caused by a germ that could be carried in the air and passed from one person to another. Although Koch does not discover a successful vaccine for TB, he does develop a simple skin test to determine if a person is infected. **(See also 1907 and 1944)**

1884 · Discovery of tetanus bacterium. Tetanus bacterium is discovered and first described by German physician and bacteriologist Arthur Nicolaier (1862–1942). A serious infectious disease that causes severe contraction of the muscles, tetanus is caused by a bacterium called *Clostridium tetani* that lives in soil and enters the bloodstream through breaks in the skin, especially deep puncture wounds. Tetanus can be fatal if not treated.

1884 · Phagocytosis in animals is discovered. Phagocytosis in animals is discovered by Russian-French physiologist Élie Metchnikoff (1845–1916). In this phenomenon, amoeba-like cells engulf foreign bodies such as bacteria and act as the first line of defense against acute infection. Metchnikoff names them phagocytes from the Greek words meaning "devouring cells." In humans, these phagocytes are known as leukocytes or white corpuscles. Metchnikoff's work offers what becomes a fundamental tenet of the science of immunology (the study of the immune system).

1885 · First use of rabies vaccine. The first use of a successful vaccine for rabies is made by French chemist Louis Pasteur (1822–1895). Although not a common disease in the nineteenth century, rabies was a fatal, viral disease with no cure, and its victims died a horrible death after much suffering. It was known that saliva from the bite of an infected animal could transmit the disease to humans. Pasteur was able to make a weakened germ by passing it through different species of animals until its strength had lessened. Hesitant to try his vaccine on humans, Pasteur had his mind changed by a badly mauled boy named Joseph Meister. Pasteur gave his vaccine to a doctor to administer to the boy (Pasteur was not a physician and had no license to practice). The boy received twelve inoculations over several days and eventually recovered. In 1940 when the Nazis occupied Paris, Meister was a gatekeeper at the Pasteur Institute, and when ordered by the Germans to open Pasteur's crypt, he killed himself rather than dishonor the man who saved his life.

1886 · Appendicitis and its symptoms are described. Reginald Heber Fitz (1843–1913), an American surgeon, first describes the symptoms and clinical features of appendicitis. He details how a physician can diagnose the condition and prescribes when an operation is required. After correlating his bedside observations with his extensive autopsy findings, he shows that what had been called "inflammation of the bowel" was usually a severe infection (peritonitis) that followed a ruptured (or burst) appendix.

1887 · Electrical activity of the human heart is recorded. French physiologist Augustus Desire Waller (1856–1922) first records the electrical activity of the human heart and lays the foundation for future electrocardiography. While using electrical methods to study emotional states, he discovers that the heart's electric currents or regular beat can be recorded by connecting electrodes placed on the surface of the body with a capillary electrometer. This is essentially the first electrocardiogram. **(See also 1903)**

1890 · Sterile rubber gloves are introduced into the operating room. American surgeon William Stewart Halsted (1852–1922) introduces the use of sterile rubber gloves into the operating room. As an early convert to antiseptic ideas, he introduces antiseptic procedures into American operating rooms. (Antiseptic procedures prevent the growth of possibly harmful microorganisms.) Halsted's use of very thin rubber gloves that allow the surgeon to retain his delicate touch is a major innovation toward the goal of totally sterile (free from microorganisms) operating conditions.

December 28, 1895 • Discovery of X rays. German physicist Wilhelm Konrad Röntgen (1845–1923) first communicates his discovery of X rays in his paper, "über eine neue Art von Strahlen." This discovery not only heralds the age of modern physics but revolutionizes medicine as well, and one of the earliest applications of X rays is in medical diagnosis and therapy. Physicians realized almost immediately that with this new tool their diagnostic powers had taken a quantum leap. They could now detect bone fractures and see foreign objects in the body as well as dental cavities and diseased conditions such as cancer. Therapeutically, they would also use X rays to stop the spread of malignant growths.

1896 • Mercury sphygmomanometer is invented. The mercury sphygmomanometer—the precursor of the modern blood-pressure instrument—is invented by Italian physician Scipione Riva-Rocci (1863–1903). His device uses an armband that is inflated until the blood flow through the arteries is no longer detected. Air is then released from the band, and when the pulse reappears, the pressure is measured on a mercury manometer (pressure gauge). This device proves accurate but limited, since it only measures systolic pressure (pressure within the artery when the heart is contracting or working). The later use of a stethoscope to listen to both the sound of maximum (systolic) and minimum (diastolic) pressure (pressure within the artery when the heart is at rest between contractions) is suggested by Russian physician Nikolai Korotkoff.

1899 • Aspirin is introduced. Aspirin, or acetylsalicylic acid, is introduced on the market by the German pharmaceutical firm Färbenfabriken Bayer. This mild analgesic (pain reliever) relieves headache and muscle and joint aches. It also reduces fever and reduces swelling associated with arthritis. Its blood-thinning properties make it useful for many heart patients. It is available without a prescription and is probably the most widely used of drugs.

1900 • Human blood types are discovered. The different types of human blood are discovered by Austrian-American physician, Karl Landsteiner (1868–1943). He finds that there are different blood groups, which differ in their capacity to agglutinate or clump together. By 1902 Landsteiner has clearly divided human blood into four main groups that he names A, B, AB, and O. Once this is done, it becomes a simple task to show that in certain combinations transfusions would work, while in others, the red cells would clot and possibly have fatal results. With the ability to blood-type both patient and donor, blood transfusions become safe.

1900 ▪ Founding of orthodontics. The first specialized course on orthodontics (dentistry that deals with teeth irregularities and their correction with mechanical aids) is offered by American orthodontist Edward Hartley Angle (1855–1930). Considered to be the founder of the modern practice of orthodontics, he devises the first simple and logical classification system for malocclusions (teeth coming together improperly) and pioneers the movement against the routine extraction (pulling) of permanent teeth. Angle founds the first school and college of orthodontia, organizes the American Society of Orthodontia in 1901, and founds the first orthodontic journal in 1907.

1901 ▪ Yellow fever is studied. American military surgeon Walter Reed (1851–1902) proves that yellow fever, the sometimes fatal infectious disease of tropical and subtropical areas, is transmitted by a mosquito and is preventable. Reed had carefully studied the disease, which killed more American soldiers in Cuba during the Spanish-American War in 1898 than had Spanish guns, and believed that it was not transmitted by bodily contact or by clothing or bedding but rather by mosquitos. To prove this, he runs a controlled experiment using volunteers who live under the same conditions except that one group is protected from mosquitos. The unprotected group contract the disease while the protected group remains healthy. When a campaign to locate and destroy the breeding sites of the *Aedes* mosquito is conducted, the disease all but vanishes from Havana, Cuba.

1903 ▪ Invention of the string galvanometer. Willem Einthoven (1860–1927), a Dutch physiologist, invents the string galvanometer from which the electrocardiograph is derived. Knowing that the healthy heart works with a regular rhythm that can be sensed electrically, he guesses that a departure from that normal electric rhythm might indicate when something is wrong. He then builds a string galvanometer (an instrument for detecting small electric currents) as a diagnostic tool consisting of a delicate conducting thread stretched across a magnetic field. A current

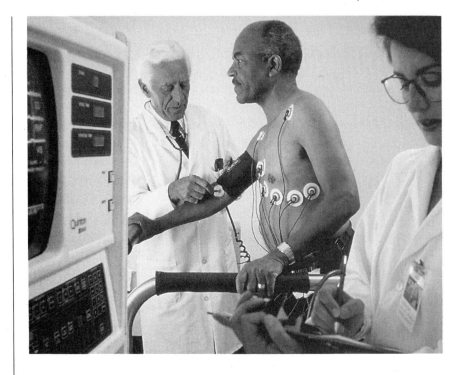

In modern electrocardiogram testing, sensors attached to the patient relay information about the heart's activity to the computer display.

flowing through the thread causes it to move at right angles to the magnetic lines of force, with the distance it moves equal to the strength of the current. His device is sensitive enough to record graphically the varying electrical potential of the heart's contracting muscles. He coins the term "electrocardiogram" to describe this process.

1904 ▪ Novocaine developed as anesthesia. Novocaine is first developed as a safe substitute in local anesthesia. Also known as procaine hydrochloride or simply procaine, it is a synthetic organic chemical generally used in a 1 to 10 percent saline solution and administered by injection. Unlike cocaine, it is not toxic, addictive, or irritating. It is used today primarily as a dental anesthesia.

1905 ▪ Discovery of syphilis bacterium. The bacterium responsible for syphilis is discovered by German zoologist Fritz Richard Schaudinn (1871–1906) and German dermatologist Erich Hoffmann. They discover the organism to be *Spirochaeta pallida*, later called *Treponema pallidum*, and contribute significantly to the control of this sexually transmitted disease. In 1906 the first diagnostic blood test for syphilis is introduced by German bacteriologist August von Wasserman (1866–1925). He develops a test for the antibody produced by persons infected with *Spirochaeta pallida*, and the "Wasserman test" soon becomes a standard procedure.

1907 • Skin reaction test for TB. The first cutaneous or skin reaction test for the diagnosis of tuberculosis (TB) is introduced by Clemens Peter von Pirquet (1874–1929), an Austrian physician. His diagnostic TB test consists of scratching a small area of skin and introducing a drop of tuberculin and watching for a reddened reaction. Pirquet also is the first to suggest the word "allergy" to denote hypersensitivity or a capacity for reaction to some substance.

1909 • Transmission of typhus fever. Charles-Jean-Henri Nicolle (1866–1936), a French bacteriologist, shows that typhus fever is transmitted by the body louse. He is intrigued by the fact that while typhus is easily contracted outside of a hospital, after patients are hospitalized they are found to be no longer contagious. He suspects body lice as carriers when he realizes that patients are stripped and scrubbed when admitted. His experiments prove him correct.

1910 • Chemical treatment for syphilis. The first effective chemical treatment for syphilis is discovered by German bacteriologist Paul Ehrlich (1854–1915) and Japanese bacteriologist Sukehachiro Hata (1873–1938). When Hata finds that an arsenic-based compound appears to kill spirochetes, the microorganism that causes syphilis, the two scientists continue testing and find that the drug attacks the syphilis germs but does not harm healthy cells. Ehrlich names the new drug "Salvarsan," using the Latin words for "preserve" and "health," and it is later known as arsphenamine. Modern chemotherapy (the use of chemicals in treating diseases) begins with Ehrlich and Salvarsan.

1918 • First blood and serum banks. The first blood and serum banks are established in Europe during World War I (1914–18). Austrian-American physician Karl Landsteiner's (1868–1943) discovery of the human blood groups made blood transfusions safe and practical (see 1900: Human blood types are discovered), and the massive numbers of casualties caused by this long war makes transfusions a necessity. Many lives are saved because of these blood banks.

1921 • Discovery and isolation of insulin. The discovery and isolation of the hormone insulin is achieved by Canadian physician Frederick

Grant Banting (1891–1941), Canadian physiologist Charles Herbert Best (1899–1978), Scottish-American physiologist John James Rickard Macleod (1876–1935), and Canadian biochemist James Bertram Collip (1892–1965). They develop a method of extracting insulin from an animal pancreas and then injecting it into the blood of diabetics to lower their blood sugar. (Diabetics have the disease diabetes and cannot process sugar properly.)

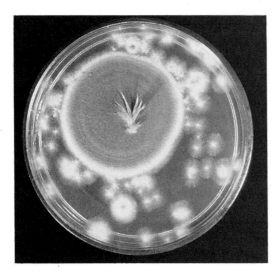

A penicillin culture.

1927 • Measles serum is introduced.

American scientist Ruth Tunnicliff (1876–1946) first introduces a serum to be used against measles. Also called rubeola, measles is an infectious disease caused by a virus and primarily infects children. A red rash on the face, neck, trunk, hands, and feet accompanies a high fever, headache, and cough. Despite Tunnicliff's efforts, an effective live-virus vaccine is not developed until after the 1954 isolation of the measles virus. **(See also 1954: Development of measles vaccine)**

1928 • Invention of the Pap test.

Greek-American physician George Nicholas Papanicolaou (1883–1962) invents the Pap test, a simple and painless smear procedure for the early detection of cervical and uterine cancer. After making a microscopic study of vaginal discharge cells in pigs, he conducts human studies and observes cell abnormalities in a woman with cervical cancer. This leads him to develop a method of detecting cancer cells through cytology or microscopic cell examination. By 1943 his method wins wide acceptance because it allows for detection of cancer in an early stage when the disease can best be treated.

September 1928 • Penicillin is discovered.

The first of the wonder drugs, penicillin, is discovered by Scottish bacteriologist Alexander Fleming (1881–1955). While searching for a safe antibacterial substance, Fleming grows staphylococcus cultures in petri dishes that he accidentally leaves uncovered overnight. When he returns next day, he notices that a spore of mold has entered the culture and grown on it. His scientist's eye, however, also notices that dead and dying staphylococcus microbes lie in a ring around the mold. He then isolates the mold and identifies it as one called *Penicillium notatum,* closely related to what grows on stale bread.

He also finds that as the mold grew, it produced some type of substance that destroyed bacteria. He calls this substance penicillin. When he tries to isolate and identify this substance, however, Fleming meets with no success. Since he is unable to obtain much help in his search, his discovery of what is the first antibiotic goes unexploited until his colleague, Australian-English pathologist Howard Walter Florey (1898–1968), at Oxford's School of Pathology takes up Fleming's cause and isolates penicillin ten years later. **(See also 1938)**

1935 · External pump as an artificial heart. American surgeon John Heysham Gibbon Jr. (1903–1974) demonstrates for the first time that life can be maintained by an external pump acting as an artificial heart. During his research on a heart-lung machine, he finds that roller pumps are gentle enough to minimize both clotting and damage to blood cells. He also learns that centrifugal force can be used to spread the blood in a layer thin enough to absorb the required amounts of oxygen. He accomplishes this during surgery on a dog, laying the groundwork for future work on humans. **(See also July 3, 1952)**

1935 · First lobotomy is performed. António Caetano de Abreu Freire Egas Moniz (1874–1955), a Portuguese surgeon, performs the first lobotomy. Also called a leukotomy, this operation cuts into the skull and severs the nerve fibers connecting the patient's thalamus with the frontal lobes of the brain. This procedure opens an entirely new field called psychosurgery in which mental disturbances are treated by means of brain surgery. This surgery is applied to patients showing chronic mental conditions that result in severe distress, depression, or aggressiveness, as well as to relieve pain caused by an incurable illness. It is usually employed as a last resort and eventually is done away with once tranquilizers and other mind-affecting drugs are discovered.

1936 · Reichstein isolates cortisone. Cortisone is first isolated by Tadeus Reichstein (1897–1996), a Polish-Swiss chemist. During his work on hormones of the brain's adrenal cortex, he describes and names "substance F." This proves identical with a substance found by American biochemist Edward Calvin Kendall (1886–1972), who at the same time isolates nine related steroid hormones from adrenal cortical extracts, one of which is later named cortisone. Cortisone is found to have anti-inflammatory properties, and by 1948 is used in the treatment of rheumatoid arthritis. Continued research has limited some of its major side effects, and it

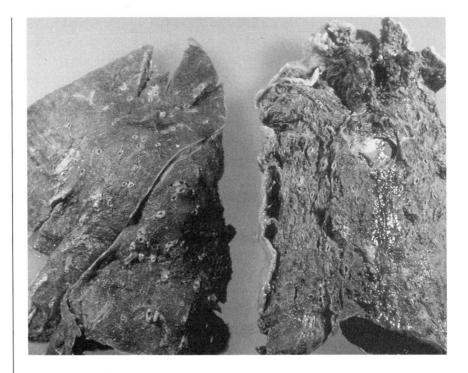

A normal healthy lung (left) and the lung of a cigarette smoker (right).

becomes an important drug to organ transplantation by helping to prevent rejection.

1937 · Discovery of antihistamines. Antihistamines are discovered by Swiss-French-Italian pharmacologist Daniele Bovet (1907–1992). Histamines in the body are the cause of allergic reactions, and Bovet searches for a natural counteragent to them. Finding that none exists, he investigates structurally similar compounds and identifies what neutralizes them. This research pays off and he synthesizes the first antihistamine, thymoxydiethylamine. This proves too toxic for humans, and in 1944 he succeeds with an antihistamine (pyrilamine) that effectively reduces allergic reactions. This work lays the basis for the safe, effective synthesis of antihistamines.

1937 · Lung cancer from smoking is described. Lung cancer in cigarette smokers is first described by American surgeons Alton Ochsner (1896–1981) and Michael Ellis DeBakey (1908–), who suggest that smoking causes cancer. At this point in time, smoking is already a worldwide phenomenon. Despite increasingly strong social, religious, and medical arguments, the use of tobacco creates a major American industry. By the

1980s, however, cigarette smoking is associated with not only lung cancer but also coronary artery disease, chronic bronchitis, lip cancer, and emphysema. By the 1990s the connection to lung cancer is absolute, and it is demonstrated that nicotine and related alkaloid substances supply the narcotic effects of smoking and make it addictive. During these years, the U.S. federal government bans smoking from its buildings and facilities, and all life insurance companies have separate and much higher rates for individuals who jeopardize their health by smoking.

1938 ▪ Penicillin is isolated and purified. Howard Walter Florey (1898–1968), an Australian-English pathologist, and Ernst Boris Chain (1906–1979), a German-English biochemist, isolate and purify penicillin, originally discovered by Scottish bacteriologist Alexander Fleming (1881–1955) in 1928. While searching for antibacterial substances, they obtain a culture of Fleming's original mold and are able to extract and purify the penicillin. Tests on animals reveal that it is nontoxic as well as an effective antibiotic. Subsequent trials with humans are so successful that the United States sponsors an efficient method of mass-producing penicillin to treat wounded soldiers during World War II (1939–45). Penicillin proves to be a true miracle drug, and is the most powerful of the antibiotics—being used to treat syphilis, meningitis, and pneumonia. **(See also September 1928 and February 1, 1941)**

February 1, 1941 ▪ First use of penicillin to treat a human. Penicillin is first given to a human to treat a condition. An American policeman with an advanced staphylococcus infection complicated by streptococcus is given penicillin for five days. Despite his desperate condition, the infection is temporarily arrested and his condition improves. He soon dies, however, when his doctors run out of the new drug and cannot make more fast enough. It becomes clear that given in massive doses, penicillin can deal with the most difficult infection, but also that it must be administered until the disease is eliminated.

1941 ▪ Anticoagulant drug dicumarol. The anticoagulant drug dicumarol is first identified and synthesized by American biochemists Mark Arnold Stahmann, Karl Paul Link, and C. F. Huebner. During the 1920s a cattle disorder was discovered in which livestock that had eaten hay from spoiled sweet clover bled to death. During the 1930s it was found that a substance in the clover reduced the activity of prothrombin, a clotting factor in the blood. Once this clotting factor was isolated, the American team was able to synthesize it as dicumarol. The availability to medicine of this and other anticoagulants allows them to be used to keep blood transfusions from clotting, to treat conditions involving dangerous blood clots, such as cerebral thrombosis and coronary heart disease, and during surgical operations on heart valves.

1944 ▪ Discovery of streptomycin. Streptomycin, the first antibiotic effective against tuberculosis (TB), is discovered by Russian-American microbiologist Selman Abraham Waksman (1888–1973). Until Waksman discovered this important antibiotic, the only treatment for TB was prolonged bed rest and nutritious food. The drug proves so safe and effective that it nearly eliminates the disease in the United States. Streptomycin is found to be active against seventy different bacteria that did not respond to penicillin, including infections of the abdomen, urinary tract, pelvis, and meninges (membranes that cover the brain and spinal cord).

1945 ▪ Invention of kidney dialysis machine. The kidney dialysis machine is invented by the Dutch-American surgeon Willem Johan Kolff (1911–). His artificial kidney machine keeps patients with kidney failure alive by filtering out urea from their blood. Kolff's machine diverts blood from an artery, usually the wrist, and brings it into contact with one side of a membrane. As this happens, dissolved substances in the blood, such as urea and inorganic salts, pass through into a sterile solution on the other side. The blood's red and white cells, as well as its platelets and proteins, cannot penetrate the membrane because they are too large. Dialysis is soon improved using ultrafiltration, and becomes a common procedure for patients with temporary or chronic kidney failure. Today, it buys time for those awaiting a transplant organ.

1950 ▪ Terramycin is discovered. A. C. Finlay and microbiologist Gladys Lounsbury Hobby (1910–1993) of the United States discover the antibiotic drug oxytetracycline, later given the trade name Terramycin. Unlike penicillin, an antibiotic developed from a mold, the family of which Terramycin is a part (which also includes erythromycin and aureomycin) is developed from bacteria. The tetracycline group of antibiotics are broad-spectrum drugs that can have side effects and are used more carefully than the penicillin groups.

1950 ▪ Kidney transplantation a temporary success. The first human to survive a kidney transplantation is Ruth Tucker, a forty-nine-

Historic cardiac pacemaker fueled by radioactive plutionium 238.

year-old American woman dying from chronic uremia. American surgeon Richard Lawler of Chicago transplants a kidney from a cadaver (dead body) into his patient who survives for a short time. Lawler finds, upon autopsy, that the new liver has not only stopped functioning but has turned into a shriveled mass of dead tissue. This is the result of immunological rejection in which the body's white cells attack and destroy a graft of "foreign" tissue. **(See also December 23, 1954)**

1951 ▪ First successful oral contraceptive. The first successful oral contraceptive drug is introduced. American biologist Gregory Pincus (1903–1967) collaborates with American biologist Min-Chueh Chang (1909–1991) and American physician John Rock (1890–1984), and employs a synthetic hormone that renders a woman infertile without altering her capacity for sexual pleasure. They use a synthetic progesterone called progestin and find that it suppresses ovulation (the release of an egg from the ovary). Clinical trials begin in 1954, and in 1960 the U.S. Food and Drug Administration approves progestin as an oral contraceptive. It soon is marketed in pill form and effects a social revolution because it can remove from the sex act the possible consequences of pregnancy.

377

1952 · First practical cardiac pacemaker. American cardiologist Paul M. Zoll introduces the first practical cardiac pacemaker. Zoll theorizes that he can use the heart's natural responsiveness to electrical stimulation to treat cases of heart block (when the cardiac muscle responsible for sending impulses to the heart suddenly stops). He develops an external pacemaker that sends an electric shock to the heart through electrodes placed on the patient's chest. Although correct in principle, his early pacemaker requires that both the patient and the device be close to an electrical outlet. The shocks are also painful to the patient's chest muscles. Pacemakers eventually become practical with the invention of the transistor which allows the pacemakers to be so reduced in size as to be implantable by 1970. Today's pacemakers adjust themselves to the patient's exercise level and have microprocessors that are even reprogrammable using radiofrequency signals.

July 3, 1952 · First mechanical heart pump. The first mechanical heart pump is used successfully on a human being undergoing heart surgery. Designed by American surgeon Forest D. Dodrill with help from General Motors engineers, the portable electric pump performs the heart's functions while it is undergoing surgical repair. It takes two years of work to design and build a pump that is durable and dependable yet gentle, since blood is very fragile and easily destroyed. This breakthrough marks the beginning of today's increasingly sophisticated cardiac bypasses, valve repairs, and even transplants.

1952 · Pioneering use of electric shock treatment for heart attacks. American cardiologist Paul M. Zoll develops the technique of external heart stimulation by electric shock in cases of cardiac arrest. During some heart attacks, a condition occurs in which various muscle groups in the heart beat independently and without any rhythm, meaning they pump no blood despite their rapid quivering. This is called fibrillation, a usually fatal condition. In 1956 Zoll introduces the external defibrillator, a device that provides an external electrical impulse to the chest and shocks the muscles back into uniform, rhythmic beating.

September 1952 · First artificial heart valve. Charles Anthony Hufnagel, an American surgeon, inserts the first artificial heart valve. Heart valves are tissue flaps inside the heart that open only one way and allow blood to flow from one chamber to another and then close to prevent any blood from leaking back. Valve disease or failure can cause stress on the

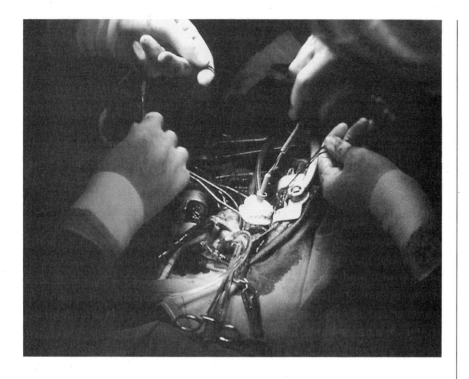

Open heart surgery to replace the mitral heart valve. The replacement valve is made from tissue of a porcupine pericardium. The tubes carrying blood are connected to a heart-lung machine.

heart and result in eventual cardiac failure. The only effective treatment in these cases is valve replacement. Hufnagel's breakthrough invention to prevent backflow is a tube-and-float device inserted in a patient's descending aorta.

February 1952 ▪ Bevis develops amniocentesis process. Douglas Bevis, an English physician, publishes an article describing his use of amniocentesis in Rh-factor cases. This process uses a needle to obtain samples of amniotic fluid (in which the fetus floats) from a mother's womb. Bevis chemically analyzes the iron and urobilinogen content of the fluid to determine whether the unborn child has this blood disease. After Bevis shows the feasibility of diagnosing by amniocentesis, others improve it and can determine the sex of the fetus as well as know whether a fetus is affected by Down's syndrome. Today, hundreds of hereditary diseases can now be diagnosed through amniocentesis.

May 6, 1953 ▪ First open-heart surgery. The first successful open-heart operation using a heart-lung machine is conducted by American surgeon John Heysham Gibbon Jr. (1903–1974). Gibbon spends years develop-

The polio virus

Polio is an acute infectious viral disease that invades the body through the mouth, targets the neurons of the spinal cord and brain and destroys them, often resulting in muscle paralysis or death. In 1894 the first major polio epidemic in the United States broke out. In 1916 twenty-seven thousand Americans developed polio, nearly seven thousand of whom died. In 1950 alone more than 33,000 people—the majority of whom were children—contracted polio.

In 1949, in a race to find a vaccine to immunize the terrified public against the epidemic, scientists found that the polio virus could be grown in embryonic tissue, allowing large scale research efforts. The first vaccine was developed by American virologist Jonas Edward Salk in 1952. His vaccine introduced a killed polio virus into the system. At about the same time, Polish/Russian-American virologist Albert Bruce Sabin developed a live-virus—and orally administered—vaccine. Fear of introducing live polio virus into a child prevented Sabin's vaccine from being used for several years. In the meantime over four hundred thousand children were vaccinated with Salk's live-virus. By 1955 Salk's vaccine was effective in almost 90 percent of the cases. By 1957 more than two hundred million doses of the Salk vaccine had been administered, and by mid-1961 a 96 percent reduction in the number of cases of polio in the United States was reported. In 1958 Sabin's live-virus vaccine replaced Salk's in the United States, proving more potent, longer lasting, and easier to administer; innoculation efforts spread rapidly. In 1994 the elimination of polio in the Western Hemisphere was announced. According to the Pan American Health Organization, mass immunization has wiped out polio as a health menace in North and South America.

ing his pump-oxygenator that diverts blood from the veins through a catheter (tube) to a machine that supplies the blood with oxygen and then pumps it back into the arteries. He uses this machine to keep a patient alive while he operates directly on her heart, closing an opening between her atria (heart chambers). The era of open-heart surgery begins with this operation.

December 23, 1954 ▪ First successful organ transplant. American surgeon Joseph Edward Murray (1919–) conducts the first successful organ transplant as he transfers a kidney of one twin to another. Murray makes a bold application of the principle, known since the 1930s, that identical twins share a common genetic identity, and that an organ from one is not considered to be "foreign" tissue and thus is not rejected. **(See also April 5, 1962)**

1954 ▪ Development of measles vaccine. The first vaccine for measles is developed by John Franklin Enders (1897–1985), an American microbiologist, and Thomas Peebles, an American pediatrician. This infectious disease of childhood is caused by a virus. Along with symptoms of high fever, headache, cough, and a red rash, complications can arise if there is a secondary bacterial infection. After Enders isolates the measles virus he is able to find an attenuated (weakened) strain that is suitable for a live-virus vaccine. Although an immunization program using this vaccine is started, a truly practical and successful vaccine is not achieved until 1963.

1954 ▪ Polio vaccine is developed. The first safe and effective antipoliomyelitis vaccine that prevents paralytic polio is developed by Jonas Edward Salk (1914–1995), an American virologist. Working on polio since 1949, Salk confirms that there are three virus types responsible for the disease and then experiments with ways to kill the viruses yet retain the ability to produce an immune response. By 1952 he produces a dead virus vaccine that works against all three. He then tests the vaccine on monkeys, then on children who have had the disease, and finally on his own children, none of whom ever had polio. His vaccine is tested nationally this year and proves between 60 and 90 percent effective. Soon thereafter, Polish-American virologist Albert Bruce Sabin (1906–1993) develops a live virus vaccine that is also the first oral vaccine. This proves more effective than Salk's dead virus vaccine and has longer-lasting immunity. Sabin's oral vaccine is still used today.

c. 1955 ▪ X-ray screening for breast cancer in women. The first physician to advocate the wide use of X rays to screen women for breast cancer is American physician and radiologist Jacob Gershon-Cohen. He begins a five-year study of more than thirteen hundred women and finds that women diagnosed early through mammography (X-ray imaging of the breast) have a better recovery rate than those whose disease is discovered at a later date. Mammography is introduced as a widely used diagnostic tool in 1967 and becomes a standard screening method advocated by the National Cancer Institute in the United States.

1955 · Drugs are used to treat schizophrenia. Chlorpromazine is first used to treat psychiatric disorders. Also called Thorazine, this powerful drug is used primarily to treat schizophrenia (a severe emotional disorder marked by a person's inability to tell what is real and what is not). Developed by a French pharmaceutical company, chlorpromazine is found to alter profoundly a patient's mental awareness, giving previously agitated individuals an almost detached sense of calmness. Along with lithium and other powerful antipsychotic drugs, chlorpromazine initiates the age of tranquilizers (drugs used to reduce mental disturbances). The development of chlorpromazine marks the first time a drug is discovered that specifically targets the central nervous system without profoundly affecting other behavioral or muscular functions.

1957 · Antibodies are found to act only against bacteria. Scottish virologist Alick Isaacs (1921–1967) demonstrates that antibodies act only against bacteria. Antibodies are special proteins in the blood that lock on to a foreign substance and make it harmless. This important discovery means that antibodies are not one of the body's natural forms of defense against viruses. This knowledge leads eventually to the search for how the body attempts to defend itself against a virus, and to the discovery of interferon this same year by Isaacs and his colleague, Jean Lindenmann of Switzerland. They find that in most living things, the generation of a small amount of protein is the first line of defense against a virus. Lindenmann and Isaacs describe this protein as an "interfering protein" and give it the name "interferon." Unlike antibodies that take several days to form, interferon is produced within hours of a viral invasion. Although interferon holds great promise in the treatment of viral diseases, it is found to be species-specific (only human interferon will work on people) and is produced by the body in minute quantities. The goal of interferon research is a large-scale, genetically engineered product that can be targeted to fight cancer and specific viral diseases.

1958 · CPR used for first time. The first use is made of closed-chest (external) heart massage combined with mouth-to-mouth respiration for cardiac resuscitation. Now popularly known as CPR (cardiopulmonary resuscitation), this technique provides a way to keep a stricken individual's heart pumping oxygenated blood to the brain. It becomes standard procedure used by rescue and emergency crews in cases of heart attack or life-threatening situations such as drowning or electric shock in which a person's heart stops. These crews carry special ventilation bags or airway tubes to avoid contracting disease. Proper CPR techniques are now taught to increasing numbers of people.

1958 ▪ Ultrasound makes debut. Ultrasound is first used in obstetrics (the branch of medicine dealing with pregnancy and childbirth) to examine an unborn fetus. In use after World War II (1939–45) primarily to test machine parts by using beams of high frequency sound waves to detect cracks, ultrasound is believed by English physician Ian Donald to have a future in obstetrics as a replacement for X rays. By 1957 he builds and tests an ultrasonic device for medical use, which he tests successfully by using sound waves to correctly diagnose a patient's heart condition. Ultrasonics works with sound waves of very high frequencies (from 1 to 10 megahertz) that penetrate tissue harmlessly. Because different types of tissue reflect sound waves back to the source differently, physicians can compile a picture of what exists inside. Improvements in ultrasound techniques have made it the most common method for examining a fetus and have helped obstetricians gain valuable information in treating pregnancies.

1961 ▪ Cryosurgery is first used. Irving S. Cooper, an American neurosurgeon, first uses a freezing technique known as cryosurgery to freeze and destroy damaged tissue within the brains of patients with Parkinson's disease. Using liquid nitrogen, extremely low temperatures of about -130° C (-200° F) are achieved that quickly destroy any tissue touched. As an alternative to traditional surgery, cryosurgery can usually be used without general anesthesia and can be applied to difficult to reach areas.

1962 ▪ First eye surgery using a laser. The first eye surgery with a laser is performed. A laser is a device that produces an extremely concentrated beam of light capable of generating intense heat when focused at close range that can destroy or otherwise alter the targeted tissue. Lasers are used to operate on the eye's retina (the part of the eye that receives the image) to repair tears in it or to remove unwanted, diseased tissue. Comparing a laser incision in the cornea to that made by a surgical instrument, the edge of the laser wound is smooth and regular, showing little disruption of tissue. The cut made by a razor-sharp surgical blade, however, is ragged and

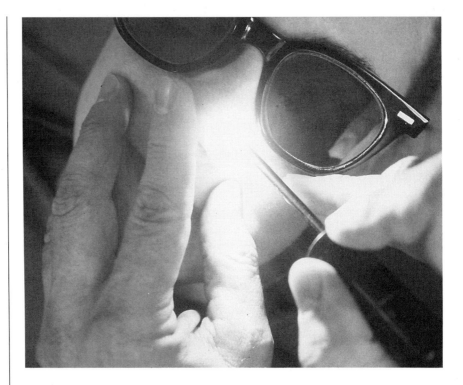

Cosmetic laser surgery. The intense heat of the laser beam can destroy or alter the targeted area without damaging surrounding tissue.

irregular. A new concept to appear in the mid-1990s is the prospect of using lasers to reshape the cornea (the transparent covering over the pupil and iris) to correct farsightedness, nearsightedness, and astigmatism.

April 5, 1962 · First kidney transplant between unrelated people. American surgeon Joseph Edward Murray (1919–) uses a kidney from a cadaver (dead body) and transplants it into a living human subject. This is the first successful renal allograft (a kidney transplant between unrelated subjects). His patient lives for seventeen months. This is also the first time that chemical immunosuppression (decreasing the body's natural resistance) is used with the drug azathioprine.

1963 · First human liver transplant. The first human liver transplant is performed by American surgeon Thomas Earl Starzl (1926–). The recipient survives for twenty-three days. Such operations are experimental at this time, since the problem of suppressing the body's immune system in order to prevent organ rejection is not yet solved. **(See also July 1976)**

1963 · Valium is developed. Valium, the world's most widely used tranquilizer (a drug used to reduce mental disturbance), is first developed.

As a barbiturate, it is a mood-altering drug that manipulates the central nervous system. It is a minor tranquilizer, often prescribed to calm people and help them sleep while they are trying to cope with a traumatic event. Excessive use, however, may hinder a person's coping skills, and the mixing of Valium and alcohol can prove fatal.

1967 • First coronary artery bypass surgery using a vein. The first coronary artery bypass surgery using a vein is performed by Argentine surgeon René Geronimo Favaloro (1923–). When the coronary arteries that supply the heart with blood become blocked by plaque, severe chest pain and in some cases heart attack can occur. Favaloro devises a method of grafting a vein from the patient's leg to bypass a blocked portion of a coronary artery, creating an alternative blood-supply pathway. This technique takes advantage of new developments in arteriography (images of the heart) and microsurgery. This procedure becomes very popular in the 1970s.

December 3, 1967 • First successful human heart transplant. The first successful human heart transplant is performed by South African surgeon Christiaan Neethling Barnard (1922–) in South Africa. The recipient, a fifty-three-year-old grocer named Louis Washkansky, lives for eighteen days. He receives the heart of a twenty-five-year-old woman who had been killed by an automobile. Barnard performs four more heart transplants over the next few years, and although one patient lives 593 days, none is considered really successful since each dies of infection after receiving massive doses of immunosuppressants (which decrease the body's natural resistance to transplants). Although Barnard masters the surgical techniques of implanting a new heart to replace a diseased one, he stops performing the operation until the problem of a safe immunosuppressant drug is resolved. **(See also July 1976)**

April 1969 • First artificial heart. The first artificial heart is implanted in a human being. Denton Arthur Cooley (1920–), an American surgeon, implants a mechanical heart made of silicon. This temporary plastic device keeps the patient alive for sixty-five hours until a human heart is implanted to replace it. The patient dies thirty-eight hours after this second operation due to pneumonia and kidney failure. Since the heart and its functions can be viewed primarily as a pump that circulates blood throughout the body, many believe at this time that an artificial heart will be superior to organ transplantation. The results of repeated implantation of several different types of artificial hearts, however, reveal what appear to be insurmountable complications: infections, patient immobility, and stroke-causing blood clots.

April 3, 1969 ▪ Vaccine to prevent rubella. The first license for a vaccine to prevent rubella is granted. Also called German measles, this fairly mild viral infection generally affects children and young adults. Although not usually dangerous to them, it can cause birth defects if contracted by a woman during the first three months of her pregnancy. The rubella virus was first propagated in a laboratory culture by American physician Thomas Huckle Weller (1915–) in the 1960s. After this success, researchers from Harvard University and the Walter Reed Army Medical Center develop an attenuated (weakened) virus suitable for a vaccine. This early vaccine eventually is improved to the point where it is included in the standard MMR (measles, mumps, rubella) vaccinations required of all school-age children in the United States.

c. 1969 ▪ CAT scan debuts. The first computerized axial tomography device (CAT scan) is constructed by South African-American physicist Allan MacLeod Cormack (1924–). His initial model uses a thin beam of X rays aimed at one internal section of the body but repeated from many different angles, producing a three-dimensional view. He lacks a system, however, to process the huge amounts of data produced. In 1971 English biomedical engineer Godfrey Newbold Hounsfield (1919–) uses computers to collate the X-ray data and create a tomographic image that offers a detailed, sharp map of a particular cross-section of the body. Assembling a complete picture involves a huge amount of information, since CAT machines use up to three hundred X-ray scanners taking three hundred snapshots each, resulting in almost ninety thousand X-ray "slices." CAT scans are nearly one hundred times more efficient than X-ray machines and significantly reduce the need for dangerous, exploratory surgery, particularly of the brain.

1972 ▪ First satisfactory artificial hip. English orthopedic surgeon John Charnley (1911–1982) designs the first satisfactory artificial hip. He spends years searching for a successful method of replacing hip joints made painful from rheumatoid arthritis. Early attempts at hip replacements were far from satisfactory, and Charnley tests new materials, achieving initial success in the 1960s with low-friction Teflon (an artificial resin containing fluorine). He continues to improve his artificial hip, and in 1972 he perfects his technique by using high-density polyethylene (a polymer made from ethylene resin) to build the hip socket. This operation is performed on a regular basis today, with new materials such as titanium contributing to its effectiveness. In the early 1990s, a professional athlete, American football and baseball player Bo Jackson (1962–), undergoes a hip replacement and returns to actively compete in professional baseball for a time.

1974 · Introduction of Heimlich maneuver. The Heimlich maneuver is introduced as first aid for choking. Developed by American chest surgeon Henry Jay Heimlich (1920–), this method of dislodging an obstruction in a person's throat is a recognized life-saving technique. When a person is choking and able to stand, the rescuer stands behind the victim, encircles the victim's waist with his arms, and places the thumb side of his fist above the choker's navel and below his rib cage. The rescuer then grasps his fist with his free hand and thrusts upward into the victim's abdomen. The procedure can also be performed on people who are seated or lying on their backs. Dislodging an obstruction quickly is crucial, since within four minutes, brain anoxia (insufficient oxygen reaching the brain) can result in permanent brain damage or death.

July 1976 · Immunosuppressant cyclosporin A is developed. Jean François Borel, a microbiologist at the Swiss pharmaceutical firm Sandoz, announces a new immunosuppressant (which decreases the body's natural resistance) called cyclosporin A. This leads to clinical trials of a drug that halts the body's rejection of a new organ while still allowing its immune system to function normally and fight general infection. After analyzing soil samples containing a fungus (cyclosporin) from southern Norway in 1969, Borel's tests reveal that it acts to inhibit the immune system's T-lymphocyte activity (that detects and attacks foreign invaders). That is, it selectively interferes with only one subpopulation of the immune system, allowing the rest to do their work. In 1983 the U.S. Food and Drug Administration approves the drug for use in all transplant operations, and successful transplantations become commonplace. The drug must be taken indefinitely and can, in high doses, produce lymphomas (tumors) and have a toxic effect on the kidneys, but it has proven to be a life-saver to thousands.

1977 · First-known AIDS victims. The earliest-known AIDS (acquired immune deficiency syndrome) victims in the United States are two homosexual men in New York who are diagnosed as suffering from a cancer called Karposi's sarcoma. In addition to an increase in this rare type of cancer, physicians in New York and California report a variety of infections including pneumonia among previously healthy young homosexual men. All these diseases are associated with a failure of the immune system, which leads epidemiologists (medical scientists who study diseases) to search for a common link. **(See also 1981: AIDS is officially recognized)**

1978 ▪ First test-tube baby. The first test-tube baby (conceived by in vitro fertilization) is born in England. This is the first human being conceived outside the human body to be born. Patrick Steptoe (1913–1988) and Robert G. Edwards, English physicians, develop a method of stimulating ovulation (the release of eggs from the ovary) with hormone treatment, then retrieving the nearly mature ova (eggs) and placing them in culture to mature. The physicians then add male sperm to the petri dish containing the eggs, and fertilization takes place. After undergoing division, the eight-celled embryo is implanted in the mother's uterus and develops normally. The first human being produced by this technique is a baby named Louise Brown.

1978 ▪ MRI of human head is taken. The first magnetic resonance image (MRI) of the human head is taken in England. Invented by American physicist Raymond Damadian (1936–) in 1971, this new imaging technology is called "nuclear magnetic resonance spectroscopy" and is first used to study the molecular structures of chemicals. Later experiments on parts of the body revealed that, linked with a computer, the device produced a vivid, three-dimensional cross section showing layers of skin, muscle, and bone and was apparently harmless to patients. It is found to be especially useful for imaging the brain.

1980 ▪ Human interferon is first genetically engineered. Charles Weissmann of Switzerland produces the first genetically engineered human interferon, making large-scale production possible. Interferon is produced in the body as a response to a virus. Interest in interferon is strongly revived following the discovery that it slows or stops tumor growth in mice, and the demand for it increases significantly. This technique indicates one way of making it in large enough quantities. **(See also 1957)**

February 7, 1980 ▪ Breaking up kidney stones with shock waves. Shock waves are first used successfully on a human patient to break up kidney stones. Called "extracorporeal shock wave lithotripsy," it is developed and performed by a team in West Germany. After the patient is placed in a tub of water and the location of the stone is identified with an X ray, a series of shock-wave pulses strike the stone and are reflected, causing mechanical stress and fracturing. The stone is broken into small enough pieces to be passed through the urinary tract, thus avoiding the need for surgery.

1981 ▪ AIDS is officially recognized. AIDS (acquired immune deficiency syndrome) is officially recognized by the U.S. Centers for Disease Control, and the first clinical description of this disease is made. It soon becomes recognized that AIDS is an infectious disease characterized by a failure of the body's immune system and caused by a virus that is spread almost exclusively by infected blood or body fluids. The virus in question comes to be known as HIV (human immune deficiency virus) for which there is still no cure or vaccine.

1981 ▪ First successful heart-lung transplant. The first successful combined heart-lung transplant is achieved by American surgeons Norman Edward Shumway (1923–) and Bruce A. Reitz. In three previous attempts at a heart-lung transplant, the longest survival was twenty-three days. The surgeons use the new immunosuppressive drug cyclosporin on their forty-five-year-old patient who survives and returns to a normal life. **(See also July 1976)**

December 2, 1982 ▪ Jarvik-7 artificial heart is implanted. The first Jarvik-7 artificial heart is implanted by American surgeon William C. DeVries. The gravely ill patient, Barney Clark, lives for 112 days. This procedure is the first total heart replacement intended for permanent use. The replacement heart is designed by American physician Robert K. Jarvik (1946–) and is a plastic and titanium pump powered by compressed air delivered through two tubes inserted in the patient's abdomen. After Clark dies, four other Jarvik-7 implants are carried out. Each patient dies, including William Schroeder who lives for 620 days. The Jarvik-7 and other artificial hearts soon fall out of use as surgeons concede that transplants are far superior solutions.

1983 ▪ Discovery that a bacterium causes ulcers. Researchers uncover evidence that a bacterium causes ulcers of the stomach and small intestine. This leads to a major reevaluation of the factors once thought to cause ulcers, such as stress and diet, and of the appropriate treatment. Ten years later, the medical community believes that the common peptic ulcer is most likely caused by a bacterium, *Heliobacter pylori*, which can be treated with antibiotics.

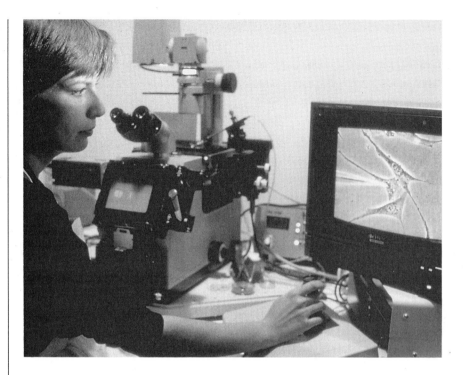

A scientist performs gene therapy by the microinjection of a corrective gene into a white blood cell. The scientist controls the injection by means of the joystick in her right hand.

1984 ▪ First successful surgery on a fetus. William H. Clewall, an American surgeon, performs the first successful surgery on a fetus. With the ability to diagnose prenatal problems has come the ability to correct some of them while the fetus is still being carried by the mother. Some of the correctable anatomic malformations are urinary tract obstruction, diaphragmatic hernia, and hydrocephalus.

1985 ▪ Lasers are used to unblock clogged arteries. Lasers are used for the first time to unblock clogged arteries. A laser is a device that produces an extremely concentrated beam of light capable of generating intense heat when focused at close range. Research on the use of lasers in medicine began around 1962, and lasers became useful for delicate eye surgery, removing birthmarks from the skin, and sealing blood vessels during operations to prevent bleeding. Now they are used to reopen blocked arteries by vaporizing fatty deposits.

September 1990 ▪ First use of human gene therapy. The first patient to receive human gene therapy to treat a genetic defect is a four-year-old American girl suffering from adenosine deaminase (ADA) deficiency. Because of this disease, her immune system is unable to fight infection. She receives a series of intravenous infusions of her own immune cells that have been "gene-corrected" by the introduction of normal genes. The treatment has to be repeated once a month because, like all body cells, lymphocytes (infection-fighting cells) die and must be replaced. The altered cells succeed in raising the girl's immune function to near normal levels. **(See also October 20, 1995)**

1992 ▪ Baboon liver is transplanted into a human. For the first time, a baboon's liver is transplanted into a man whose liver was destroyed by the disease hepatitis B. The patient dies of an infection seventy-one days later. When a second patient, a sixty-two-year-old man, dies in February 1993, twenty-six days after receiving a baboon's liver, there are many demands for such experiments to stop. Both are completed under the direction of American surgeon Thomas Earl Starzl (1926–). Starzl is a pioneer in organ transplantation and argues that the future of transplants lies in using animal parts. This may mark the beginning of animal-to-human transplants.

October 20, 1995 ▪ Success of gene therapy is reported. The first success of gene therapy is reported in an article published in *Science*. Written by American researcher R. Michael Blaese of the National Center for Human Genome Research, the article details how, five years after two young girls were given immune system genes they lacked, they are healthy and thriving. Gene therapy is a technique in which doctors give patients healthy genes to replace the defective ones inherited from their parents, or to enhance the action of genes they already have. **(See also September 1990)**

January 22, 1997 ▪ Mad cow disease is discovered. Discovery of "mad cow" disease (bovine spongiform encephalopathy) in Germany compels the government to order the killing of some fifty-two hundred cows thought to be at risk. Since herds in England had the highest incidence of this disease and had to be slaughtered, the German government decided to take no risks. Earlier, British scientists had announced the discovery of a possible link between mad cow disease and Creutzfeldt-Jakob disease, a fatal human brain ailment. This led to a global ban of British beef.

Physics

c. 2650 B.C. ▪ Building of the Step Pyramid. The first great stone tomb, the Step Pyramid, is built by Imhotep, an Egyptian scholar and architect. As the first of the pyramids and the oldest-known monument of hewn stone, it is 200 feet high with a base 388 feet by 411 feet. Its successful completion on the ancient site of Memphis, Egypt, demonstrates the ability of ancient engineers and their familiarity with the basics of mechanics.

c. 600 B.C. ▪ Magnetism is studied systematically. The first to systematically study magnetism is Greek philosopher Thales of Miletus (c. 625–c. 547 B.C.). He is also the first to notice the electrification of amber by friction, finding that when amber is rubbed, it becomes capable of picking up light objects. This process becomes known as triboelectrification. The Greek name for amber is *elektron*, and it gives rise to many words we use today in connection with electricity. Thales also writes one of the earliest studies on physics and proposes water as the basic substance of the universe.

c. 475 B.C. ▪ Theory on matter is suggested. The first to suggest that matter can be neither created nor destroyed is Greek philosopher Parmenides. This is an anticipation of the modern law of conservation of energy. Parmenides holds that the multiplicity of existing things, as well as their changing forms and motion, are but an appearance of a single eternal reality. This gives rise to the Parmenidean principle, "All is one."

c. 450 B.C. ▪ Rule of causality is first stated. The first to state the rule of causality, that every natural event has a natural cause, is Leucippus, a Greek philosopher. He is also credited with being the creator of atomism since he is the teacher of Greek philosopher Democritus (c. 460–c. 370 B.C.). Leucippus believes that every substance is a gathering of atoms or countless, small bodies of varying size and form. These are eternal, unchanging, and indivisible. **(See also c. 425 B.C.)**

c. 425 B.C. ▪ Expansion of atomic theory. The first fully stated atomic theory, that all matter consists of infinitesimally tiny particles that are indivisible, is offered by Greek philosopher Democritus (c. 460–c. 370 B.C.). He states that these atoms are eternal, uncaused, and unchangeable, although they can differ in their properties. They can also recombine to form new patterns. Democritus's intuitive ideas contain much that is found in modern theories of the structure of matter and foreshadow theories of the indestructibility of matter and of the conservation of energy.

c. 350 B.C. ▪ Offering of motion theory. A theory of motion is put forth by Greek philosopher Aristotle (384–322 B.C.), stating that a continuous force is required for an object to remain moving. He also states that a heavier object will fall faster than a lighter one. Both of theses ideas are incorrect but influence thinking for the next thousand years. His rejection of atomism also condemns that correct notion. **(See also c. 1350)**

Democritus, Greek philosopher and first to state the atomic theory of matter.

c. 220 B.C. ▪ Discovery of buoyancy principle. The principle of buoyancy is discovered by Greek mathematician and engineer Archimedes (c. 287–c. 212 B.C.). In his *Treatise on Floating Bodies*, he tells of his discovery of this principle with which he is able to determine if a crown is pure gold or not. He measures the amount of water the crown displaces (when the water level rises) and compares it to the quantity displaced by an equal amount of actual gold. He also works out mathematically the principle of the lever, showing that weights and distances are in inverse proportion, and develops the notion of a center of gravity. With all of this, he is

regarded as the founder of the science called "statics," which is the study of the forces acting on bodies that do not move.

c. A.D. 50 ▪ Steam-power principle is established. The principle of the motive power of steam is established by Greek engineer Hero, who builds many steam-powered devices. His most famous device is a hollow sphere to which two bent tubes are attached. When water is boiled in the sphere, steam escapes through the tubes and the sphere rapidly whirls about. This is a demonstration of what we now recognize as the law of action and reaction. Hero also writes about various simple machines, describing the lever, pulley, wheel, inclined plane, wedge, and screw. Writing on the nature of air, he shows that it is a substance and that it is compressible and takes up space. It will be another fifteen hundred years until these ideas are known again.

c. 1025 · First correct theory of vision. The first to maintain the correct theory of vision or human sight is Arabian physicist Alhazen (965–1039). He rejects the prevailing idea that people see because their eyes send out a light that reflects back from the object, and argues that light comes from the sun or another source and reflects from the object into the eye. He works with lenses and attributes their magnifying effect to the curvature of their surfaces and not to any inherent property of the substances of which they are composed. He also studies all aspects of light, especially reflection (light bouncing off) and refraction (light rays bending), and also discusses the rainbow.

A magnetic compass.

1269 · Converting magnetism to kinetic energy. The first suggestion that magnetism might be converted to kinetic energy (energy possessed by a body because of its motion) is made by Petrus Peregrinus, a French scholar also called Pierre Le Pèlerin de Maricourt. He speculates that a motor that uses magnetic force might be constructed to keep a planetarium moving. This year he writes a small study on the compass titled *Epistola de magnete* (Letter on magnetism) and discusses the nature and fundamental properties of magnetism. This is believed to be the first full, Western account of a compass and its workings.

c. 1350 · Theory of motion is revised. The first major revision of Greek philosopher Aristotle's (384–322 B.C.) theory of motion is made by Jean Buridan (1300–1358), a French philosopher. He refutes the Aristotelian notion that an object in motion requires a continuous force, and maintains that only an initial impetus is required. His impetus theory states that the mover imparts to the thing being moved a power, proportional to the speed and mass, which keeps it moving. He also correctly theorizes that air resistance progressively reduces the impetus, and that weight can add or detract from speed.

1473 · Early work is translated to Latin. The first Latin translation is made of *De rerum natura* (On the nature of things) written by the Roman philosopher and poet Lucretius (c. 95–c. 55 B.C.). Through this translation the atomism of Greek philosopher Democritus (c. 460–c. 370

B.C.) becomes known in the West. Lucretius holds that all things are composed of atoms, including the mind, the soul, and even the gods. He also argues that mankind lives in an evolutionary universe in which the gods play no real role. **(See also c. 425 B.C.)**

c. 1500 · Description of capillary action. The first to describe capillary action (the rise of a liquid in a narrow, open-ended tube) is Italian artist Leonardo da Vinci (1452–1519). Also called capillarity, it is caused by forces of attraction or adhesion between the molecules of water and the glass walls and among the molecules of water themselves. In 1709 English physicist Francis Hauksbee (c. 1666–1713) is the first to study capillary action experimentally. In his *Physico-Mechanical Experiments on Various Subjects*, he makes the first accurate observations of the effects involving the attractive forces that cause water to rise within thin tubes and to spread over a flat surface.

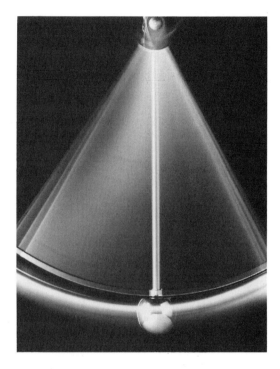

1581 · Discovery of the regularity of the pendulum. The principle of isochronism or the regularity of the pendulum is discovered by Italian astronomer and physicist Galileo Galilei (1564–1642). He observes a hanging lamp that is swinging back and forth and notes that the amount of time it takes the lamp to complete an oscillation (back-and-forth motion) remains constant, even as the arc of the swing steadily decreases. He then suggests that this uniform principle of the pendulum may have an application in regulating clocks. **(See also 1673)**

The time it takes a pendulum to complete an oscillation remains constant, even as the arc of the swing decreases.

1586 · Declaration of the law of inclined planes. The law of inclined planes is first stated by Belgian-Dutch mathematician Simon Stevin (1548–1620). An inclined plane is like a ramp (in the shape of an unequal triangle), and his law states that the shorter the length of the plane, the stronger the force is pulling something down it. Stevin shows that if a chain were draped over two unequal sides of a triangle, that less weight on its steep slope would balance more weight on its gentler slope. His work on displacement (water rising when something is placed in it) is the first since antiquity, and he also founds hydrostatics (the study of fluids at rest and objects immersed in fluids) by stating that the pressure by a liquid on the bottom of the vessel containing it depends only on the size or area of the surface under pressure and the amount or height of liquid above it (and not upon the shape of the container that holds it). This becomes a fundamental principle of hydraulics.

1587 ▪ Demonstrating the law of falling bodies. The law of falling bodies is first stated by Italian astronomer and physicist Galileo Galilei (1564–1642) who shows that the rate of fall of a body is independent of its weight. He uses a gently sloping inclined plane to demonstrate this once and for all and later states correctly that all objects will fall at the same rate in a vacuum (an area in which all matter has been removed). He also demonstrates that a body can move under the influence of two forces at one time. He proves these and many other of his claims using the geometric methods of the Greeks and contributes much to the eventual downfall of Aristotelian physics.

1600 ▪ First use of electrical terms. The first to use the terms "electric attraction," "electric force," and "magnetic pole" is English physician and physicist William Gilbert (1544–1603). This year he publishes his *De magnete* (On the magnet), which is a full account of his extensive investigations on magnetic bodies and electrical attraction, and is considered the first great work on physical science produced in England. Gilbert suggests that the Earth itself is a great, round magnet, and he actually builds a model or *terrella*. This "little Earth" is a lodestone ground into a spherical shape that functions as a model from which he is able to transfer his findings directly to the Earth itself.

1611 ▪ Laws of refraction. The laws of refraction are first stated by German astronomer Johannes Kepler (1571–1630) in his *Dioptrice* (Dioptrics). Refraction is the way in which light rays bend as they enter or leave a transparent substance. With this work, Kepler founds the science of modern optics (the study of light). He also studies the newly invented telescope and applies geometric optics to the study of lenses and combinations of lenses, making a true theory of the telescope possible.

1621 ▪ Refraction and mathematics. The mathematics of the refraction (bending) of light is discovered by Dutch mathematician Willebrord Snel (1580–1626). He finds that when a ray of light passes obliquely from a rarer into a denser medium (such as from air into water), it is bent toward the vertical. Although this was known more than fifteen hundred years ago by the Greeks, Snel offers a general mathematical relationship to express this refraction of light by relating the degree of the bending of light to the properties of the refractive material. This is a key discovery in optics but it goes unpublished.

1638 · Modern mechanics foundations are laid. The foundations of modern mechanics (the study of the effects of forces upon objects) are laid by Italian astronomer and physicist Galileo Galilei (1564–1642) in his *Discorsi e dimostrazioni mathematiche intorno a due nuove scienze* (Mathematical discourses and demonstrations relating to two new sciences). In this work he formulates what comes to be known as the first law of motion (or the law of inertia), as well as the laws of cohesion and strength of materials. He is the first to show that if a structure continues to increase in all its dimensions equally it will grow weaker. Using what is known as the square-cube law, he shows that if a deer grows to the size of an elephant and keeps its exact proportions, it would collapse, for its legs would have to be thickened far out of proportion to support its great body. He also provides a definition of momentum (the mass of an object multiplied by its velocity or speed).

1643 · Sustained vacuum is first created. The first to create a sustained vacuum is Italian physicist Evangelista Torricelli (1608–1647). He creates this first artificial vacuum in the process of inventing the barometer. He fills a 4-foot-long glass tube with mercury and turns it upside-down onto a dish of mercury. He observes that not all the mercury flows out and that over time, the level remaining in the tube goes up or down a bit. He concludes correctly that these changes are caused by atmospheric pressure. He further theorizes correctly that a vacuum was created above the mercury in the tube and that the mercury is held at a given level not by the vacuum, but by the pressure of air pushing down on the mercury outside in the dish. With this one experiment, he demonstrates the existence of a vacuum, explains why pumps can move liquids up only to a certain height, and creates an instrument capable of measuring air pressure, the barometer. **(See also 1648)**

1644 · Descartes publishes his principles of philosophy. Cartesian physics is first fully stated as French philosopher and mathematician René Descartes (1596–1650) publishes his *Principia philosophiae* (Principles of philosophy). At the core of its incorrect principles (among which are the nonexistence of the vacuum and the infinite speed of light) is an essentially mechanistic view of the world. He attacks and rejects most Aristotelian physical concepts and sees the entire universe acting as a great machine.

1648 ▪ Demonstration of the variability of atmospheric pressure. Variability of atmospheric pressure (the amount of air pushing down on a surface) is first demonstrated by French mathematician and physicist Blaise Pascal (1623–1662). Pascal conceives and directs this test, which demonstrates that air pressure decreases as altitude increases. He sends two barometers up a mountain, and their columns of mercury drop as he predicts. This means that if the mercury column is actually held up by air pressure, if one climbs higher, then there should be less air above to push down on the mercury outside the vacuum, and the column should therefore drop. Pascal's experimenters show that the mercury does indeed drop 3 inches in a 1 mile ascent. This is an experimental verification of the barometric principles discovered in 1643 by Italian physicist Evangelista Torricelli (1608–1647). **(See also 1643)**

1650 ▪ Creating a vacuum with first air pump. German physicist Otto von Guericke (1602–1686) constructs the first air pump that can create a vacuum. He conducts several experiments using evacuated (emptied) spheres that show a vacuum's properties. He demonstrates that animals cannot live in a vacuum nor will a candle burn or a bell be heard. The pump he devises is something like a water pump, but has its parts well-fitted to be reasonably airtight.

1660 ▪ First generation of an electrical charge with a machine. The first machine to generate an electrical charge is invented by German physicist Otto von Guericke (1602–1686). He invents a frictional (rubbing) electrical device that generates static electricity. His hand-rotated globe of sulfur mechanizes the act of rubbing and accumulates static electricity. Since it can be discharged and recharged indefinitely, he is able to conduct several electrical experiments with it, generating sizable electric sparks. Perhaps his largest contribution is simply the enthusiasm for electrical experimentation that his work creates.

1662 ▪ Studying the compressibility of air. Robert Boyle (1627–1691), a British physicist and chemist, discovers the law that air is

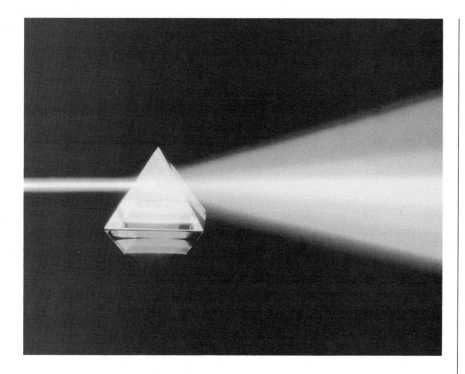

This prism is diffracting light as it enters, producing a spectrum of colors as it emerges.

not only compressible (able to be squeezed or condensed) but that this compressibility varies with pressure according to a simple inverse (opposite) relationship. He conducts his experiments by trapping air in the short, closed end of a J-shaped, 17-foot-long glass tube into which he pours mercury to close off the bottom. He discovers that by adding more mercury, the additional weight of the fluid squeezes the trapped air more closely together and that its volume decreases. He then finds that the volume varies inversely with the pressure, so that if he doubles the mercury weight, the volume shrinks to one-half. The implications of Boyle's law are that air and other gases have atoms that normally are widely spread apart.

1665 ▪ Diffraction of light is discovered. Discovery of the diffraction of light is revealed in a posthumous (after death) publication by Italian physicist Francesco Maria Grimaldi (1618–1663). Diffraction is the bending of light rays as they pass outward from the edge of a gap. Grimaldi describes an experiment in which he lets a beam of light pass through two narrow openings, one behind the other, and then onto a blank surface. When he notes that the band of light on the last surface is slightly wider than it should be, he concludes that the light has been bent slightly outward. He names this phenomenon diffraction. This is a major discovery, since light could only behave this way if it traveled in waves and was not composed of particles. His work is ignored for over a century.

1672 · Experimentations with light. English scientist and mathematician Isaac Newton (1642–1727) publishes his letter on light in the Royal Society's *Philosophical Transactions*. This letter, which is his first scientific publication, details his prism experiments of 1666 and offers findings that reveal for the first time the true nature of light. Newton recounts how he let a ray of sunlight enter a darkened room through a small hole and then passed the ray through a prism onto a screen. The ray was refracted (bent away) and a band of consecutive colors in rainbow order appeared. He then passed each separate color through another prism and noted that although their light was refracted, the color did not change. From this he deduces that sunlight (or white light) consists of a combination of these colors. Later he elaborates further on this groundbreaking experiment in his 1704 book, *Opticks*.

1673 · Regulation of clocks with the principle of isochronicity. The principle of isochronicity is first applied to regulate a clock by Dutch physicist and astronomer Christiaan Huygens (1629–1695). This year he publishes his *Horologium oscillatorium* (The oscillating clock) in which he details his invention of the pendulum or "grandfather" clock. He employs the principle stated by Italian astronomer and physicist Galileo Galilei (1564–1642) in 1581—that a back-and-forth motion of a pendulum remains constant even as the arc of the swing steadily decreases—and ingeniously adapts it to the inner workings of a clock. Huygens's device begins the era of accurate timekeeping that is so important to the advancement of physics.

1676 · Boyle's law is improved upon. French physicist Edme Mariotte (c. 1620–1684) independently discovers Boyle's law and adds an important qualification to it. Like English physicist and chemist Robert Boyle (1627–1691), Mariotte notes that air expands with a rising temperature and contracts with a falling temperature, but he adds that the inverse (opposite) relationship between temperature and pressure only holds if the temperature is kept constant. Because of this, Boyle's law is called Mariotte's law in France. **(See also 1662)**

1684 · Newton and his theory of gravitation. English scientist and mathematician Isaac Newton (1642–1727) provides the first summary explanation of his theory of gravitation. When asked by his friend, English astronomer Edmond Halley (1656–1742), how he thought the planets would move if there were a force of attraction between bodies that weakened as the square of the distance (distance multiplied by itself), Newton tells Halley they would move in ellipses (a stretched-out egg shape), and that he had already calculated this in 1666. Halley urges Newton to resume work on this problem, and Newton soon expands this after eighteen months of work into his landmark 1687 book. **(See also 1687)**

1687 · Newton publishes work on theoretical physics. The first systematic work on theoretical physics is English scientist and mathematician Isaac Newton's (1642–1727) *Philosophiae Naturalis Principia Mathematica* (The mathematical principles of natural philosophy). In it, Newton states his three laws of motion. The first is the principle of inertia. A body at rest remains at rest and a body in motion remains in motion at a constant velocity as long as outside forces are not involved. The second law defines force as the product of mass (the amount of matter in an object) and acceleration. This gives the first clear distinction between the mass of a body and its weight. The third law of motion states that for every action there is an equal and opposite reaction. From these laws, Newton arrives at his law of universal gravitation. He shows that gravitation is directly proportional (an equal ratio) to the product of the masses of two bodies (Earth and Moon) and inversely proportional (opposite ratio) to the square of the distance between their centers. This landmark work opens the era of classical mechanics (the study of the effects of forces upon objects).

1690 · Wave theory of light is proposed. The wave theory of light is stated by Danish physicist and astronomer Christiaan Huygens (1629–1695). He argues in his *Traité de la lumière* (Treatise on light) the unpopular theory that considers light as a longitudinal (running lengthwise) wave that undulates in the direction of its motion much as a sound wave does. He is opposed by English scientist and mathematician Isaac Newton (1642–1727) who argues that light is a particle because there is a vacuum between the Earth and the Sun, and he cannot see how a wave can travel where there is nothing to wave. Huygens counters by saying that there must be some sort of very subtle fluid in space.

1714 · Accurate thermometer is invented. The first very accurate thermometer is invented by Daniel Gabriel Fahrenheit (1686–1736), a German-Dutch physicist. His use of mercury in his thermometer instead of alcohol means that temperatures far above the boiling point of water and well below its freezing point can be measured (since alcohol has a low boiling point). He also invents the Fahrenheit temperature scale at which the freezing point of water is 32° and the boiling point is 212°. He arrives at these by adding salt to water to find the lowest freezing point, which he calls zero. Physicists and other scientists now possess a precision instrument for measuring temperature.

1738 · First statement of Bernoulli's principle. Bernoulli's principle is first stated by Swiss mathematician, Daniel Bernoulli (1700–1782). In his comprehensive work on fluid flow, *Hydrodynamica* (Hydrodynamics), he demonstrates the principle that as the velocity (speed) of fluid flow increases, its pressure decreases. Bernoulli also becomes the first to attempt to explain the behavior of gases when changes in pressure and temperature occur.

1742 · Celsius creates new temperature scale. A new temperature scale is described by Swedish astronomer Anders Celsius (1701–1744). He applies a new scale to his thermometer by dividing the temperature difference between the boiling and freezing points of water into an even hundred degrees (with 0 at the freezing point and 100 at the boiling point). Compared to the Fahrenheit scale whose freezing and boiling values are the oddly chosen 32 and 212, the simplicity of a system in which a positive reading means water and a negative value means ice is obvious and attractive to all. His system is adopted initially as the "centigrade" scale (from the Latin for "hundred steps"), but is eventually converted to the "Celsius" scale by international agreement in 1948. Oddly, the United States is the lone exception—as the entire world adopts Celsius, the United States alone retains Fahrenheit.

1744 · Least action principle is stated. The principle of least action is first stated by French mathematician Pierre-Louis Moreau de Maupertuis (1698–1759). This year he publishes a paper in which he states that physical laws include a rule of economy in which action is a minimum. Maupertuis argues that this principle shows that nature chooses the most economical path for moving bodies, rays of light, and other things.

1745 · Discovery of the Leyden jar. The Leyden jar is discovered by Dutch physicist Pieter van Musschenbroek (1692–1761). This device for storing electricity is also discovered independently this same year by German physicist Ewald Georg von Kleist (1700–1748). Musschenbroek makes his accidental discovery when he places water in a glass bottle suspended by insulating silk cords. He then leads a brass wire connected to an electrical (frictional) machine through a cork into the water. One of Musschenbroek's students, named Cunaeus (or Cuneus), picks up the container while touching the brass wire and nearly dies from the electric shock he receives. This startling demonstration shows just how much of an electric charge can be stored in this bottle or jar. Kleist has a similar shocking experience and retires from any further such work. Because Musschenbroek continues to experiment and further popularize his discovery, and because he does his work at the University of Leyden, this electricity-storing device comes to be called a "Leyden jar."

1751 ▪ Theoretical book on electricity is published. The first major theoretical work on electricity is written by Benjamin Franklin

Benjamin Franklin experimenting with lightning.

(1706–1790), American statesman and scientist. He publishes a two-volume work, *Experiments and Observations on Electricity Made at Philadelphia in America,* in which he formulates a theory of general electrical "action" also called his single fluid theory of electricity. His theory is adopted as are several of the terms and concepts he introduces, such as positive and negative charge. **(See June 1752)**

June 1752 ▪ Franklin conducts electrical experiment. The first to prove that electricity in the atmosphere is identical with that generated artificially on Earth is American statesman and scientist Benjamin Franklin (1706–1790). He flies a kite carrying a pointed wire in a thunderstorm and attempts to test his theory that atmospheric lightning is an electrical phenomenon similar to the spark produced by an electrical frictional machine. To the kite's point he attaches a silk thread with a metal key at the other end, and as lightning flashes, he puts his hand near the key, which sparks just as a Leyden jar (a type of electrical condenser) would. He proves his point in this extremely dangerous experiment. Franklin is wise enough to connect a ground wire to his key. Two other scientists attempting to duplicate the experiment neglect this ground wire and are killed when they are struck by lightning.

1781 ▪ Introduction of specific heat concept. The concept of specific heat is independently introduced by Scottish chemist Joseph Black (1728–1799) and German physicist Johann Carl Wilcke (1732–1796). This theory states that different bodies of equal masses require different amounts of heat to raise them to the same temperature. Specific heat is the ratio of the quantity of heat required to raise the temperature of a body 1° to that required to raise the temperature of an equal mass of water 1°. In the early nineteenth century, it is discovered that measurements of specific heats of substances will allow calculation of their atomic weights. Atomic weight is a quantity that tells the relative atomic mass (or how much matter there is) of a substance.

1785 ▪ Establishment of the basic laws of electrostatics and magnetism. The first of seven papers is published in which the basic laws of electrostatics (static electricity) and magnetism are established by French physicist Charles-Augustin de Coulomb (1736–1806). Using his newly invented torsion balance, he determines that English scientist and mathematician Isaac Newton's (1642–1727) law of inverse squares also applies to electrical and magnetic attraction and repulsion. Newton's law states that the intensity of a wave varies inversely (opposite) with the square of its distance from its source. Coulomb's law states that electrical forces obey a rule similar to that of gravitational forces.

1787 · Quantitative relationships of sound are explored. The first to discover the quantitative (measurable) relationships that rule the transmission of sound is German physicist Ernst Florens Friedrich Chladni (1756–1827), who publishes *Theorie des Klanges* (Theory of sounds) this year. He also creates "Chladni's figures" by spreading sand on thin plates and vibrating them, producing complex patterns from which much is learned about vibrations. He is considered the father of acoustics.

1791 · Theory of animal electricity is proposed. "Animal electricity" is first proposed by Italian anatomist Luigi Galvani (1737–1798). Observing that the muscles of a dissected frog will twitch when touched by an electric spark from a Leyden jar (a type of electrical condenser), he concludes after years of experimentation that animal tissue contains an unknown vital force. He calls this force "animal electricity," and says that it activates nerve and muscle when touched by metal probes. He builds an entire anatomical theory around animal electricity. Although he is proved partly wrong by Italian physicist Alessandro Giuseppe Antonio Anastasio Volta (1745–1827), Galvani is a pioneer in the field of electrophysiology (electrical phenomena associated with the function of the body).

1801 · Human eye sees only three colors. The first to demonstrate that the human eye sees only three colors is English physicist and physician Thomas Young (1773–1829). He shows that all other colors to the eye are combinations of red, green, and blue. This three-color theory is later refined by German physiologist and physicist Hermann Ludwig Ferdinand von Helmholtz (1821–1894) and is referred to as the Young-Helmholtz three-color theory. Today's color photography and color television make use of this theory.

1801 · Discovery of spectrum's ultraviolet region. The ultraviolet region of the spectrum is discovered by German physicist Johann Wilhelm Ritter (1776–1810). Knowing that silver chloride darkens in the presence of light, he also knows that the blue end of the spectrum (the display of colors in the arrangement that occurs when a beam of is refracted by a prism) brings this about more efficiently than the red. He then explores the region beyond the blue or the violet (where nothing is apparent to the eye), and finds that an invisible light also blackens silver chloride. He concludes that radiation must exist that is invisible to the eye. This section of the spectrum next to the violet is now called "ultraviolet" for "beyond the violet."

1802 ▪ Nature of light is demonstrated to be waves. The first demonstration of the wave nature of light is provided by English physicist and physician Thomas Young (1773–1829). He performs his classic experiment on interference (the way in which two light rays combine together) in which sunlight is made to pass through two pinholes in an opaque screen. He then allows the two separate beams of light that emerge from the holes to overlap, and finds that when they spread and overlap, the overlapping region forms a striped pattern of alternating light and dark. This phenomenon can only happen, he argues, if light—like sound—is a wave and not a particle. Streams of particles simply cannot produce interference effects. With a wave interpretation of his observations, he is also able to make the first quantitative (measurable) values of the length of light waves.

1807 ▪ Modern scientific definition of energy. English physicist and physician Thomas Young (1773–1829) first uses the word "energy" in its modern scientific sense meaning the property of a system that makes it capable of doing work. He also states that it is proportional (in the same ratio) to the product of the mass of a body (how much matter it contains) and the square of its velocity (its speed times itself).

July 1820 ▪ Demonstration of magnetic field created by a current of electricity. Danish physicist Hans Christian Ørsted (1777–1851) experiments with a compass and electricity and demonstrates that a current of electricity creates a magnetic field. After bringing a compass needle near a wire through which a current is passing, he observes the needle slightly deflect. By moving his compass needle around the wire, he discovers that the magnetic field is circular and that the needle always points at a right angle to the field. This is the first time a real connection can be shown between electricity and magnetism, and it founds the new field of electromagnetism.

August 1820 ▪ Application of advanced mathematics to electrical and magnetic phenomena. The first to apply advanced mathematics to electrical and magnetic phenomena is French mathematician and physicist André-Marie Ampère (1775–1836). Within a week of hearing about the discovery made by Danish physicist Hans Christian Ørsted (1777–1851), Ampère conducts experiments that allow him to extend Ørsted's work and formulate one of the basic laws of electromagnetism. Ampère discovers that two parallel wires each carrying a current attract each other if the currents are in the same direction, but repel each other if in the opposite direction. He then concludes that magnetism is the result of electricity in motion. His mathematical theory is able to explain a magnet's properties and behavior, and essentially founds the science of electrodynamics (now called electromagnetism).

1821 ▪ Determining the wavelength of light. The first to determine the wavelength of light is Joseph von Fraunhofer (1787–1826), a German physicist and optician. He describes his method of using closely spaced thin wires or gratings to refract (bend) light. He goes on to detail how wavelengths can be measured via a mathematical relation between the wavelength of diffracted light and the distance between the wires. Fraunhofer is the first person to take an analytical approach toward the construction of these diffraction gratings. He is credited with making them into a precision instrument for obtaining the spectrum of light (splitting it into a band of its component colors). He proceeds to measure the positions of the more prominent lines he observes and proves that they always fall in the same portion of the spectrum whether the light source is direct or reflected sunlight. These lines come to be called Fraunhofer lines.

1824 ▪ Relationship of heat and work. The first to consider quantitatively (measurably) the manner in which heat and work are interconverted is French physicist Nicolas-Léonard-Sadi Carnot (1796–1832) in his *Réflexions sur la puissance motrice du feu* (Reflections on the motive power of fire). Attempting to understand the behavior of heat so as to be able to maximize a steam engine's efficiency, he proposes an equation stating that the maximum efficiency of any heat engine depends only on the difference between the hottest and coolest temperatures within the engine. Carnot's theory is recognized as the first true theory of thermodynamics (the study of heat movement), and although this work founds the science of thermodynamics, it is neglected for ten years. Carnot also makes a major contribution to physics by defining work as "weight lifted through a height." The modern restatement of this important concept defines work as any force applied through a distance against resistance.

1825 ▪ Invention of electromagnet. The electromagnet is invented by English electrical engineer William Sturgeon (1783–1850). Beginning with the work of French mathematician and physicist André-Marie Ampère

(1775–1836), Sturgeon wraps a wire many times around an iron core that is shaped like a horseshoe. When he sends a current through the wire, each coil reinforces the other since they form parallel lines with the current running in the same direction. The resulting strong magnetic force can lift 9 pounds, or twenty times its weight, and only works while the current is running.

Electricity arcing over the surface of ceramic insulators.

1827 ▪ Proposal of Ohm's law. Ohm's law is proposed by German physicist Georg Simon Ohm (1789–1854). Experimenting with various conductors (a substance through which electricity can flow), he uses wires of different length and diameter and discovers that a long, thick wire passes less current than a short, thin wire. He continues to experiment and finally states what becomes his law: that the amount of current passing through a wire is inversely proportional (opposite) to the length and directly proportional (same) to the thickness. Once accepted by the scientific community, his law makes it possible for scientists to calculate the amount of current, voltage, and resistance in circuitry, thus eventually establishing the science of electrical engineering.

1829 ▪ Work and kinetic energy get modern scientific definitions. The first to introduce the modern scientific definitions of the terms "work" and "kinetic energy" is French physicist Gaspard-Gustave de Coriolis (1792–1843). In his *Du Calcul de l'effet des machines* (On the calculation of mechanical action), he defines the kinetic energy (the energy possessed by a body because of its motion) of an object as half its mass times the square of its velocity. Work (the transfer of energy) that is done upon an object is equal to the force upon it multiplied by the distance it is moved against resistance. Coriolis's later research concerning motion on a spinning surface results in his observations of the circular motions of winds and ocean currents. The effect of Earth's rotation on the circulation of air and water at or near the Earth's surface comes to be known as the Coriolis force.

August 1831 ▪ Discovery of electromagnetic induction. Electromagnetic induction (the use of magnetism to produce electricity) is discovered by English physicist and chemist Michael Faraday (1791–1867). After laboring for ten years to achieve the opposite of what Danish physicist Hans Christian Ørsted (1777–1851) had done—convert magnetism into electricity—Faraday finally produces for the first time an induction current in a metal object by using a magnet. Further work leads to the generation of a continuous current by rotating a round copper disk between two poles of a horseshoe magnet. This is the forerunner of both the dynamo (electric generator) and the transformer (a device that changes the voltage and current of electricity). In August 1830 American physicist Joseph Henry (1797–1878) actually discovered the principle of electromagnetic induction, but put off more work until the following August. Henry is later shocked to learn that Faraday had already announced his own discovery.

1840 · Photovoltaic effect is shown. The photovoltaic effect is demonstrated by French physicist Alexandre-Edmond Becquerel

Engraving of Michael Faraday lecturing.

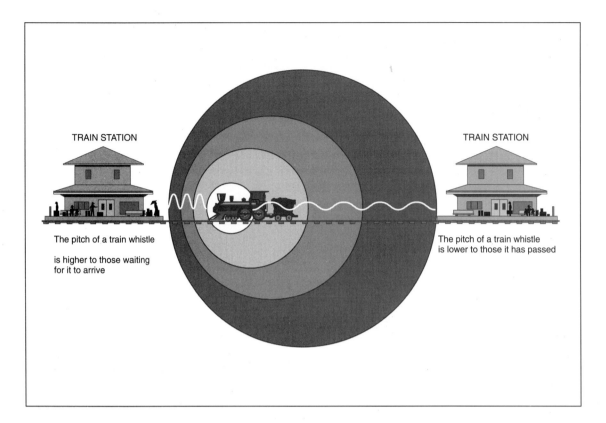

TRAIN STATION

TRAIN STATION

The pitch of a train whistle

is higher to those waiting
for it to arrive

The pitch of a train whistle
is lower to those it has passed

The Doppler effect.

(1820–1891). While investigating the solar spectrum and electricity and magnetism, he discovers that when light induces certain chemical reactions it can produce an electric current. This leads him to invent a device that can measure light intensity by determining the strength of the current it produces between two metal plates. Today's solar cells, which turn sunlight into electricity, employ the photovoltaic effect.

1842 · First time Doppler effect is stated. The Doppler effect is first stated by Austrian physicist Christian Johann Doppler (1803–1853). He studies a common but unexplained phenomenon—that the pitch of a sound varies as the source moves away from or toward the listener. Knowing that sound waves exist and that pitch depends on how far apart those waves are, he theorizes that if a sound source were moving toward a listener, the waves in front of the source would be squeezed together, creating a higher frequency. Similarly, the waves behind would be lengthened, creating a lower frequency. Doppler is then able to work out the mathematical formula that governs this shift, and once demonstrated, it becomes known as the Doppler effect. Later, both sonar and radar employ this principle, as do astronomers who prove that light can undergo a Doppler shift.

1843 ▪ Joule defines value of the mechanical equivalent of heat.

The first accurate value for the mechanical equivalent of heat is given by English physicist James Prescott Joule (1818–1889). After scores of experiments measuring heat produced by all manner of substances and processes, he determines exactly how much work is required to increase the temperature of 1 gram of water by 1° C. This value is called the mechanical equivalent of heat and is now represented by the letter J for Joule. Joule's argument that the various forms of energy—mechanical, electrical, and heat—are basically the same and can be changed, one into another, forms the basis of the law of conservation of energy (also called the first law of thermodynamics). **(See also 1847)**

1847 ▪ Conservation of energy concept is explained. The first detailed and clear explanation of the concept of conservation of energy is offered by German physiologist and physicist Hermann Ludwig Ferdinand von Helmholtz (1821–1894). He considers the sun the source of all energy and demonstrates that energy cannot be created spontaneously nor can it simply vanish, but that it is either used or released as heat. In stating that the total amount of energy in the universe is constant—meaning that it can be neither gained nor lost (although it can be converted from one form to another)—he offers science one of the most basic laws of nature. The law of conservation of energy is also known as the first law of thermodynamics.

1848 ▪ Absolute zero concept is introduced. The concept of absolute zero is introduced by Scottish mathematician and physicist William Thomson, Baron Kelvin (1824–1907). He confronts the dilemma posed by Charles's law—which states that when a gas is cooled from 0° C, its volume decreases by 1/273 for every degree drop. The dilemma is if the temperature were reduced to -273°, then the volume of the gas would be reduced to zero, and no one can explain how matter can take up no volume. Thomson explains this by stating that it is not the volume that reaches zero but the motion of the gas's molecules that stops at zero, and it effectively takes up no space. Thomson then names -273 as absolute zero since no further reduction in temperature can occur. He also introduces a new temperature scale with this ultimate low point as its zero. On his Kelvin scale, the freezing point of water is 273° K and the boiling point is 373° K.

1850 ▪ Second law of thermodynamics. The second law of thermo-dynamics is offered by German physicist Rudolf Julius Emanuel Clausius (1822–1888). This law states that heat can never pass of its own accord from a colder to a hotter body. As the French physicist Nicolas-Léonard-Sadi Carnot (1796–1832) showed in 1824, some of the energy generated by a steam engine is lost as heat and is not turned into useful work. Clausius finds, mathematically and not experimentally, that this is true of any ener-gy conversion. He says that some energy is always lost as heat and that heat can never be converted completely to any other form of energy. This second law of thermodynamics implies theoretically that at some point in a far distant future the universe may simply have no useful energy left at all. Clausius later calls this "entropy." **(See also 1865)**

1851 ▪ Experiment to prove that Earth rotates. The first experi-mental proof of the Earth's rotation is given by French physicist Jean-Bernard-Léon Foucault (1819–1868). After realizing that a pendulum has a tendency to stay swinging in one plane, he conceives a brilliant experiment to prove that the Earth moves. He conducts a spectacular demonstration before a huge crowd at the Pantheon in Paris, France, in which he sus-pends a large iron ball from a wire that is more than 200 feet long. After the pendulum is set swinging, a spike on the bottom of the ball scratches a line in the sand on the floor. As times passes, the line shifts and the crowd real-izes that since the pendulum could not arbitrarily change direction once it began to move, then the shift had to be the result of the Earth rotating. The spectators gasp at the realization that they are watching the Earth rotate under the pendulum.

1852 ▪ Invention of the gyroscope. The gyroscope is invented by French physicist Jean-Bernard-Léon Foucault (1819–1868). Learning from his pendulum experiment of the year before, he finds that just as a pendu-lum swings in an unchanging plane, so a large sphere in rotation has a simi-lar tendency to maintain the direction of its axis. Foucault then sets a wheel within a heavy rim spinning and finds that it not only holds its axial direction, but when tipped, it is set right again by the force of gravity. This suggests that a gyroscope can be used like a compass as an indicator of true north.

1855 ▪ Geissler tubes are made possible. The first Geissler tubes become possible as German inventor Johann Heinrich Wilhelm Geissler (1815–1879) devises a mercury air pump with no moving parts. The pump can remove the air from a chamber more thoroughly than anything to date. By moving a column of mercury up and down, the vacuum above the column is used to very slowly suck out the air in an enclosed vessel until the vacuum within the vessel approaches that above the mercury. With this new pump Geissler is able to produce highly improved vacuum tubes. Called Geissler tubes, they make possible a more advanced study of electricity and eventually of the atom. They lead to the discovery of the cathode-ray tube and the electron. **(See also 1858)**

1858 ▪ Using Geissler tubes in experiments. The first successful experiments with Geissler tubes are conducted by German mathematician and physicist Julius Plücker (1801–1868). Using the new improved vacuum tubes, he forces an electric current through a vacuum and observes fluorescent effects. This bright, streamlike glow between the electrodes is brighter than anything produced before. Plücker also finds that the glow responds to a magnetic field and actually shifts position. This discovery proves extremely important because it suggests that the stream crossing the vacuum is composed of particles and not rays. This is the first suggestion of an awareness of subatomic particles. It is also the beginning of the cathode-ray tube (in which a beam of electrons lights up a screen).

1859 ▪ First stating of Kirchhoff's law. Kirchhoff's law is first stated by German physicist Gustav Robert Kirchhoff (1824–1887). Using a spectroscope (which separates light into a spectrum of colored bands), he discovers that when various elements are heated to incandescence (so they emit light), each produces light of only certain wavelengths. He realizes that each element produces its own spectral lines, which it absorbs when cool and not incandescent (not producing light). This becomes known as Kirchhoff's law and it is eventually used to analyze light from any source—including the sun and the stars, and to identify its constituent elements (since the pattern of lines is different for each element).

1865 ▪ Entropy is defined. The term "entropy" is introduced by German physicist Rudolf Julius Emanuel Clausius (1822–1888) who further refines his second law of thermodynamics. Defining entropy as the ratio of heat content in a closed system to its absolute temperature, he states that the heat given off will not be reconverted into usable energy and that all of the energy will eventually be used up, filling the system with waste heat. Modern theorists have explored this concept with varying results. Some say it implies the inevitable heat-death of the universe, while others say that we have no way of knowing if the laws of physics that we understand even apply to the rest of the universe. Clausius selects the word "entropy" from the Greek word for transformation. **(See also 1850)**

1873 · Electromagnetic theory is stated. The electromagnetic theory is stated by Scottish mathematician and physicist James Clerk Maxwell

(1831–1879). After linking magnetism and electricity and then proving that they are distinctly related, he calculates mathematically the transmission speed of both electromagnetic and electrostatic waves. When his calculations indicate that both are around 186,300 miles per second, he realizes instantly that this is coincidental with the speed of light. Maxwell then makes the theoretical leap and identifies light as a form of electromagnetic radiation that travels in waves. Although unable to prove his theory at this time, he nonetheless uses it to make unheard of predictions. His idea that there are wavelengths below infrared will be proven by radio waves and radar, and his reference to wavelengths above ultraviolet will be demonstrated once X rays and gamma rays are discovered. This year he publishes his unification of the three main fields of physics—electricity, magnetism, and light—in his landmark, two-volume work, *A Treatise on Electricity and Magnetism.*

James Clerk Maxwell, pioneer in unifying electricity, magnetism, and light theory.

1876 · Cathode rays get their name. The first to use the name "cathode rays" is German physicist Eugen Goldstein (1850–1930). He applies the name to the luminescence produced at the cathode in a vacuum tube. In 1886 he also is one of the first to observe the positive rays produced when an electrical current is passed through a gas in a glass ("cathode") tube. He names these rays *Kanalstrahlen,* and they are called "channel rays" or "canal rays" in English. The study of canal rays leads to the eventual discovery of the proton.

1877 · Liquefying gases is achieved. The first to successfully liquefy gases is Louis-Paul Cailletet (1832–1913), a French physicist. By combining low temperatures with high pressure, he produces small amounts of liquid oxygen, nitrogen, and carbon monoxide. He begins by compressing a gas and then cooling it as much as possible. He allows it to expand, which makes it cool drastically. He then uses what is called the "cascade" process, which reduces temperature step by step. With this method, one liquefied gas is used to cool a second gas that has a lower critical temperature, and then the second gas, when liquefied, is used to cool another gas with an even lower critical temperature, and so on.

1880 ▪ First view of electrons. Electrons are first seen (but not recognized) by English physicist William Crookes (1832–1919). In 1875 Crookes had invented the Crookes tube, a greatly improved version of the Geissler tube (see 1855). While experimenting with his own Crookes tubes, he observes a green glow that appears when an electric current is introduced and the tube evacuated (emptied of air). He also notes that when he places a pivoting vane in the tube, it turns slightly, as if it were in the current of an invisible stream. Although he explains this effect as being caused by negatively charged particles, he cannot explain what these particles are. In 1897 English physicist Joseph John Thomson (1856–1940) proves these to be electrons. **(See also 1897)**

1880 ▪ Discovery of piezoelectricity. Piezoelectricity is discovered by French chemist Pierre Curie (1859–1906), who collaborates with his brother, Jacques. Working with crystals, they note that certain crystals (such as quartz) when compressed or stretched, create an electric charge proportionate to the amount they are stressed. The Curies then discover that when a current is applied to certain faces of a quartz crystal it expands. The crystal also vibrates when an alternating current is applied. They name this generation of electricity by stress "piezoelectricity," from the Greek word for "to press." Crystals with piezoelectric properties soon are used as an important part of sound-based electronic devices like microphones and record players.

1883 ▪ First description of the Edison effect. The Edison effect is first described by American inventor Thomas Alva Edison (1847–1931). After inserting a small metal plate near the filament of a light bulb, he finds that the plate draws a current when he connects it to the positive terminal of the light bulb circuit, even though the plate is not touching the filament. This passage of electricity from a filament to a plate of metal inside an incandescent (glowing) light bulb eventually comes to be called thermionic emission. Although Edison patents this idea in 1884 and describes it in the technical literature, he can find no immediate practical use, so he does not pursue it. This turns out to be Edison's one purely scientific discovery and it becomes a major factor in the invention of the vacuum tube as well as an important phenomenon in the study of the structure of matter during the next decade. **(See also May 7, 1911)**

1887 · Mach and the speed of sound. The first to note the sudden change in the movement of the airflow over a moving object that occurs as it approaches the speed of sound is Austrian physicist Ernst Mach (1838–1916). He conducts extensive aerodynamic experiments studying the conditions that occur when a solid object and air are in rapid motion relative to each other. The speed of sound is the natural rate at which the air's molecules move, and when an object is moving through the air at speeds higher than that natural rate, the molecules in the air literally get shoved aside faster than they want to go. This creates a bunching up of sound waves that then expand to produce a sudden clap. Because of his discovery, the speed of sound in air (under certain temperature conditions) is called Mach 1. Mach 2 is twice that speed and so on.

1887 · Ether experiment "fails". Nonexistence of ether in space is demonstrated by the failure of the Michelson-Morley experiment. German-American chemist Albert Abraham Michelson (1852–1931) collaborates with American chemist Edward Williams Morley (1838–1923) to test the age-old hypothesis that Earth moves through ether, a supposedly invisible, motionless, light-carrying element that exists outside or above the Earth's atmosphere. They use Michelson's interferometer—which splits a beam of light in two, sends each part on a different path, and then reunites them—to test out this idea. If the ether exists, Michelson states that one of the beams traveling against the ether would be slowed. When Michelson and Morley conduct their beam-splitting experiment, they can detect no difference in the velocity of light in any direction under any circumstances. Since Michelson strongly believes in the existence of the ether, he considers the experiment a failure. What it is, however, is the evidence needed to overturn the old ether theory once and for all. It also forces others to recognize that an explanation for the unchangeability of the speed of light is needed. **(See also June 30, 1905)**

1888 · Generation of first radio waves. Radio waves are generated for the first time by German physicist Heinrich Rudolph Hertz (1857–1894). Devising a simple wire loop detector that can detect and measure an electromagnetic wave, he is able to prove experimentally the 1873 prediction of Scottish mathematician and physicist James Clerk Maxwell (1831–1879) that electricity is propagated in wave formations, and to verify his hypothesis that light is an electromagnetic phenomenon. The work of Hertz not only discovers radio waves and leads eventually to radio communication, but brings together the three main fields of physics—electricity, magnetism, and light.

1889 · Photoelectric cell is made practical. The first practical photoelectric cells that can measure the intensity of light are developed by Johann Philipp Ludwig Julius Elster (1854–1920) and Hans Friedrich Geitel (1855–1923), both German physicists. Further study of the photoelectric effect (when an electric current is created upon the exposure of certain metals to light) leads to their invention of the modern photoelectric cell by modifying a cathode-ray tube. Their affordable cell eventually makes it possible for many industries to develop photoelectrical technology and leads directly to the development of television.

1892 · Invention of the thermos bottle. The first thermos bottle is built by Scottish chemist and physicist James Dewar (1842–1923). Studying the liquefaction of gases, he faces the problem of keeping the gases cold long enough to analyze them. Since liquid oxygen kept in a flask absorbs heat from the air and turns back to a gas, he puts the flask with liquid gas in it inside a larger flask and creates a vacuum between them. He finds that the vacuum prevents the transfer of energy that occurs through conduction (transmission through another medium) or convection (transfer of heat by circulation), and that heat will not penetrate, nor will cold escape. Dewar continues to improve his device and it comes to be known as the Dewar flask. Since his flasks also keep hot liquids hot and cold liquids cold, they become adapted to everyday use and are known as the thermos bottle.

April 25, 1894 · Marconi builds radio wave receiver. Italian electrical engineer Guglielmo Marconi (1874–1937) uses the method of producing radio waves invented by German physicist Heinrich Rudolph Hertz (1857–1894) and builds a receiver to detect them. After experimenting with Hertz's spark-gap generator and building an improved detector, Marconi succeeds in sending his first radio waves 30 feet to ring a bell. The next year, his improved system can send a signal $1\frac{1}{2}$ miles.

November 5, 1895 · Accidental discovery of X rays. X rays are discovered accidentally by German physicist Wilhelm Conrad Röntgen

A nine and a half pound button of uranium-235, which will be manufactured into a nuclear weapons component.

(1845–1923), initiating the modern age of physics and revolutionizing medicine. While experimenting with cathode-ray tubes (in which a beam of electrons lights up a screen), he notices that a nearby sheet of paper that is coated with a luminescent substance glows whenever the cathode-ray tube is turned on. Röntgen becomes especially intrigued when he sees that the paper is glowing despite being blocked by a piece of cardboard. Further experimentation reveals to him that some sort of radiation is emerging from the cathode-ray tube that is highly penetrating but invisible. Having no idea what is the nature of these rays, he calls them X rays for unknown. He experiments for seven weeks, and near the end of the year feels prepared to report publicly the basic properties of these unknown rays. **(See also December 28, 1895)**

December 28, 1895 · Report on X rays. The discovery of X rays is announced by German physicist Wilhelm Conrad Röntgen (1845–1923), who submits a paper documenting his discovery. He tells how this unknown ray or radiation can affect photographic plates, and that wood, paper, and aluminum do not block it. It also can ionize gases (giving them an electric charge) and does not respond to electric or magnetic fields nor exhibit any properties of light. This discovery leads to such a stream of groundbreaking discoveries in physics that it has been called the beginning of the second Scientific Revolution.

1896 ▪ Cloud chamber is first developed. The first cloud chamber is developed by Scottish physicist Charles Thomson Rees Wilson (1869–1959). Trying to duplicate cloud effects, he devises a way of allowing moist air to expand in a closed container. This expansion cools the air so that it becomes supersaturated. Following the discovery of X rays, Wilson introduces radiation to the chamber and discovers that charged particles make useful tracks that can be photographed and studied. These tracks or fog trails reveal whether the charge is positive or negative and how massive the particle is. They also indicate collisions of particles with molecules or other particles.

March 1, 1896 ▪ Natural radioactivity. The first observation of natural radioactivity is made by French physicist Antoine-Henri Becquerel (1852–1908). While studying fluorescent materials to see if they might emit the newly discovered X rays, Becquerel discovers instead that uranium produces a natural ray. He finds this out when he uses potassium uranyl sulfate (containing uranium atoms) as the fluorescent material and discovers that it fogs photographic film on a sunless day. He realizes that whatever rays the material is giving off have nothing to do with either sunlight or fluorescence. In 1898 Polish-French chemist Marie Sklodowska Curie (1867–1934) studies these rays and names the phenomenon "radioactivity."

1897 ▪ Invention of the oscilloscope. The oscilloscope is invented by Karl Ferdinand Braun (1850–1918), a German physicist. He modifies a cathode-ray tube (in which a beam of electrons lights up a screen) so that the streaming electrons are affected by the electromagnetic field of a varying current. This results in the green fluorescent spot formed by the stream of speeding particles shifting with the electromagnetic field set up by a varying current. This modified cathode-ray tube is known as the oscillograph or oscilloscope. Its ability to show the changing voltage of an electrical signal as a curved line on a screen makes it the first step toward television and radar.

1897 ▪ Discovery of the electron. The electron is discovered by English physicist Joseph John Thomson (1856–1940). An electron is a tiny, negatively charged particle that moves in a path around the nucleus of an atom. Thomson produces cathode rays in a much-improved vacuum tube he builds and is able to deflect them with an electric field as well as a magnet (proving they are negatively charged). He then conducts further cathode-ray experiments and concludes that these "electrons" are smaller in mass than hydrogen atoms, the smallest particle then known. The electron is the first subatomic particle to be discovered.

1899 ▪ Intensity of radiation is studied. Johann Philipp Ludwig Julius Elster (1854–1920) and Hans Friedrich Geitel (1855–1923), German physicists, demonstrate together that external effects do not influence the intensity of radiation. Elster and Geitel are also the first to characterize radiation as being caused by changes that take place within the atom. Until their work, it was not known whether radiation was an effect caused only by uranium or whether it could be found elsewhere in nature. They show that radiation can be found at varying levels nearly everywhere in the universe.

1900 ▪ First proposal of quantum theory. Quantum theory is first proposed by German physicist Max Karl Ernst Ludwig Planck (1858–1947). In his revolutionary paper, he tells of his discovery that light or energy is not found in nature as a continuous wave or flow but is emitted and absorbed discontinuously in little packets or "quanta." Further, each quantum or packet of energy is indivisible. Planck's entirely new notion of the quantum seems to contradict the mechanics of English scientist and mathematician Isaac Newton (1642–1727) and the electromagnetics of Scottish mathematician and physicist James Clerk Maxwell (1831–1879), and to replace them with new rules. In fact, Planck's quantum physics are the new rules of a new game of physics—the game of the very fast and the very small. His theory is soon applied by German-Swiss-American physicist Albert Einstein (1879–1955) and incorporated into physics by Danish physicist Niels Henrik David Bohr (1885–1962) and becomes the watershed mark between all physics that comes before it (classical physics) and all that is after it (modern physics).

1900 ▪ Discovery of radon. Radon is discovered by German physicist Friedrich Ernst Dorn (1848–1916). He demonstrates that the newly discovered element radium gives off a radioactive gas he calls "radium emanation" (radon), as well as producing radioactive radiation. This proves to be the first demonstrable evidence that in the radioactive process, one element is actually transmuted (essentially converted) into another.

1900 · First description of gamma rays. Gamma rays are first described by French physicist Paul Ulrich Villard (1860–1934). While studying the radiation given off by uranium, he notes that along with the already-discovered alpha and beta rays, a third type of radiation exists. Further analysis shows that it is unaffected by a magnetic field and is more energetic than beta rays. He also finds that where alpha rays are stopped by a few centimeters of air, and beta rays by a few centimeters of aluminum, gamma rays are unusually penetrating and can only be stopped by a relatively thick piece of lead. It is some time before it is realized that since the wavelengths of gamma rays are like very short X rays, they are a form of electromagnetic radiation.

December 12, 1901 · First transatlantic radio transmission. The first transatlantic radio transmission is achieved by Italian electrical engineer Guglielmo Marconi (1874–1937), who successfully sends a radio signal from England to Newfoundland, Canada. Although the system is still only useful for sending Morse code, its achievement generally is considered by most as the day radio is invented. Marconi proves his many critics wrong in their belief that since radio waves seem to travel in only straight lines, they would travel no farther than the horizon. He sends his signals more than 2,000 miles and demonstrates that radio is viable for vast distances and will become an important form of communication.

1904 · First suggestion of Lorentz transformation. Lorentz transformations are first suggested by Dutch physicist Hendrik Antoon Lorentz (1853–1928). Considering the negative results of the 1887 Michelson-Morley experiment (see 1887: Ether experiment "fails"), Lorentz attempts to explain its results by assuming that matter, consisting of electrons, decreases in length as it moves. The faster it moves, the more the matter is shortened. While this is not noticeable at everyday velocities, speeds approaching that of light make this an important phenomenon. One consequence of this theory is that nothing can exceed the speed of light since no object can have a negative length (although it can have a zero length, which it has at exactly the speed of light). These mathematical formulas that he uses to describe the increase of mass, shortening of length, and dilation of time are called Lorentz transformations. They eventually serve to form the basis of German-Swiss-American physicist Albert Einstein's (1879–1955) special theory of relativity.

1904 · Concept of boundary layer is first proposed. Boundary layer concept is first offered by German physicist Ludwig Prandtl

(1875–1953). He discovers that as liquid flows in a tube, a film layer forms next to the wall that does not flow as fast as the rest of the liquid. Called the viscous boundary layer, this concept also applies to the surface of a body moving in air or water. This, in turn, eventually leads to an understanding of skin friction drag and of the way in which streamlining reduces the drag of airplane wings and other moving bodies. Prandtl's work becomes the basic material of aerodynamics (the study of the movement of objects in air).

Albert Einstein

March 17, 1905 · Einstein and the dual nature of light. The dual nature of light is first stated by German-Swiss-American physicist Albert Einstein (1879–1955). Assuming that light travels in quanta (see 1900: First proposal of quantum theory)—following the new theory of German physicist Max Karl Ernst Ludwig Planck (1858–1947)—Einstein says light therefore also has particle-like properties, as well as those of a wave. Thus, prior to stating his special theory of relativity, he states that light has a dual, wave/particle quality.

June 30, 1905 · Special theory of relativity. Special theory of relativity is offered by German-Swiss-American physicist Albert Einstein (1879–1955). His theory states that motion or movement is relative and not absolute. Since there is no one, fixed point in the universe, we cannot say that some things are moving and others are not. All we can say is that things move "relative" to each other. Einstein also says that the only known absolute in the universe is the speed of light (since it is independent of both the light source and the motion of the observer). This is a fundamentally new and revolutionary way to look at the universe, and this new world picture soon replaces the old Newtonian system. **(See also September 27, 1905)**

September 27, 1905 · E = mc² is first suggested. The equation $E = mc^2$ is posited by German-Swiss-American physicist Albert Einstein (1879–1955). In his second paper on relativity, he includes this famous equation stating the relationship between mass and energy (E is energy, m is mass, and c is the velocity of light). This equation changes the traditional concept of mass as a fixed, inert thing into something that can be transformed into energy, since mass and energy are but different aspects of the same phenomenon. Coupled with his earlier special theory of relativity, Einstein abolishes concepts of absolute space and time and revolutionizes physics to its core, altering its most primary conceptions. **(See also June 30, 1905)**

1905 ▪ Stating of third law of thermodynamics. The third law of thermodynamics is stated by German physical chemist Walther Hermann Nernst (1864–1941). Also described as the determination of chemical equilibrium, it proves to be a powerful tool for determining the attainability of many chemical reactions. After working for eleven years on the fact that chemical reactions behave very differently near absolute zero (the lowest possible temperature), Nernst succeeds in approaching absolute zero to within 1 degree and finds that all matter tends toward random motion and all energy tends to dissipate. Since he knows that at absolute zero the motion of particles in all substances will stop, Nernst holds this to be a proof of the impossibility of attaining absolute zero and hails this as the third law of thermodynamics. His law has wide applications and supports the emerging theories of quantum physics.

1908 ▪ Development of the Geiger counter. The first Geiger counter is developed by German physicist Johannes Hans Wilhelm Geiger (1882–1945) and British physicist Ernest Rutherford (1871–1937). Rutherford's research on energetic particles that are emitted by radioactive substances is made much easier as his assistant, Geiger, invents the first successful device to detect and later record these particles. Geiger builds a cylinder containing a gas under high electric potential. When a high-energy subatomic particle enters, it sets off a mass of ionization (an atom gaining an electron) that produces a momentary electric discharge (designed to give a click sound). This first successful counter of individual alpha rays is improved by Geiger in 1913 (so as to count beta particles as well), and again in 1928 in collaboration with Walther Müller, to produce a more sensitive all-particle detecting device with a longer lifetime.

1910 ▪ First evidence of the existence of isotopes. The first indication that ordinary elements may also exist as isotopes is given by English physicist Joseph John Thomson (1856–1940). An isotope is a different version of the same element (having a different number of neutrons). Isotopes are produced in radioactive transformations. While measuring deflections

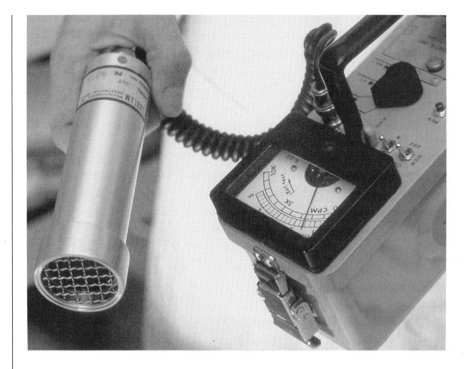

A hand held Geiger counter.

of positive rays in a cathode tube and calculating the masses of various atoms, Thomson obtains results suggesting that there are two different types of neon gas. This is the first confirmation that isotopes are possible, as predicted by English chemist Frederick Soddy (1877–1956). **(See also February 18, 1913)**

1911 ▪ Phenomenon of superconductivity is discovered. The superconductivity phenomenon is discovered by Dutch physicist Heike Kamerlingh Onnes (1853–1926) as he studies the properties of certain metals subjected to the low temperatures of liquid helium. Aware that metals tend to lessen their resistance to an electric current as the temperature drops, Kamerlingh Onnes finds that some metals, such as mercury and lead, undergo a total loss of electrical resistance at temperatures close to absolute zero and can be called "superconductors."

May 7, 1911 ▪ Nuclear atom theory is stated. The theory of the nuclear atom is announced by British physicist Ernest Rutherford (1871–1937). He states that the atom contains a very small, positively charged nucleus at its center and that the nucleus also contains all the protons of the atom, and therefore virtually all of its mass. The nucleus is surrounded by negatively charged electrons that are very light and pose no barrier to the passage of alpha particles. This concept replaces the old idea of the atom as a featureless, indivisible sphere and lays the foundation for the development of nuclear physics.

1913 • Moseley proposes atomic numbers. Atomic numbers of the elements are first proposed by English physicist Henry Gwyn Jeffreys Moseley (1887–1915). After comparing the wavelengths of more than fifty elements to their respective atomic weights (which tells how much matter there is in a substance), Moseley discovers that these wavelengths all decrease regularly and in an orderly pattern as their atomic weight increases. He then discovers that this means that a particular element has the same number of electrons as its nuclear charge (which he calls "atomic number"), and that the position of an element in the periodic table might be indicated by its nuclear charge as well as by its atomic weight. He also realizes that arranging the elements by atomic number will give scientists, for the first time, foreknowledge of how many elements remain to be discovered and where in the periodic table they would fall.

1913 • Applying quantum theory to the atom. The first application of quantum theory to the atom is made by Danish physicist Niels Henrik David Bohr (1885–1962). His idea offers an entirely different theoretical model for the hydrogen atom. Searching to understand how an atom radiates light, he incorporates the quantum concept of German physicist Max Karl Ernst Ludwig Planck (1858–1947) and states that electrons orbit the nucleus in fixed orbits, giving off quanta (separate packets of energy) when jumping from one orbit to another. When an electron loses energy, it will drop to a lower orbit nearer the nucleus, and when it absorbs energy, it will rise to a higher orbit. This is the first reasonably successful attempt to explain the internal structure of the atom via spectroscopy (which analyzes substances by examining the colors in the light they give off). **(See also Chemistry: 1911)**

February 18, 1913 • Isotopes get their name. Isotopes are named by English chemist Frederick Soddy (1877–1956). He observes that an atom that loses an alpha particle or a beta particle changes in a very predictable way into another kind of atom. According to what it loses, the atom's charge changes and it occupies a different but predictable place on the periodic table. Thus an atom in position 90 on the table could have been produced by an alpha decay of element 92 (since an alpha has a 2 charge) or a beta decay of element 89 (charge of 1). This means that atoms with the same number can still have different atomic weights. Soddy calls this phenomenon "isotopes," meaning roughly, "the same place." Today, isotopes are considered forms of an element that have the same atomic number (the same number of protons) but different atomic weights (different number of neutrons).

Ernest Rutherford, the founder of nuclear physics.

1919 ▪ Creation of first man-made nuclear reaction. The first man-made nuclear reaction is created by British physicist Ernest Rutherford (1871–1937). When he bombards nitrogen gas with alpha particles, the nitrogen atoms that are struck are converted to oxygen atoms and protons (hydrogen nuclei), thus achieving the first form of artificial fission (the splitting of nuclei to release energy). Rutherford succeeds in altering an atomic nuclei and thus in transforming one element into another. For investigating radioactivity, discovering the alpha particle, and developing the nuclear theory of atomic structure, Rutherford becomes known as the father of nuclear physics.

1925 ▪ Naming of cosmic rays. Cosmic rays are named by American physicist Robert Andrews Millikan (1868–1953). This year he and his associate, George H. Cameron (1902–1977), attempt to detect the background radiation that constantly bombards Earth at extremely high speeds. They lower an electroscope (an instrument that detects an electric charge) into a lake and still are able to detect radiation that is more powerful than any known emission. Measurements taken from different locations assure them that the source is from outer space, and Millikan thus chooses to call this unexplainable radiation "cosmic rays." Today, we know that cosmic rays are not rays but fast-moving protons, electrons, and nuclei produced by the sun and stars.

October 1926 ▪ Origin of photon. The term "photon" is introduced by American chemist Gilbert Newton Lewis (1875–1946) to describe the minute, discrete energy packet of electromagnetic radiation that is essential to quantum theory. The concept comes into general use after American physicist Arthur Holly Compton (1892–1962) demonstrates in 1923 the corpuscular (particle-like) nature of X rays. Photons are subatomic particles that travel at the speed of light, have no electric charge, and are carriers of the electromagnetic field. The term comes from the Greek *photos*, for light.

1927 ▪ Uncertainty principle is advanced. The uncertainty principle is put forward by German physicist Werner Karl Heisenberg (1901–1976). Also known as the principle of indeterminacy, this principle states that it is impossible to determine accurately two variables of an electron (such as its position and momentum) at the same time. More generally, it states that when working at the level of atom-sized particles, the very act of measuring such particles affects and therefore interferes with the results obtained. We cannot therefore accurately predict the behavior of particles. Philosophically, this can be a troubling notion, for it calls into question much of our traditional belief in straightforward cause and effect. Scientifically, however, it contributes to a better understanding of how the universe actually works.

September 1927 ▪ Complementarity principle is introduced. The idea of complementarity is introduced by Danish physicist Niels Henrik David Bohr (1885–1962). In general, this principle states that certain atomic phenomena can be considered in each of two mutually exclusive ways, with each way staying valid on its own terms. In physics, Bohr applies this principle specifically to the simultaneous wave and particle behavior of both light and electrons. Bohr says that although it is impossible to observe both wave and particle aspects simultaneously, together these aspects present a more complete description than either of the two taken alone. His work serves to reconcile some of the apparent conflicts between classical physics and quantum physics.

1929 ▪ Development of first successful particle accelerator. The first successful particle accelerator is developed by British physicist John Douglas Cockcroft (1897–1967) and Irish physicist Ernest Thomas Sinton Walton (1903–1995). They devise an arrangement of condensers (devices that store electrical charges) that produce a beam of protons accelerated at a very high speed. These are later made to collide with accelerated electrons traveling in the opposite direction, producing high-energy nuclear reactions and therefore new particles. Until this invention, the only means of changing one element into another was by bombarding it with alpha particles from a natural source, such as a radioactive substance.

1930 · Building of the first cyclotron. The first cyclotron is built by American physicist Ernest Orlando Lawrence (1901–1958). He invents a device that accelerates protons, electrons, and other subatomic particles by having them spin in spirals, giving them an additional boost each time around. It is the first accelerating device that uses a magnetic field to force particles into a spiral orbit of increasing sizes and energy. This first cyclotron is small, but Lawrence builds successively larger ones and gives physicists a major tool for producing high-energy nuclear reactions via collisions.

May 1931 · Existence of antiparticles is proposed. Antiparticles are first theorized by British physicist Paul Adrien Maurice Dirac (1902–1984). After his mathematical calculations indicate that an electron can have two different types of energy states—one positive and one negative—he concludes that since the electron is negatively charged, there should exist a similar, positively charged particle. Antiparticles are therefore two particles with the same mass but with opposite properties. They are later created in particle accelerators.

February 27, 1932 · Discovery of the neutron. The neutron is discovered by English physicist James Chadwick (1891–1974). After noting that bombarding light elements such as beryllium and lithium with alpha particles results in an intense but unknown form of radiation, Chadwick experiments and concludes that the radiation must consist of particles with no charge and a mass equal to that of the proton. He calls this neutral (no charge) particle a neutron. This discovery is of major importance to nuclear physicists since—unlike the proton, electron, and other subatomic particles—the neutron is not repelled by either the nucleus or the orbital electrons in an atom. It thus proves to be a much more efficient "bullet" for atomic scientists who seek to initiate nuclear reactions.

1934 · Creation of artificial radioactivity. The first example of "artificial radioactivity" is produced by French physicists Frédéric Joliot-Curie (1900–1958) and Irène Joliot-Curie (1897–1956), a husband-and-wife team. They bombard aluminum with alpha particles and discover that it contin-

A cyclotron at the University of California at Berkeley, 1947.

ues to emit radiation even after the bombardment ceases. They then find that the reaction results in a transformation, and that they have produced an isotope of phosphorus (a radioactive form of phosphorus that does not exist naturally). This shows that radioactivity is not confined only to heavy elements such as uranium, but that any element can become radioactive if the proper isotope is prepared.

1934 · Nuclear chain reaction becomes a theory. The nuclear chain reaction idea is conceived by Hungarian-American physicist Leo Szilard (1898–1964). His notion of a nuclear chain reaction is one in which a neutron induces an atomic breakdown, which then releases two neutrons, which in turn break down two more atoms, and so on. Although his method uses beryllium rather than uranium and would be impractical, it is correct in principle. He keeps it a secret, foreseeing its importance in making nuclear bombs, but it is soon discovered by others.

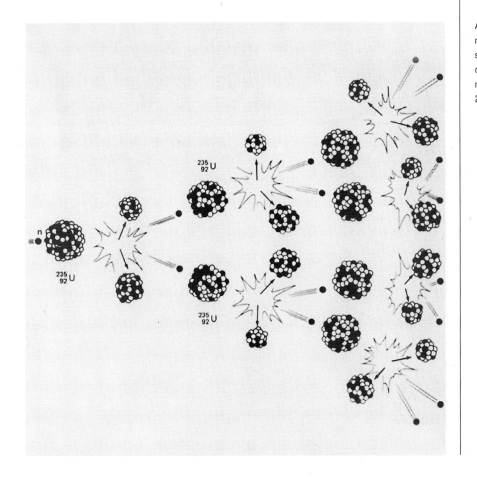

A nuclear chain reaction: the successive fissioning of ever-increasing numbers of uranium-235 atoms.

1934 · First nuclear fission reaction. The first nuclear fission reaction is produced by Italian-American physicist Enrico Fermi (1901–1954). Fission is the splitting of nuclei to release energy. Fermi bombards uranium, the heaviest-known element, with neutrons and obtains not only a new element, but also a number of other products he is unable to identify. What he eventually discovers is that he has not only created a synthetic element, number 93, but that he has also produced the first nuclear fission reaction. In addition, he finds that neutrons that pass through paraffin or water are more effective at starting nuclear reactions than those that do not because the neutrons are slowed down and spend more time in the vicinity of the target nuclei. **(See also December 2, 1942)**

Lise Meitner, co-developer of the theory of nuclear fission.

February 11, 1939 · Explanation of fission. The term "fission" is first used by Austrian-Swedish physicist Lise Meitner (1878–1968) and her nephew, Austrian-English physicist Otto Robert Frisch (1904-1979), to describe the splitting apart of the uranium nucleus and the release of energy that accompanies it. Although the discovery of this phenomenon is made by German physical chemist Otto Hahn (1879–1968) and German chemist Fritz Strassmann (1902–1980), and published the month before, they do not use the word "fission" nor actually describe the breaking apart of the uranium nucleus. Meitner and her nephew, however, develop a theory as well as a name for Hahn's discovery, and their explanation of fission proves to be an essential link in the development of the atomic bomb.

December 2, 1942 · Production of first controlled chain reaction. The first self-sustaining nuclear chain reaction is produced by Italian-American physicist Enrico Fermi (1901–1954), who heads the wartime Manhattan Project team at the University of Chicago in pursuit of producing an atom bomb. A controlled chain reaction is produced in an "atomic pile" made up of uranium and uranium oxide with graphite blocks. This pile is actually the first nuclear reactor and consists of the fuel (uranium), a moderator (graphite), and control rods (made of cadmium). Control rods absorb neutrons released during fission, and as the rods are slowly with-

The Manhattan Project: Making the Atom Bomb

Atomic bomb blast, Nagasaki, August 8, 1945.

As events propelled Europe into World War II in the early 1940s, all of the scientific discovery necessary for the construction of the atom bomb was falling into place. Many scientists recognized this and became convinced that the United States should build a bomb before Adolph Hitler and the Nazis could build one. A group of scientists persuaded Albert Einstein to present a letter to President Franklin D. Roosevelt describing the atom bomb and encouraging funding for its development.

In mid-1942 Roosevelt authorized the creation of the Manhattan Project, a team of scientists whose charge was to build the bomb and who were provided the funding to do it. One group worked out ways to produce fissionable material for the bomb, particularly trying to separate the naturally occuring but hard to obtain uranium-235 from the more common uranium-238. Another team, centered at the University of Chicago and led by Enrico Fermi, researched the atomic pile and the first chain reaction. The third team, led by J. Robert Oppenheimer, was charged with research and basic assembly. The final challenges in every area were worked out in a relatively short time. The first test of a nuclear weapon was successfully conducted near Alamagordo, New Mexico, on July 16, 1945. Within a month, two bombs were dropped on Japan, at Hiroshima and Nagasaki, killing an estimated 110,000–150,000 people and injuring 200,000 or more people.

drawn from the reactor, more and more neutrons become available to start the reaction. Once it is actually demonstrated that a nuclear reaction is physically possible, Fermi and his team are able to stop it from going out of control by reinserting the rods. With this, the atomic age begins.

1947 ▪ Concept of holography. Holography is conceived by Hungarian-British physicist and electrical engineer Dennis Gabor (1900–1979). He works out the idea of holography as lenseless, three-dimensional photography and begins to develop its basic techniques. His idea involves splitting a beam of light, resulting in a three-dimensional image that can convey far more information than an ordinary photograph. Since the light sources available are too weak or too diffuse, however, and the technology of optics has not advanced enough, he must wait until the 1960 invention of the laser to make his idea commercially feasible. **(See also May 1960)**

1952 ▪ Construction of the first bubble chamber. The first bubble chamber is constructed by American physicist Donald Arthur Glaser (1926–). While studying new "strange" particles, he finds he needs a medium of higher density than the vapor cloud available in a cloud chamber (See 1896: Cloud chamber is first developed). Glaser builds a device that is the reverse of a cloud chamber and uses a liquid ready to boil rather than a vapor ready to condense. His glass container is filled with superheated diethyl ether in which ions (atoms that carry an electric charge) form when high energy radiation passes through. This new method proves far more sensitive than cloud chambers and when improved, proves to be a powerful detection device for particle physicists.

May 1960 ▪ First working laser is built. The first working laser is constructed by American physicist Theodore Harold Maiman (1927–). He uses a ruby cylinder that emits a light that is coherent (all in a single direction) and monochromatic (a single wavelength). He finds that the light can travel thousands of miles as a beam without dispersing, and that it can be concentrated into a small, superhot spot. Laser is an acronym for "Light Amplification by Stimulated Emission of Radiation," which actually describes not the beam of light but the machine used to create the beam. Modern applications of the laser include delicate surgery—especially upon the eye—communications, and even weaponry.

February 1964 ▪ Quark concept is introduced. American physicist Murray Gell-Mann (1929–) introduces the concept of "quarks" as he theorizes the existence of unusual particles that carry fractional or partial electric charges. He proposes that protons are not themselves fundamental particles but that they are composed of quarks. Gell-Mann's models based on quarks prove useful for their predictive value. Thirty years later, quarks are still being investigated as to whether they are ultimate particles or not (although they have never been produced individually). Gell-Mann chooses the unusual name from a line in *Finnegans Wake*, written in 1939 by Irish novelist James Joyce (1882–1941), "Three quarks for Master Mark."

1974 • Development of first grand unified theory. The first grand unified theory is developed by American physicists Howard M. Georgi and Sheldon Lee Glashow (1932–). Their unified theory ties together the strong and electroweak theories and attempts to show how both forces can be thought of as manifestations of a single basic force. Georgi and Glashow's theory accounts for four fundamental forces that hold everything together—gravity, the strong nuclear force, the weak nuclear force, and the electromagnetic force. They say that each is a part of a single force that broke apart when the universe cooled down after the big bang.

1986 • Demonstration of superconductivity in ceramic materials. Superconductivity in ceramic materials is first demonstrated by Swiss physicist Karl Alexander Müller (1927–) and German-Swiss physicist Johannes Georg Bednorz (1950–). They discover an oxide combination that, at around 30° K (or 30° above absolute zero), is the highest-known temperature for superconductivity reached to date. Prior to this, superconductivity (conducting electricity without resistance) was attainable only at impractical temperatures near absolute zero (0° K).

1991 • Discovery of Nitromag. New material called Nitromag is discovered by a team of scientists in Ireland. Belonging to the generation of permanent magnetic alloys (a mixture of metals), Nitromag's composition ($Nd_2 Fe_{17} N_3$) is such that magnets made of this material remain useful at much higher temperatures, allowing them to be used in more severe environments.

1995 • Scientists produce new state of matter. A new state of matter, a Bose-Einstein condensate, is first produced by American physicists Carl Wieman and Eric Cornell. By producing conditions that are extremely close to absolute zero (the lowest possible temperature at which the motion of particles in all substances will stop), Wieman and Cornell produce this new state of matter that appears as only a brief blob on a television screen. This single, fuzzy megaparticle is what happens to atoms when put in temperatures of 20 nanokelvins, which is 36 billionths of a degree Fahrenheit above absolute zero. This is the coldest temperature ever produced, and at this state, atoms slow down and smear. This means that while the speed of atoms is able to be determined, their location is indefinite since they become wavelike.

Transportation

c. 7500 B.C. ▪ Reed boats and dugout canoes are developed.
Reed boats are first developed in Mesopotamia and Egypt, while in north-western Europe, dugout canoes are used. Reed boats are made from the stem of the papyrus plant. These reeds are bound together to make boats, probably spool-shaped, with their bows (front) pointed and curved upwards. A dugout canoe is made from a log that is hollowed out by burning, chipping, and scraping. Its outer edges are sometimes streamlined in shape. Both are used only for inland waters.

c. 5000 B.C. ▪ Early ship illustration is found. The earliest-known ship illustration is found at Hierakonpolis in Egypt. It shows a reed boat with a steering oar that works from the port (left) side. The earliest illustration of a sail dates from around 3500 B.C. Painted on the outside of a funeral vase found near Luxor, Egypt, the illustration shows a ship with a sail fixed to a single mast and a shelter aft or toward the rear. Square sails made of reed matting and later square and rectangular ones of rough cloth made good use of the wind well before this date.

c. 4500 B.C. ▪ Oldest long-distance highway. The oldest long-distance highway begins to be regularly used. Later known by the Persians as the Royal Road, it takes travelers on a 1,755-mile (2,825-kilometer) journey beginning in Susa (now in Iran) to the Turkish ports of Ephesus and

Smyrna. A relay system of royal messengers could make the entire trip in nine days, although normal travel was about three months. Alexander the Great (356–323 B.C.), king of Macedonia, uses this road in his successful invasion of the Persian Empire.

c. 4000 B.C. ▪ Early use of yokes on draft animals. The yoke is used, possibly for the first time, in the Near East. This wooden bar or frame rests on the shoulders or withers (the ridge between the shoulder bones of a work animal) of draft animals and is tied to their neck or horns to assure that they pull together. Around 2300 B.C., bridles (straplike headgear an animal wears so it can be controlled) and bits (the hard part of a bridle that is held in the animal's mouth) made of horn or bone are first introduced in Mesopotamia. Oxen are guided by a rope or ring through their nose.

c. 3500 B.C. ▪ Invention of the wheel. The wheel is invented at the dawn of the Bronze Age (era of human history characterized by the use of bronze, dating roughly between 4000 B.C. and 1000 B.C.). No one knows exactly when and where the principle of the wheel was discovered. The first wheeled vehicles are believed to have appeared in Sumer (now Iraq) at this time since there exist temple drawings of wheeled vehicles that date to this period. The wheel for transport may have evolved from a rolling log as well as from the potter's wheel.

c. 3500 B.C. ▪ Chinese imperial road system is developed. The imperial road system begins to be developed in China. Totaling about 2,000 miles of road, it is well-built, often surfaced with stone, and distinctive in its crookedness. Around 1900 B.C., the earliest roads in Europe, called the "Amber Routes," begin to be made and are used by Etruscan and Greek traders to transport amber (a hard, yellow-brown translucent stone) and tin from north of Europe to the Mediterranean and Adriatic Seas (the Etruscans were the people of Etruria, an ancient country in central Italy). Four separate routes have been identified.

c. 3000 B.C. ▪ Slide-car is used to carry objects. The slide-car, a type of improved and more permanent travois or Y-sled, is used to carry objects. It has two poles or shafts that are attached to an animal's side, with its other ends dragging on the ground. The poles are kept apart by crossbars and the cargo is carried on them.

A Prsewalski's horse, one of the last remaining species of wild horses. Horses have been used by humans for work and transportation since around 2000 B.C.

c. 2650 B.C. ▪ Cheops burial ship. The oldest known remains of a complete ship, known as the Cheops burial ship, is discovered in modern times and dated to this period. A wood-planked ship over 43 meters (141 feet) long, its refinement indicates substantial experience with timber construction. Cheops, also known as Khufu, was an Egyptian king and builder of the Great Pyramid at Giza.

c. 2250 B.C. ▪ Babylonians use principle of a railway. The principle of a railway, as a track that guides vehicles along it, is first known and used by the ancient Babylonians, who build grooved stone wagon-ways about 5 feet (1.5 meters) wide. Around 200 B.C., "rut" roads first are built on the island of Malta. They consist of two V-shaped grooves about 4.5 feet (1.4 meters) apart cut into the coral sandstone of the island. The wheels of pulled carts fit in the grooves.

c. 2000 B.C. ▪ Nomads tame horses. Horses are tamed by the nomads in the steppes (level, treeless areas) of what is now Iran. Although not as strong as an ox and difficult to harness, horses prove well-suited to pulling a light, wheeled vehicle that becomes the chariot. Horses are eventually trained to allow men to ride on their backs.

1352 B.C. ▪ Chariots are buried with King Tutankhamen. Egyptian King Tutankhamen (c. 1370–1352 B.C.) dies and is buried with his chariots. When the intact tomb is discovered in 1922 by English archaeologist Howard Carter (1873–1939), working parts of dismantled wooden chariots are found. The chariot was introduced to Egypt around 1600 B.C. by neighboring Middle Eastern invaders, the Hyksos. It usually resembled a two-wheeled cart in which the driver stood and held the reins of the horses pulling it. Chariots maneuvered well on flat battlefields and were the equivalent of modern tanks.

c. 1000 B.C. ▪ Kite is invented. The kite is invented in China. As the true ancestor of the airplane, the kite can be considered the first type of heavier-than-air device to fly. Since the propulsion is supplied by the kite being tilted or inclined to the wind, it is really a tethered glider.

681 B.C. ▪ Bireme ships are in use. The first recorded illustration of a bireme (a ship with two banks of rowers) is found in the ruins of King Sennacherib's palace in Assyria. At about this time, the Phoenicians also had bireme war galleys in which oarsmen, sitting inside the hull, worked a lower row of oars while others on benches pulled an upper tier of oars. The Phoenicians are the most enterprising sea travelers of this age.

c. 600 B.C. ▪ Greek galley is introduced. The Greek galley is introduced as the major fighting ship of this time. It is a long, low, sleek vessel that is lightly built and propelled by oars. The later biremes (two rows of oarsmen) and triremes (three rows with different length oars) are larger versions of this ship. As fighting ships, their main offensive weapon is a ram made of hard wood that projects from the bow and sometimes under the waterline. Around 400 B.C., the *cercurus* type of ship first appears in Greek waters. This light, fast, round-bottomed boat becomes the standard cargo carrier of the time. Its mast carries a large, square sail and it is aided by a single bank of twenty oars.

c. 325 B.C. ▪ Early horseshoes. Alexander the Great (356–323 B.C.), king of Macedonia, is reported to have used "boots" or "sandals" on his horses' feet to protect them in rough terrain. These are an early form of horseshoes. About 50 B.C., the Roman poet Catullus (c. 84–c. 54 B.C.) mentions U-shaped metal plates that protect a horse's hooves. Around A.D. 900, real horseshoes made of iron begin to appear. These increase a horse's speed and extend the distance a horse can cover.

312 B.C. ▪ Construction of Appian Way Begins. Construction begins on the "Via Appia" or Appian Way under the direction of the Roman censor and dictator Appius Claudius or Caecus (the Blind). One of twenty-nine great military roads that radiate from Rome, it divides in two at Beneventum (ancient name for the town of Benevento, Italy, located about 34 miles northeast of Naples, Italy) and eventually extends 410 miles (660 kilometers) down the coast of the Adriatic Sea. Probably the most famous road of all time, it embodies the heights reached by the Romans—the first scientific road builders.

280 B.C. ▪ First recorded lighthouse. The first recorded lighthouse, the Pharos of Alexandria, is built. Ptolemy II (308–246 B.C.), king of Egypt, called Ptolemy Philadelphus, erects a 400-foot (122-meter) marble tower on top of which a fire is kept burning for ships. Scholars believe it took twenty years to build the lighthouse, considered one of the seven wonders of the ancient world. It was destroyed by an earthquake. In 1157 the first lighthouse of medieval times is built by the Pisans at Meloria, Italy.

A.D. 100 ▪ Appearance of rigid saddles. Rigid saddles without stirrups first appear in the West in Roman Gaul, probably introduced from the East (Asia). Until this time, horses were usually ridden with simple cloths or blankets. The rigid saddle makes it easier for a rider to keep his seat. **(See also c. 450)**

c. 200 ▪ Dhow's first appearance. A traditional Arab trading vessel called a "dhow" first appears. It is equipped with fore-and-aft (front and back) sails of the triangular, lateen type (see c. 700) that allow it to sail across the direction of the wind as well as with the wind behind it. Supposedly modeled on the shape of a whale, the dhow is an efficient and speedy vessel.

c. 450 ▪ Stirrups appear. Stirrups are first used by the Mongolian armies of Atilla the Hun (king of the Huns from 434 to 453). The great advantage provided by these hanging slings or rings into which horse riders can put their feet is that the stirrups provide a more comfortable, secure ride. In terms of combat, however, stirrups revolutionize infantry tactics and are the technological basis for shock combat. With the lateral (side) support provided by the stirrup, the horse and rider become one. Riders can use their hands to do battle and can deliver fearsome blows that have the entire weight of horse and rider behind them. With their feet securely held, the opponent riders themselves will not be knocked off by such blows.

500 · Modern harness is first depicted. The modern harness or horse collar is first depicted in frescoes in Kansu, China. This device goes over an animal's head and neck and sits on its shoulders rather than pressing on its windpipe, allowing the animal to throw all its weight into pulling. Around 800 the modern harness or horse collar appears in Europe, having been introduced there from Asia.

c. 500 · Clinker-built ships debut. Clinker-built ships first appear in Scandinavia. They are distinguished by having planks that overlap one another. This results in strength but also inefficient streamlining. Clinker ships are made to weather high seas and are typically boats of northern European waters. They are distinguished from later carvel-built ships used in southern Europe that have planks placed edge-to-edge against an already-built framework. Carvel construction is smooth and streamlined, but takes a long time to complete and results in weak hulls.

c. 700 · Lateen sail becomes established in the Mediterranean. The lateen or triangular sail becomes established in the Mediterranean. Its evolution was pioneered by the Arabs (see c. 200). As a "loose-footed" sail or one with great flexibility of movement, it can be adjusted quickly to a large variety of angles to better catch the wind. In a sea with no trade winds, such as the Mediterranean, this type of sail proves ideal.

984 · First canal lock. The first canal or water lock for which there is clear evidence is built by Chinese engineer Ch'iao Wei-Yo on the Grand Canal. A lock is a chamber enclosed by movable gates and is placed between two stretches of water that vary in height from each other. Water is then admitted or drained through the sluices or gates to raise or lower the boat to the proper new canal level. Although the lock is invented in China, it is little-used there and its later development occurs mainly in the West. **(See also 1373)**

c. 1000 · Whiffletree makes appearance in Europe. Whiffletree, a horizontal transverse (lying across) bar that joins the harnesses or collars of two animals, first appears in Europe. Also called a whippletree, this crossbar device helps to equalize the pull of draft (load-pulling) animals and prevents a wagon from overturning.

c. 1100 · Incan road system begins. The road system of the Inca empire in South America begins as the Incas establish themselves at Cuzco (Peru) and start two parallel roadways extending from what is now Quito, Ecuador, to points south. As the Incas do not have the wheel, their road traffic consists entirely of people on foot and pack animals (llamas). They have a swift courier (relay-messenger) system and also build suspension bridges with wool or fiber cables.

1295 · Marco Polo describes the junk (Chinese sailing vessel). The junk, a classic Chinese sailing vessel and probably the first ship to have a central stern rudder (to steer), is described by Italian adventurer Marco Polo (1254–1324) upon his return to Venice from China. As a flat-bottomed ship with a high stern (end) and forward-thrusting bow, the junk is considered the most aerodynamically efficient of all the large oceangoing sailing ships.

1373 · First canal lock in Europe. The first lock for canal navigation in Europe is built at Vreeswijk in the Netherlands where a canal from Utrecht enters the river Lek. It consists of two sluice gates, one behind the other, enclosing a basin or chamber and forming what is essentially a lock. It is within this lock or basin that the water level (and thus the boat) is raised or lowered to overcome the difference in water height.

A canal in Delft, the Netherlands, today. The first network of canals was built in the thirteenth and fourteenth centuries in the Netherlands.

1388 · Queen Anne invents the sidesaddle. Sidesaddle is invented by Queen Anne of England (1366–1394), the wife of King Richard II (1367–1400). Since it is considered scandalous for a woman to straddle a horse as a man would, the queen's new saddle allows a woman to sit with both legs on the same side of the horse. Prior to this, whenever women rode horses, they usually rode behind a man, sitting on pillions—little side seats placed directly behind the man's saddle. The inventive queen basically adapts stirrups to the pillion and does away with the man and his saddle.

c. 1400 · Danzig Ship appears. A new type of sailing ship, the "Danzig Ship," first appears in north European waters. The strengthened hull is more streamlined and a crow's nest (platform used as a lookout) is added to the mast. It is still single-masted and has a single square sail. At about this time, the "carracks" are dominating the Mediterranean (in southern Europe). These are three-masted ships with the tallest (square) sail in the middle. They also have a high forecastle (the forward part of the upper deck) thrusting out over the bow (in front) and an even higher poop deck in the stern (rear).

1578 ▪ Submarine is described by William Bourne. English mathematician William Bourne publishes the first detailed description of a submarine in his *Inventions or Devices*. Although it contains no illustrations, his text is remarkably detailed. He never builds one himself. In 1620 Dutch inventor Cornelius Jacobszoon Drebbel (1572–1633) invents the first navigable submarine. His "diving boat" is made of wood and is propelled in the Thames River in England by oars. Air is supplied by two tubes that use floats to keep one end above water. **(See also September 7, 1776)**

1600 ▪ Land vehicle propelled by the wind. The first land vehicle that does not use muscle power of any sort as the source of its propulsion is built by Belgian-Dutch mathematician Simon Stevin (1548–1620). His wind-propelled *zeylwagen* or sail wagon is built of wood and canvas and is a kind of two-masted ship on wheels. It is steerable and is said to cover 50 miles (80 kilometers) in only two hours.

1610 ▪ Four-wheeled coach debuts. The hackney coach, a four-wheeled coach drawn by two horses and seating six people, first appears in England. It is used primarily as a taxi. Around 1650 steel-springed coaches first appear in England. This technical breakthrough does much to ensure a smoother, sway-free coach ride. In 1667 a light, two-wheeled carriage called a cabriolet makes it first appearance. This doorless, hooded, one-horse carriage is first used in France and becomes very popular in the eighteenth century. It is often used as a cab for hire.

c. 1650 ▪ Post horns used by stagecoaches. The continuous sound of the post horn is heard for the first time. This horn is blown, playing the same six-note tune, by stagecoaches throughout Europe, warning every other vehicle that they have the right of way. Stagecoaches get their name by going "in stages" to their destination, using fresh horses at each stage. Horses are changed every 10 miles (16 kilometers) to keep up the speed.

March 18, 1662 · The first buses. The first "bus" begins operations in France. This scheduled service operates horse-drawn vehicles that seat eight. It is owned by a company formed by French scientist and philosopher Blaise Pascal (1623–1662). The service's vehicles leave regularly and on time, whether full or empty. In 1669 a similar "Flying Coach" service begins between London and Oxford, England.

May 1681 · Languedoc Canal opens. The Languedoc Canal in France, also known as the Canal du Midi, opens and links the city of Toulouse with the Mediterranean. This 150-mile (240-kilometer) waterway is considered to be the greatest feat of civil engineering between Roman times and the nineteenth century. It has one hundred locks, three long aqueducts, and one tunnel. It becomes the pioneer and model of the modern European canal.

November 14, 1698 · First Eddystone Lighthouse. The first Eddystone Lighthouse is built and becomes the first such structure to be exposed to the full force of the sea. Designed by English engineer Henry Winstanley (1644–1703), it marks the dangerous submerged reef off Plymouth, England. Built of timber, the lighthouse is destroyed in a violent storm on November 26, 1703. The second is built in 1708 by English engineer, John Rudyard. Anchored firmly to the reef with iron rods driven deep into rock, it stands until destroyed by fire in 1755. The third is built by English engineer John Smeaton (1724–1792) in 1759. Made out of interlocking stones, its new design revolutionizes lighthouse and tower design, and it stands until erosion forces its replacement in 1882. That year, a fourth is completed by James N. Douglass of England who generally follows Smeaton's design, although making it taller. It still stands today.

1713 · American schooner-type ship is first used. The first American schooner-type ship (a sailing craft with both fore and aft sails and with two to four masts) is built by American Andrew Robinson in Massachusetts. These slim, fast vessels come to be called Baltimore clippers, since that city in Maryland is where most are built. They are used as freighters and fishing vessels, and by smugglers and slavers.

c. 1750 · Conestoga wagons in common use. Conestoga wagons become the preferred vehicle for hauling freight in America. They travel only by day and do not change their six heavy horses. Conestogas have large hoops, strong hemp covers, curved-up floors, and a dory or boat shape. They originate in Lancaster, Pennsylvania, and have a very high body that makes fording streams easier. A descendant of the Conestoga was the prairie schooner used by American pioneers to transport their possessions westward. It had a flat body and lower sides than the Conestoga.

1751 ▪ Pennsylvania Road important to colonial America. The Pennsylvania Road becomes the most important sunrise-to-sunset pathway connecting the eastern American colonies with the west territories. Like most early American roads, it is transformed from an old Native American trail and fur trader's path into a larger thoroughfare. Beginning in 1792, it is surfaced with broken stone and gravel and its "turnpiking" or stone surfacing is completed in 1820.

1757 ▪ First oscillating lighthouse. The first oscillating lighthouse light is built by Swedish inventor Jonas Norberg (1711–1783). In order to distinguish the Swedish lighthouse at Korso from a nearby light, he builds a mechanism that turns the light horizontally, giving the effect of a flashing light. On February 15, 1781, Norberg installs the first revolving lighthouse light in the Carlsten Lighthouse near Marstrand in Sweden. It emits flashes at regular intervals using an arrangement of oil lamps and reflectors that are rotated by clockwork.

1764 ▪ Founder of modern road technology. French civil engineer Pierre-Marie-Jérôme Trésaguet (1716–1796) becomes the engineer of roads and bridges at Limoges. He goes on to become the founder of modern road technology and introduces the notion that road building can be improved by using the methods of experimental science.

1769 ▪ First self-propelled vehicle. The first self-propelled vehicle is designed by French inventor Nicolas-Joseph Cugnot (1725–1804). He builds a steam-fueled car or truck for transporting the French army's cannons. Commissioned by the government, this huge, three-wheeled vehicle is able to go about 2.5 miles (4 kilometers) per hour and has to stop every fifteen minutes for its boiler to be refilled. It is the first such vehicle built for actual, practical use and not for experimentation. It proves nearly impossible to steer.

September 7, 1776 ▪ First operational submarine. The first operational submarine is commanded by American Ezra Lee under New York Harbor. Designed by American inventor David Bushnell (c. 1742–1824), this unique turtle-shaped vessel is intended to be propelled underwater by an operator who hand-turns its propeller. Made of oak and covered with tar, it submerges by taking on water, and its air supply lasts about thirty minutes. Lee tries to screw a mine into the hull of a British ship to blow it up in the harbor, but is unable to do so. Despite this military failure, Lee demonstrates the feasibility of a submarine.

1777 ▪ First cast-iron bridge. The first cast-iron bridge opens in Coalbrookdale, England. Built by two English ironmasters, Abraham Darby III and John Wilkinson, this bridge crossing the Severn River consists of a single 140-foot (43-meter) semicircular arch made up of five arched ribs. Iron will soon replace stone in bridge-building.

1782 ▪ Aimé Argand revolutionizes lighthouse illumination. Lighthouse illumination is revolutionized as Swiss physicist and inventor Aimé Argand (1755–1803) builds an oil lamp whose circular wick and glass chimney give a brilliant flame. Combined with the parabolic (curved) reflectors coming into use—whose hundreds of mirror fragments are set in a curved plaster of Paris mould—lighthouses can for the first time produce a beam of very high intensity from a relatively small light source.

June 4, 1783 ▪ Montgolfiers demonstrate their hot-air balloon. French inventors Joseph-Michel Montgolfier (1740–1810) and his brother Jacques-Étienne (1745–1799) give the first public demonstration of their hot-air balloon by sending up a large model made of linen lined with paper. The balloon is 30 feet (9 meters) in diameter when inflated and open at the bottom so it can be filled with hot air from a ground fire. It rises about 6,000 feet (1,850 meters) and stays up for ten minutes. **(See also November 21, 1783)**

November 21, 1783 ▪ First untethered human flight. The first free or untethered human flight takes place when French physicist Jean-François Pilâtre de Rozier (1756–1785) and French soldier and aeronaut François d'Arlandes (1742–1809) fly as high as 500 feet (150 meters) and travel 5 miles (8 kilometers) in a Montgolfier hot-air balloon, floating for about twenty-five minutes across Paris. This marks the real beginning of aviation. **(See also June 15, 1785)**

December 1, 1783 ▪ Charles makes first hydrogen balloon flight. French physicist and chemist Jacques-Alexandre-César Charles

(1746–1823) and his colleague Nicolas Robert make the first flight in a hydrogen balloon (instead of hot air), going 27 miles (about 43 kilometers) from Paris. Modern ballooning derives many of its features from Charles, who fits his balloon with a valve, a suspended basket or car, ballast or weight for stability and control, and a barometer (a device used to measure the pressure of the air) to act as an altimeter (to gauge altitude).

January 7, 1785 ▪ First air crossing of the English Channel. The first crossing by air of the English Channel is accomplished by French aeronaut Jean-Pierre-François Blanchard (1753–1809) and American physician John Jeffries (1744–1819). They fly from Dover, England, to Calais, France, in a nightmarish, two-hour crossing during which their balloon is at times hitting waves. Blanchard later becomes the first to make a balloon flight in England and in North America, and is a pioneer of the parachute.

June 15, 1785 ▪ First balloon fatalities. The first balloon fatalities occur as physicist Jean-François Pilâtre de Rozier (1756–1785) and Pierre Ange de Romain, both of France, are killed near Boulogne, France, while attempting a France-to-England crossing of the Channel. Twenty-five minutes after taking off, the balloon catches fire and crashes. Pilâtre de Rozier, who was the first man to fly less than two years before (see November 21, 1783), is now also the first to die.

July 1786 ▪ First successful American steamboat. The first successful American steamboat makes a short trip on the Delaware River. Built by American inventor John Fitch (1743–1798), this small vessel is a barge with a steam engine that operates, using linking beams, six vertical oars or paddles on each side. In 1790 the first regular steamboat service begins as Fitch operates a one-boat line between Pennsylvania and New Jersey. During its brief summer run, his steamboat totals between 2,000 and 3,000 miles (3,200 and 4,800 kilometers) and reaches speeds as high as 7–8 miles (11–13 kilometers) per hour. The service does not make a profit, however, and Fitch never has a chance to try again.

1803 ▪ Trevithick builds first steam locomotive. The first steam locomotive is built by English engineer Richard Trevithick (1771–1833). It has a single, horizontal cylinder mounted inside the boiler and has flat wheels designed to run on rails. There is no evidence that it actually runs at this time.

1804 · Amphibious vehicle is invented. Oliver Evans (1755–1819), American inventor, builds an amphibious (able to move on land or water) steam-powered dredge (a barge with nets or buckets for plowing up river or lake beds) he names the *Orukter Amphibolos*. He drives it 1.5 miles (2.4 kilometers) through the streets of Philadelphia, Pennsylvania, and then into the Schuykill River. More than a self-propelled vehicle, it looks like a flat-bottomed boat with wheels and serves as a working dredge, equipped with chain buckets, digging devices, and paddles to move it through the water. Since Evans drives this device on land, it is the first powered road vehicle to operate in the United States.

1806 · First vehicle powered by internal combustion engine. Isaac de Rivaz (1752–1828) of Switzerland builds the first vehicle powered by an internal combustion engine. His four-wheel wagon has a single, vertical cylinder powered by hydrogen carried in a tank over the rear wheels. He reasons correctly that a controlled explosion inside an open-top cylinder will power the vehicle's axles. His car runs slowly although it stalls frequently. He builds a similar, improved version in 1813.

August 1807 · Fulton's steamboat begins its trials. The first practical, reliable steamboat begins its trials on the Hudson River. Built by American engineer and inventor Robert Fulton (1765–1815), the 150-foot (46-meter) *Clermont* steams from New York to Albany in thirty-two hours. This is compared to the four days required by a sailing sloop. The steam engine has a single vertical cylinder which, through cranks and gears, drives two 15-foot (4.6-meter) paddle wheels, one on each side of the hull. Commercial trips start in September, and they prove so successful that Fulton builds another steamboat.

1817 · Bicycle's forerunner is patented. The forerunner of the bicycle is patented by Carl von Drais de Sauerbraun (1785–1851) of Germany. Called a *Laufmaschine* or a "running machine," it is little more than a curved wooden beam set above two wooden wheels. The front wheel is steerable and the vehicle scoots along as the rider pushes off the ground with his feet. The vehicle becomes all the vogue for a while in Paris and London and is called a *Draisienne* in French and a hobby horse or pedestrian curricle in English. **(See also 1839)**

1822 · Pencil-beam of light for lighthouses. A strong pencil-beam of light that is ideal for lighthouses is first produced by the French physicist Augustin-Jean Fresnel (1788–1827), whose work on the nature of light leads

A steam locomotive.

to new lenses. His prism system, which replaces the older method of mirrors, results in all the light that is emitted from a source being refracted (bent) into a horizontal beam. This revolutionizes the effectiveness of lighthouses.

February 1825 ▪ American debut of steam locomotive that runs on rails. The first steam locomotive to run on rails in the United States is built by American inventor John Stevens (1749–1838). He builds a half-mile (.08-kilometer) circular track in his backyard in Hoboken, New Jersey, and experiments with his new machine. Stevens is one of the first to be convinced that railroads and not canals are the overland transport system of the future for America.

September 27, 1825 ▪ First steam-powered, public passenger train. The first steam-powered, public passenger train opens the Stockton & Darlington Railway in England. English engineer George Stephenson (1781–1848) uses one of his improved locomotives to steam 21 miles (34 kilometers) pulling twelve wagons of goods and twenty-one wagons carrying nearly six hundred passengers. For the first time in history, land transportation is possible at a rate faster than any horse can run. Stephenson's line turns a profit and his locomotives begin a transportation revolution throughout the world. On May 5, 1826, the first modern railway system (in that it is operated entirely by steam locomotives) is incorporated. It is with this line—the Liverpool & Manchester Railway—that the railroad becomes established as a means of regular public transport that rivals and finally passes the coach and canal companies. The entire railway opens on September 15, 1830, has double tracks, and operates passenger trains on a timetable. It still runs today.

October 26, 1825 ▪ Opening of the Erie Canal. The Erie Canal, stretching more than 350 miles (550 kilometers) from Buffalo on Lake Erie to the Hudson River at Albany, New York, officially opens. This first, great American engineering work is organized by New York mayor DeWitt Clinton (1769–1828), and built by American civil engineer James Geddes (1763–1838). It has eighty-two locks, takes eight years to build, and costs seven million dollars. When finished, it connects by boat the Atlantic Ocean and the Great Lakes.

1826 ▪ American buggy debuts. The first American "buggy" is made. This is the most typical American horse-drawn carriage and the best known. Modeled after a German wagon design, it owes its extreme lightness to its frame and wheels being made of hickory wood. It has four small wheels and elliptical springs, front and rear, mounted at right angles to the front. These springs absorb energy and shock.

1831 ▪ First railroad tunnel in the Western Hemisphere. The first railroad tunnel in the Western Hemisphere, the Staple Bend Tunnel, is begun near Jamestown, Pennsylvania. It is part of a railroad/canal transportation route that runs from Philadelphia to Pittsburgh. It still stands today but has not been used since 1852. In 1870 the first vehicular tunnel in the United States, the Washington Street Tunnel in Chicago, Illinois, is opened. It is built under the Chicago River and serves the city as the only cross-river connection after the Great Chicago Fire burns down all the bridges in 1871.

1832 ▪ First American urban streetcar. The first urban streetcar in the United States is built by American wagon builder John Stephenson, and goes into operation in New York. This thirty-passenger, stagecoach-on-rails is pulled by horses. Similar horsecar services are begun in Boston, Massachusetts (in 1856), and Philadelphia, Pennsylvania (in 1858). The first such streetcar was built in England in 1755.

1833 · Launch of first clipper ship. The first clipper-ship style vessel, the American *Ann McKim*, is launched at Baltimore, Maryland. Clipper ships do not have one particular design, but are faster, bigger sailing ships and are built to "clip" days off a voyage and thus compete with steamships. Their major design development is the bow (forward part) change from a blunt "U" to a sharp "V."

1836 · Invention of the hansom carriage. The English "hansom" carriage is invented by Joseph Aloysius Hansom (1803–1882). This horse-drawn carriage is a light, open two-seater that is driven from a highly elevated box placed behind the passengers. Hansom carriages replace the hackney coaches (see 1610). In 1838 the first brougham coach is made in England by Robinson and Cook for Lord Brougham (1778–1868). This ancestor of many nineteenth century coaches has several innovations, one

A variety of nineteenth-century bicycles.

of which is its extremely low-slung center body that permits easy entrance from ground level.

1836 • Double-screw ship propeller is invented. Swedish-American engineer John Ericsson (1803–1889) patents a double-screw propeller for ships that is successfully tested on a ship in England. In 1838 the first sizable seagoing vessel to be driven by a screw propeller is the 237-ton *Archimedes*, designed by English engineer Francis Pettit Smith (1808–1874). It has a single 7-foot (2-meter) propeller that is later replaced by a two-bladed screw.

1839 • Bicycle on way to becoming a vehicle. The first step in the development of the bicycle from the wooden hobby horse to a mechanically moved, two-wheeled vehicle is made by Scottish blacksmith Kirkpatrick Macmillan. He appears to be the first to discover that two wheels placed in line could be balanced and could be propelled by treadles or cranks fitted to one of the axles. **(See also 1861)**

June 15, 1844 • Goodyear patents vulcanization process. American inventor Charles Goodyear (1800–1860) patents the process for "vulcanizing" rubber. While experimenting on how to prevent rubber from becoming stiff in the cold and soft and sticky in hot weather, he accidentally drops some India rubber mixed with sulfur on a hot stove and discovers that it becomes dry and flexible in either temperature. His name and his discovery live today in the major use of rubber for automobile tires.

1852 • Horse-drawn streetcar rails are flush with the street. Émile Loubat, a French engineer, invents the system of placing horse-drawn streetcar rails within the street pavement itself, making them flush with the street and posing much less of an obstacle to coach and wagon traffic. By 1860 horse-drawn railcars are rapidly replacing the omnibuses or coaches, since they are a more efficient use of horsepower. A team of horses can pull vehicles of two tons or more with up to fifty passengers on rails. This is double the weight and number of a horse-drawn omnibus (without rails).

1852 • Otis invents safety elevator. The "safety" elevator is invented by American inventor Elisha Graves Otis (1811–1861). Otis designs a safety brake that will keep an elevator from falling even if the cable holding it is completely cut. His first safety guard consists of a used wagon spring on

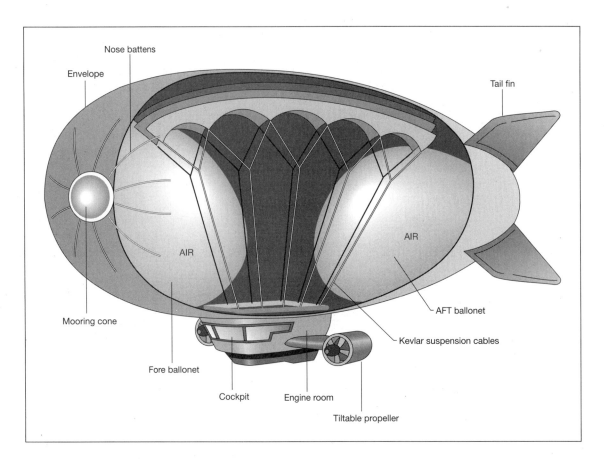

Nose battens

Envelope

Tail fin

Mooring cone

AIR

AIR

AFT ballonet

Kevlar suspension cables

Fore ballonet

Cockpit

Engine room

Tiltable propeller

The internal structure of an airship.

top of the hoist platform and a ratchet bar attached to the guide rails. If the cable snaps, the tension is released from the spring and each end immediately catches the ratchet, locking the platform in place and preventing a fall.

September 24, 1852 · First powered, manned airship. The first powered, manned airship (dirigible) is flown by its builder, French engineer Henri Giffard (1825–1888). Powered by a steam propeller, the airship flies at about 5 miles (8 kilometers) per hour and covers 17 miles (27 kilometers) from Paris to near Trappes, France. This craft marks the beginning of the practical airship.

March 6, 1855 · Railway suspension bridge. The first train to cross a span suspended by wire cables goes over the Niagara Bridge. This is the first successful railway suspension bridge in the world. Designed and built by German-American engineer John Augustus Roebling (1806–1869), its two decks are suspended from four cables which rest atop two masonry towers.

September 1, 1859 ▪ Pullman railroad sleeping car debuts. The first Pullman railroad sleeping car begins service on an overnight trip between Minnesota and Illinois. It is invented by George Mortimer Pullman (1831–1897), an American cabinet maker. In 1864 his newly designed sleeping car becomes the forerunner of the modern railroad sleepers.

1860 ▪ First practical internal combustion engine. The first practical gas engine or internal combustion engine is built and patented by French inventor Jean-Joseph-Étienne Lenoir (1822–1900). This type of engine burns the fuel inside its engine rather than in a separate chamber like a steam engine. Lenoir's new design is a converted double-acting steam engine with slide valves to admit the explosion mixture and to discharge exhaust products. This two-stroke cycle engine uses a mixture of coal gas and air and proves to be smooth-running and durable. His success spurs other inventors to examine the possibilities of this new engine rather than the steam engine. **(See also 1862)**

April 3, 1860 ▪ Pony Express opens overland mail service. Pony Express, the first rapid overland mail service to the Pacific coast, officially opens. Regularly changing horses and riders, the Express covers 250 miles (400 kilometers) in a twenty-four-hour period. Although famous and colorful, the system is a financial disaster and is put out of business within a year by the completion of the transcontinental electric telegraph system.

1861 ▪ Bicycle is driven directly by pedals for first time. The first to suggest driving a "velocipede" or bicycle directly by cranks or pedals attached to the front axle is Pierre Michaux, his son, Ernest, and their employee, Pierre Lallement. They set up shop in Paris, France, and in 1866 introduce a new model made of elegant wrought iron. Its front wheel is larger than the rear, so that each revolution of the front pedals will carry the rider farther. These bicycles become very popular. **(See also c. 1873)**

1862 ▪ Otto experiments with a four-cycle engine system. German engineer Nikolaus August Otto (1832–1891) experiments with a four-cycle system on his four-cylinder engine. The four cycles or movements of the piston (intake, compression, power, and exhaust) will become the basis of the internal combustion engine. Intake or induction occurs when the falling piston draws in gas and air; the rising piston then compresses or squeezes the mixture, which ignites from a spark; power results when the spark flares into flame causing gases to expand and driving the piston down; exhaust results when the rising piston expels hot gases out a valve that opens. When a modern engine is running, every cylinder goes through this same sequence of events, or cycle, hundreds of times a minute. Otto produces a practical engine in 1876, and it proves to be the ancestor of the modern gas engine.

January 10, 1863 ▪ First subway opens in London. The first subway or underground city passenger railroad opens to traffic in London, England. This underground railway uses steam locomotives that burn coke and later coal, both of which cause smoke and fumes. The subway is eventually converted to electrical power. The first practical subway line in the United States opens in Boston, Massachusetts, in 1897. On July 10, 1900, the first section of the Paris Underground (in France) called the Metro, opens, and in 1904 the largest system of all opens in New York City.

1864 ▪ Markus invents what some call the first automobile. Siegfried Markus (1831–1898), an Austrian inventor, produces a wooden cart powered by a two-cycle, internal combustion gas engine. Some claim this to be the first automobile. By 1875 he builds a greatly improved version with a four-cycle gasoline engine that drives the rear axle. It has a wheel for steering and goes only one speed since it has no gears.

1867 ▪ First elevated railroad in the United States. The first elevated railroad in the United States begins operations in New York City. This method of actually raising the tracks above street level proves to be the cheapest way of providing a right-of-way for inner suburban trains in large city centers.

January 23, 1869 ▪ Westinghouse applies for air-brake patent. American engineer George Westinghouse (1846–1914) applies for an air-brake patent. His new power-braking system uses compressed air as the operating medium and far surpasses any other method. When air pressure in the brake pipe is reduced for any reason, air is automatically admitted into the brake cylinder from reservoirs connected to it. This prevents brake failure. It is first tried out on a passenger train, and its final improvement in 1872 adds an important element of safety to train travel.

May 10, 1869 · Completion of transcontinental U.S. railroad. Transcontinental United States railroad is completed with the Golden Spike ceremony. The railroads joining the Atlantic and Pacific coasts are linked at Promontory Point, Utah, north of the Great Salt Lake. Within thirty years, four more transcontinental railroad lines will be completed, truly linking the entire nation.

November 17, 1869 · Suez Canal opens. The Suez Canal, a sea-level waterway across the Isthmus of Suez in Egypt, opens. Planned by French diplomat and engineer Ferdinand-Marie de Lesseps (1805–1894), it takes five years to organize and plan and ten years to construct. It extends 105 miles (168 kilometers), using several lakes, and is an open cut without locks. Following improvements and widening, it becomes one of the busiest canals, handling a significant portion of the world's sea traffic.

1871 · Hallidie improves design of cable cars. Andrew Smith Hallidie (1836–1900), an American engineer, invents the underground continuous moving cable and mechanical gripper for the underside of streetcars. His new electric cable car runs two to three times faster than a horse-drawn rail car and can go up the steepest grades. By 1873 his system is running cable cars in San Francisco, California, and other American cities. In 1964 this system is still running in San Francisco and becomes the first moving national historic landmark.

c. 1873 · First bicycle with rear-wheel chain-drive. The first design of a safety bicycle using a chain-drive to the rear wheel is made by H. J. Lawson of England. It has two medium-sized wheels of equal diameter, with the rear wheel being driven by means of a chain and sprockets.
(See also 1885: Ancestor of the modern bicycle)

May 24, 1874 · First steel arch bridge. The first steel arch bridge, the St. Louis (Missouri) Bridge, opens to traffic. Designed and built by American engineer James Buchanan Eads (1820–1887) to span the Mississippi River, it is the first bridge project to use pneumatic caissons (underwater enclosures with no bottoms in which compressed air keeps out the water), and also the first to build arches by the cantilever method without falsework or staging. Now called the Eads Bridge, it is also the first major construction project to use steel.

1875 · Plimsoll Line is invented. Samuel Plimsoll (1824–1898), an English politician and social reformer, invents the Plimsoll Line, which is established by the British Parliament this year. This line is a fixed mark placed on the hull of every cargo ship indicating the maximum depth to which the ship can be safely loaded. If a ship is overloaded, it will sit in the water below the mark. Plimsoll offers the idea in order to save the lives of crew members aboard "coffin ships"—unseaworthy, overloaded vessels whose owners care little about crew safety.

May 31, 1879 · First practical electric railroad. The first practical electric railroad begins operations at the Berlin Trades Exhibition in Germany. This passenger line, built by German engineer Ernst Werner von Siemens (1816–1892), operates on the exhibition grounds and can pull thirty passengers at 4 miles (6.5 kilometers) per hour. It is the first practical electric train that gets its power from a station generator.

1885 · Ancestor of the modern bicycle. The true ancestor of the modern bicycle is the Starley "Rover" Safety Bicycle. It has similarly sized wheels and is much lower and more stable than its predecessors. This rear-wheel-driven bicycle sets the new bicycle style internationally and sends the high-wheelers and tricycles into irreversible decline. It is designed by John Kemp Starley (1854–1901) of England.

1885 · Benz builds first true automobile. German engineer Carl Friedrich Benz (1844–1929) builds a two-seater tricycle powered by a four-cycle gas engine that drives very well in tests. This is the first vehicle in which the engine and chassis form a single unit and can be considered the first true automobile. Benz did not attempt to convert a carriage, but rather designed an entirely new kind of self-propelled vehicle.

1885 · Daimler and Maybach create first true motorcycle. Gottlieb Wilhelm Daimler (1834–1900) and Wilhelm Maybach (1846–1929), German engineers, build a much-improved high-speed, internal combustion engine. They install a one-cylinder, four-cycle gas version of it on a bicycle frame and create the first true motorcycle.

1887 · First successful electric trolley line. The first successful electric trolley line is built by Frank Julian Sprague (1857–1934), an American electrical engineer, in Richmond, Virginia. In 1897 he invents the multiple-unit electric train in which a single driver can control a number of motor coaches from either end of the train. It is first used on the Chicago (Illinois) South Side Elevated Railway. This invention becomes the key component of all modern short-haul passenger railways. Although popular and practical, it is limited by the location of the electric trolley poles and guideways.

1888 • Dunlop invents the pneumatic tire. Scottish inventor John Boyd Dunlop (1840–1921) first conceives the idea of pneumatic (air-filled) tires and applies it to his son's bicycle. Although invented for the bicycle whose ride they transform, pneumatic tires come along just in time for the emerging automobile. Dunlop was preceded in this idea by Scottish engineer Robert William Thomson (1822–1873), who patented the concept in 1846, but it is Dunlop who pursues it thoroughly and eventually creates an entirely new industry out of it.

1890 • Modern bicycle is produced. The modern form of the diamond frame bicycle is produced in England. Made by the Humber firm, it has all the essential features of a modern bicycle: chain-drive to the rear wheel, a moveable rear wheel set in slotted fork ends to permit chain-tension adjustment, ball bearings, steering head and fork, wheels of the same diameter, and a spring seat on an adjustable seat tube.

1891 • Invention of the escalator. The escalator is invented by Jesse W. Reno of the United States. His moving, inclined belt provides transportation to passengers riding on cleats that are attached to the belt. At first the handrail is stationary, but he builds an improved version with a moving handrail in this same year.

1893 • Henry Ford's first car. American inventor and industrialist Henry Ford (1863–1947) builds and runs his first car in Detroit, Michigan. It has a two-cylinder, 4-horsepower engine, looks like a buggy, and is the first of several experimental versions. On June 16, 1903, he organizes the Ford Motor Company and eventually establishes the moving assembly line to produce cars in volume, making them affordable to greater numbers of people. **(See also October 1908)**

1893 • First successful gas-powered car. The first successful gas-powered car in the United States is demonstrated in Springfield, Massachusetts, by American inventor and manufacturer Charles Edgar Duryea (1861–1938) and his brother, James Frank (1869–1967). It is propelled by a

Henry Ford and his first automobile.

4-horsepower, two-stroke motor and looks exactly like a buggy without a horse. The brothers set up the first American company to manufacture cars for sale in 1894.

1894 ▪ Forerunner of the modern car is designed. Emile Levassor (c. 1844–1897) and René Panhard (1841–1908), both French inventors, first design the Panhard auto, which is the forerunner of the modern car. With a front-mounted engine driving the rear wheels via a clutch and gearbox, this vehicle is the model after which nearly every auto for the next fifty years is patterned.

1896 ▪ Tsiolkovsky experiments with liquid-propellant space rockets. Russian physicist Konstantin Eduardovich Tsiolkovsky (1857–1935) begins his groundbreaking scientific work on the theoretical aspects of liquid-propellant space rockets. Within two years he designs several rockets and solves the theoretical problem of how reaction (rocket) engines can escape from and reenter the Earth's atmosphere. After his death, he becomes known as the father of space flight although he never launches anything into space.

1897 · First Stanley Steamer. The first Stanley Steamer takes to the road. Built by two enterprising American twins, Francis Edgar Stanley (1849–1918) and Freelan O. Stanley (1849–1940), this simple, carriage-looking car with a tiller for steering sells very well.

June 1897 · Parsons turbine engine powers a ship for first time. As the first ship to be powered by a Parsons turbine engine, the British *Turbinia* puts on a spectacular performance as it dashes through lines of assembled warships at a speed of 34.5 knots. A turbine is a motor in which a set of blades is spun or rotated by a moving stream of liquid or gas. Steam turbines are lighter, provide more power and higher speeds, and take up less space than other engines.

1898 · First truly practical submarine. The first truly practical submarine and the first underwater vessel accepted by the U.S. Navy, the *Holland*, is built by American inventor John Philip Holland (1840–1914). His 50-foot (15-meter) long, five-man submarine is powered by a 45-horsepower gasoline engine and achieves the first unqualified success in submarine history.

1899 · First car to exceed 60 miles per hour. The first automobile to exceed one-mile-per-minute (60 miles, or 96 kilometers, per hour) is the electric race car called "La Jamais Contente." This bullet-shaped car is powered by large, expensive batteries. Electric cars have never held another land speed record.

August 1899 · Wright brothers build their first aircraft. Wilbur Wright (1867–1912) and his brother Orville (1871–1948), American inventors, build their first aircraft—a biplane kite—and test its warping ability (the ability to twist and change its curvature, which makes for better control). Without this invention and the lessons it allows them to learn, the Wrights would not have been able to fly successfully. **(See also December 17, 1903)**

July 2, 1900 · Zeppelin airship makes debut. The first Zeppelin airship (dirigible) makes its initial trial flight in Germany. The first of the rigid, monster airships, it is 420 feet (128 meters) long and is housed in the first floating hangar. On June 22, 1910, regular passenger-carrying airship service is begun by the German firm Delag. Between 1910 and 1914, its five

Zeppelin airships carry nearly thirty-five thousand passengers over inland German routes without a fatality.

1901 · Oldsmobile is manufactured in quantity. The first American car to be manufactured in quantity is the "Curved Dash" Oldsmobile, designed by Ransom Eli Olds (1864–1950). This popular car has a two-speed gearbox with reverse, is steered by a tiller (instead of a steering wheel), and sells for about $650. This marks the real beginning of the American auto industry.

1902 · Renault invents the drum brake. French automobile pioneer Louis Renault (1877–1944) invents the drum brake. Designed to operate by pressing two semicircular brake shoes against a circular brake drum, they are soon adopted by nearly all vehicles.

1903 · Harley-Davidson produces its first motorcycle. Harley-Davidson Company of Milwaukee, Wisconsin, produces its first motorcycle. William S. Harley and Arthur Davidson are joined within a year by Davidson's brothers, William and Walter. Their first motorcycle is a single-cylinder machine with 2 horsepower.

November 12, 1903 · First fully practical airship. The first fully practical airship, the *Lebaudy*, makes a successful flight in France. Commissioned by the brothers Paul (1858–1937) and Pierre Lebaudy (1880–c. 1940), French sugar refiners, and designed by Henry Juillot and Don Simoni, the semirigid, 190-foot (58-meter) long airship flies 38.5 miles (62 kilometers).

December 17, 1903 · Wright brothers make historic flight. The first sustained, controlled, powered flight is made by American inventor Orville Wright (1871–1948) in the *Flyer* at Kill Devil Hills near Kitty Hawk, North Carolina. He and his brother and fellow inventor Wilbur (1867–1912) make four flights this day, all from level ground and without any take-off assistance. The historic first flight lasts twelve seconds and covers 120 feet (about 37 meters). The fourth and longest flight, piloted by Wilbur, lasts fifty-nine seconds and covers 852 feet (about 260 meters). The age of flight has begun.

1905 · First true hydrofoil. The first true hydrofoil is operated by its Italian inventor Enrico Forlanini (1848–1930). The hydrofoil principle eliminates drag on the hull of a boat by going fast enough so that its foils (fins

or skis attached to the hull) come to the surface and the vessel skids along the top of the water. This vehicle is powered by an airplane propeller. Today, more than one hundred hydrofoil passenger vessels are operating throughout the world.

The first successful flight of Wilbur and Orville Wright near Kitty Hawk, North Carolina.

1907 ▪ First taxis in the United States. Automobile taxicabs first appear in New York City. The standard fare for a short ride is a "jitney"—a common term for a nickel. The term soon becomes synonymous with the service itself.

November 10, 1907 ▪ Modern airplane configuration is introduced. French aviator Louis Blériot (1872–1936) introduces in France what will become the modern configuration of the airplane. His plane has an enclosed or covered fuselage (body), a single set of wings (monoplane), and a propeller in front of the engine.

November 13, 1907 · First piloted helicopter. The first piloted helicopter rises vertically in free flight in Liseux, France. Built by French engineer Paul Cornu (1881–1914), it is powered by a 243-horsepower Antoinette engine driving two rotors. Although a major achievement, the practical helicopter will not appear until the 1930s. **(See also January 13, 1942)**

1908 · Seiberling invents tire treads. Tire treads are invented by Frank Seiberling who perfects a machine that cuts grooves in the tire surfaces. Up to now, tires have smooth surfaces and provide little traction when roads are bad.

September 17, 1908 · First fatality in a powered airplane. The first fatality in a powered airplane occurs when Lieutenant Thomas E. Selfridge is killed when flying as a passenger with Orville Wright (1871–1948) at Fort Meyer, Virginia. After a propeller blade breaks and severs control wires, the airplane crashes from a height of about 75 feet (23 meters). Orville is severely injured and lives with back pain the rest of his life, but he will fly again.

October 1908 · Model T Ford Tin Lizzie is introduced. The legendary Model T Ford Tin Lizzie, the first of the "People's Cars," is introduced in the United States. It is the first Ford with left-handed steering and has a four-cylinder engine that gives 20 horsepower. Easy to drive and easy to repair, its production will continue until 1927, when total production reaches 16,536,075 vehicles—a record that stands until 1972. At the end of its run, it sells for an all-time low $260.

1909 · First production of derailleur gear for bicycles. Derailleur-type gear for bicycles is first made in France. This still-popular system consists of two or more rear wheel sprockets of different diameters, a chain looped over a mechanism which both lifts and transfers it from one sprocket to another to provide a change of gear ratios, and also a chain-tensioning device to take up the slack necessary to permit the chain transfer to take place. This extremely simple system also allows for direct drive on all gear ratios.

January 26, 1910 · First practical seaplane. The first practical seaplane flies. Built and flown by American inventor Glenn Hammond Curtiss (1878–1930), it lands and takes off in the waters off San Diego, California. In February 1911 Curtiss fits wheels to his seaplane and builds the first amphibian airplane (able to take off and land on both water and land).

March 8, 1910 ▪ First woman pilot. The first woman to become a qualified pilot is the Baroness de Laroche who receives her *brevet de pilote d'aéroplane* or pilot's license in France. She dies in 1919 in an airplane accident. On September 2, 1910, Blanche Scott becomes the first American woman to fly an aircraft solo.

1911 ▪ Invention of the electric starter for cars. An electric starter for an automobile is invented by Charles Franklin Kettering (1876–1958), an American engineer, and installed in a Cadillac. This invention finally does away with the difficult and sometimes dangerous business of hand-cranking, allowing a car to be started from inside the car with the touch of a toe. It also makes gasoline the fuel of choice over steam, since electric starters make gasoline-powered automobiles start up at once. Owners of steam vehicles must wait for them to heat to the required pressure.

1912 ▪ First diesel-powered locomotive. The first diesel-powered locomotive is built by the Swiss firm, Sulzer. It weighs 85 tons and provides 1,200 horsepower. Diesel-powered trains do not really become practical until the Germans develop a two-car, streamlined, diesel-electric in 1932. Diesel-electrics then begin to appear in the United States and elsewhere.

1912 ▪ Fuselage design appears. The first use of the monocoque fuselage (body of an airplane) is made in France. Taken from the French word meaning "eggshell," this new design is a hollow, shell-like structure in which the shell itself carries most of the plane's load and stress. Designed by the Swiss designer Ruchonnet and applied by L. Bechereau on a Deperdussin monoplane, this invention is one of the milestones in aviation since it is the fuselage design of the future.

August 15, 1914 ▪ Opening of the Panama Canal. The Panama Canal, linking the Atlantic and Pacific Oceans, officially opens. Built across the Isthmus of Panama by American army officer and engineer George Washington Goethals (1858–1928), it is really three major engineering projects in one. First an enormous dam is built to control the Chagras River and create a lake; next a deep cut is made through the hill whose top is the Continental Divide; and then giant locks are built at each end of the canal to move ships up and down the 85-foot (26-meter) difference. It takes about eight years to complete this massive, 51.2-mile (82.4-kilometer) canal. There are six sets of double locks, each 1,000 feet (1,600 kilometers) long. Like the Suez Canal (see November 17, 1869), the Panama Canal saves tremendous distances for ships—nearly 6,000 miles (9,650 kilometers) are cut off a journey from England to California; nearly 8,000 miles (13,000 kilometers) from a trip from New York to San Francisco; and more than 10,000 miles (16,000 kilometers) from San Francisco to the Strait of Gibraltar.

1918 ▪ Ethyl gasoline is introduced. Ethyl gasoline is first sold by General Motors Laboratories in the United States. This is a fluid additive put into gasoline that reduces engine knocking by slowing down the air/fuel burn rate. As a lead compound, however, it is later found to be a harmful and toxic contaminant and is no longer allowed in gasoline.

1919 ▪ Invention of the modern mobile home trailer. Glenn Hammond Curtiss (1878–1930), an American inventor, invents the modern mobile home trailer. He designs and builds his own custom trailer, called the Aerocar, which is twice as long as his car and has four Pullman berths, a kitchen, closets, running water, and a telephone to the car pulling it.

May 16, 1919 ▪ First transatlantic flight. The first transatlantic flight begins in stages by the U.S. Navy's Curtiss NC-4 seaplane flown by Lieutenant Commander Albert Cushing Read (1887–1967) and his crew. Leaving Trepassey Bay, Newfoundland, Canada, the NC-4 flies to Plymouth, England, via two stops in the Azores and Lisbon, Spain. It completes its trip on May 27. On June 14, 1919, the first direct, nonstop crossing of the Atlantic by airplane is made by a British two-man team. John William Alcock (1892–1919) and Arthur Whitten Brown (1886–1948) fly a Vickers Vimy bomber for 16 hours, 27 minutes from St. John's, Newfoundland, to Clifden, Ireland. **(See also May 20, 1927)**

1921 ▪ Prototype modern bus debuts. A prototype of the modern bus, the Safety Bus, is first introduced by the brothers Frank and William Fageol of the United States. This twenty-two-passenger, single-deck bus has an enclosed but very wide body and a low-slung chassis (frame). It has a totally new appearance and becomes very popular. In 1927 the brothers introduce another revolutionary bus design. Called the Twin Coach, it looks almost identical at the front and rear, seats forty-three, and is powered by two four-cylinder engines mounted on each side of the chassis. Its radical design has a flat front and back, and the entrance door is placed ahead of the front axle. It also has driver-controlled pneumatic (air-operated) doors. This becomes the accepted design for modern buses.

April 6, 1924 · First around-the-world flight. The first successful flight around the world begins as four Douglas World Cruisers leave Seattle, Washington. Of the four, only two complete the circumnavigation as they each fly 27,553 miles (44,430 kilometers) in 175 days, and return to Seattle on September 28. The actual flying time is 371 hours, 11 minutes.

September, 1924 · First modern highway opens. The first modern highway opens in Italy between Milan and Varese. Called the "autostrada" or automobile road, it has three undivided lanes on a 33-foot (10-meter) roadway with 3-foot (0.9-meter) shoulders. It is the forerunner of the modern, high-volume, high-speed highway. **(See also 1932: German autobahn opens)**

March 16, 1926 · Goddard launches first liquid-fueled rocket. The first free flight of a liquid-fueled rocket takes place as American physicist Robert Hutchings Goddard (1882–1945) designs a rocket that burns liquid oxygen and gasoline and successfully launches it at a farm in Auburn, Massachusetts. Launched from a 2-meter-tall (6.5-foot-tall) A-frame, it accelerates to a height of 12.5 meters (41 feet) with an average speed of 60 miles (96 kilometers) per hour in its 2.5-second flight. It lands 184 feet (56 meters) away. This brief flight is to rocketry what the Wright brothers' 12-second flight is to aviation.

May 20, 1927 · Lindbergh achieves first solo, nonstop flight across the Atlantic. American aviator Charles Augustus Lindbergh (1902–1974) leaves Roosevelt Field, Long Island, New York, and achieves the first solo, nonstop flight across the Atlantic Ocean. Navigating his Ryan monoplane, *Spirit of St. Louis*, by dead reckoning at times, he lands at Le Bourget Airfield, Paris, on May 21. He covers 3,600 miles (5,790 kilometers) in 33 hours, 29 minutes. His daring and romantic solo flight has a tremendous impact and serves to make the United States and the world more aware of the true potential of aviation.

September 18, 1928 · *Graf Zeppelin* launches passenger service. The first flight of the Zeppelin LZ-127 *Graf Zeppelin* occurs. It becomes the most successful rigid airship (dirigible) ever built and flies more than a

A 1929 photo of the *Graf Zeppelin* airship, which used lighter-than-air hydrogen.

million miles, carrying some 13,100 passengers. In October it makes a transatlantic crossing (Germany to New York) with paying passengers.

1930 · Jet engine is invented. Frank Whittle (1907–), an English inventor, takes out his first patent for the jet engine. Two years later, he prepares plans for a simple, lightweight engine for propelling aircraft at high speeds by reaction propulsion. Unlike a piston engine that turns a plane's propeller, a jet engine operates on the reaction or rocket principle by burning fuel and ejecting a jet of exhaust gas at high speed. During September 1941, a Whittle jet engine is flown from Britain to the United States and provides the model for the first practical American jet engines that will be built by General Electric. **(See also August 27, 1939)**

1930 · First deep-sea exploration vessel. The Bathysphere, the first deep-sea exploration vessel, is developed by American naturalist and explorer Charles William Beebe (1877–1962) and American engineer Otis Barton. This steel, spherical underwater vessel is capable of maintaining an interior environment of ordinary pressure when lowered beneath the sea. It has thick quartz windows and is suspended by a cable from a boat. In 1934 Beebe and Barton descend to a depth of 3,028 feet (923 meters). The

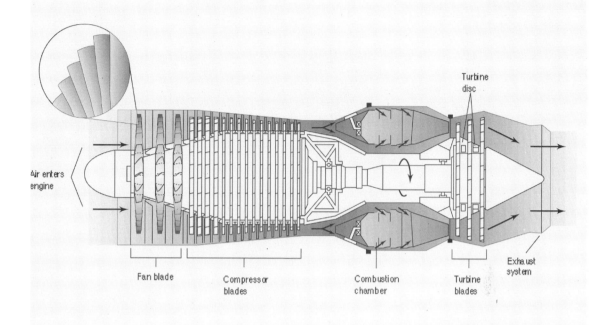

Air enters
engine

Turbine
disc

Fan blade

Compressor
blades

Combustion
chamber

Turbine
blades

Exhaust
system

bathysphere proves difficult to operate and since it is not maneuverable, it is eventually replaced by the safer, more maneuverable bathyscaphe. **(See also 1948: First modern bathyscaphe)**

1932 · German autobahn opens. The first fully modern highway system, the German autobahn network, opens to traffic. Conceived in 1926, this high-speed, limited access highway consists of dual roadways separated by a substantial median area.

May 20, 1932 · First woman to fly solo across the Atlantic. The first solo flight by a woman across the Atlantic Ocean is made by American aviator Amelia Earhart (1898–1937). She flies from Newfoundland, Canada, to Northern Ireland in a Lockheed Vega monoplane in 13 hours, 30 minutes.

February 1933 · Boeing 247 is first modern airliner. The modern airliner is born in the United States as the Boeing 247 flies for the first time. Along with the similar Douglas DC-1 and the Lockheed Electra, the Boeing aircraft revolutionizes all aspects of air transport and defines the future shape and features of airliners. Its dominating features are: all-metal, low-

A cutaway of a jet engine. It works by sucking air into one end, compressing it, mixing it with fuel, and burning it in the combustion chamber, and then expelling it with great force out the exhaust system.

wing monoplane; two powerful, supercharged, air-cooled engines mounted on the wings; variable-pitch propellers; and retractable undercarriage.

July 15, 1933 ▪ First around-the-world solo flight. The first solo flight around the world is made by one-eyed American aviator Wiley Post (1899–1935). Flying a Lockheed Vega, he covers 15,596 miles (25, 094 kilometers) in 7 days, 18 hours, 49 minutes. He also pioneers the early development of a pressure suit and proves the value of navigating instruments as well as the automatic pilot.

May 26, 1934 ▪ First American diesel-powered streamlined train. The first diesel-powered streamlined train in the United States runs the 1,015 miles (1,633 kilometers) between Denver and Chicago at an average (nonstop) speed of 77.6 miles (124.9 kilometers) per hour. This marks the beginning of the end for steam-powered trains. The efficiency of an internal combustion diesel engine that burns its fuel inside a cylinder is much greater than a steam engine that has to heat water to produce steam that then expands elsewhere.

1937 ▪ Invention of improved submarine turbine propulsion system. A submarine turbine propulsion system using oxygen generated by hydrogen peroxide is invented by the German engineer Hellmuth Walter. Prior to this system, submarines had to surface and run their diesel engines to recharge their underwater batteries. This new engine uses chemical catalysts to break down hydrogen peroxide into water and oxygen. The freed oxygen is then fed into a combustion chamber with diesel fuel to produce steam that runs a turbine. Submarines can now carry their own oxygen for power consumption.

May 7, 1937 ▪ First successful pressurized airplane cabin. The first successful pressurized airplane cabin is achieved in the experimental Lockheed XC-35. As the new generation of aircraft fly higher, passenger comfort becomes a problem, since the higher air is both extremely cold, thin, and difficult to breathe. Once the problem of making the fuselage or cabin airtight is solved, regular, high-altitude flights begin by the end of 1938. With the cabin pressurized with warm air for passenger comfort, the new generation of airliners can take advantage of high-altitude operation where maximum speed can be obtained with minimum power.

August 27, 1939 · First fully jet-propelled aircraft. The first fully jet-propelled aircraft to fly is Germany's Heinkel 178. It is powered by a centrifugal flow turbojet engine designed by Han von Ohain. Jet propulsion will revolutionize flying, but at this time, neither the Germans nor the British see its full potential, and operational jet aircraft do not appear until very late in World War II (1939–45). When they do emerge, however, they outclass everything else.

1940 · The Jeep is created for the U.S. Army. Jeep is introduced by the Bantam Car Company of the United States, which makes a four-wheel drive, light military scout car for the U.S. Army. These four-cylinder vehicles can climb a 69 percent grade fully loaded and, with special canvas sides and a snorkel, even cross streams up to six feet (1.8 meters) deep. They eventually become known as Jeeps, a variation on the abbreviation for "general purpose."

1940 · First modern automatic transmission. The first modern automatic transmission is offered as an option by General Motors on their Oldsmobile models. Called Hydra-Matic, it makes gear changes according to varying road and load conditions, without the driver having to do anything, since each gear is controlled through fluid pressure that regulates brake band clamping and engages or disengages a clutch.

January 13, 1942 · First fully practical, single-rotor helicopter. The first fully practical, single-rotor helicopter, built by Russian-American aeronautical engineer Igor Ivan Sikorsky (1889–1972), makes a successful flight. This is the first classic helicopter to use a single powered rotor to accomplish all the things that a helicopter should do: take off and land vertically; hover stationary in the air; progress through the air; and fly backwards, sideways, and forward.

1943 · Invention of the aqualung. French ocean explorer Jacques-Yves Cousteau (1910–1997) and Emile Gagnan, also of France, develop the aqualung or scuba gear. This scuba (*s*elf-*c*ontained *u*nderwater *b*reathing *a*pparatus) system allows a diver to swim freely down to about 180 feet (55 meters). It consists of three small bottles of highly compressed air that the diver wears on his or her back. The bottles are connected to a demand regulator that automatically supplies air at the correct pressure according to the diver's depth. Later, this system will be improved and divers will use a mixture of oxygen and helium rather than normal air (oxygen and nitrogen), since this will allow them to operate as deep as 1,640 feet (500 meters).

October 14, 1947 ▪ Yeager breaks the sound barrier. The first piloted aircraft to exceed the speed of sound in level flight is the Bell X-1 flown by American aviator Charles Elwood Yeager (1923–). This rocket-powered aircraft is launched or released at high altitude from a parent aircraft and reaches a speed of 670 miles (1,078 kilometers) per hour or Mach 1.015. Mach speed (the speed of sound) is relative to an airplane's altitude, so that Mach 1.0 at sea level at 15° C is 760.98 miles (1,224.42 kilometers) per hour. In the stratosphere (above 36,089 feet), Mach 1 is 659.78 miles (1,061.59 kilometers) per hour.

1948 ▪ First modern bathyscaphe. The first modern bathyscaphe, the *FNRS 2*, makes underwater trials. Built by Swiss physicist Auguste Piccard (1884–1962), this navigable diving vessel is designed to reach great depths in the ocean, and an improved version eventually descends to 13,000 feet (4,000 kilometers) in 1954. It consists of two main components, a heavy, steel crew cabin resistant to sea pressure, and a light container called a float, filled with gasoline that, because it is lighter than water, provides the necessary lifting power. On January 23, 1960, Piccard and Dons Wals of the United States make a record manned underwater descent in the bathyscaphe, *Trieste*. They descend 35,810 feet (10,915 meters) in the Mariana Trench in the Pacific Ocean.

1948 ▪ B.F. Goodrich makes reliable tubeless tires available. Reliable tubeless tires are first made available in the United States by B. F. Goodrich. These new tires require no inner tubes and are built to maintain air pressure by forming an airtight seal with a tire bead or edge and the wheel rim. Nearly all auto tires are tubeless today. This same year, the first radial-ply automobile tire is marketed by Michelin of France. Radials have their plies or inner cord material running at right angles to the beads or sides of a tire. They prove to be strong tires that give good fuel economy and better road traction than traditional-ply tires.

1952 ▪ Modern disc brakes apprear on race cars. Modern-type disc brakes, of Dunlop design, first are fitted to Jaguar entries in a European auto race. As distinct from drum brakes (whose two hinged shoes are forced apart), disc brakes are designed to operate by pressing friction pads against a rotating steel disc (like bicycle brakes that squeeze the rim). One piston brake cylinder is mounted on each side of a disc to press the pads against it. Disc brakes become common on a car's front wheels because they are not prone to brake fading.

1953 · Automobile air bag is patented. The first automobile air bag patent is registered to John Hetrick of the United States. In 1958 American inventor Harry Bertrand is granted the first patent for an automobile air bag system that uses a crash sensor. With this system, the bag inflates nearly coincidentally with the auto's impact, cushioning the driver's collision with the steering wheel and dashboard. In 1972 Ford Motor Company produces about one thousand cars with air bags, but soon drops this demonstration project. **(See also 1973)**

January 17, 1955 · First nuclear-powered submarine. The first nuclear-powered submarine, the U.S.S. *Nautilus*, is launched. Resembling a conventional submarine, this 320-foot (98-meter) long vessel has an underwater range that is nearly unlimited, being measured in years rather than miles. This can be considered the first true submarine, since all of its predecessors were really surface ships capable of brief underwater operations. The steam to run its two turbine engines is provided by a nuclear reactor.

1956 · United States begins interstate highway system. The United States enacts the Federal-Aid Highway Act of 1956 and begins its interstate highway program known formally as the National System of Interstate and Defense Highways. It is intended to be a 41,000-mile (66,000-kilometer) network of modern freeways spanning America and linking together and serving more than 90 percent of all the cities with a population over fifty thousand.

1957 · First monorail passenger train. The first monorail passenger train opens for service in Japan in Ueno, Tokyo. This new system has the passenger compartments unsupported from the bottom or sides, and hung from wheeled axles that run on a single electric rail. Later monorail trains use a bottom-supported system in which the car has a grooved bottom that straddles the single rail.

June 2, 1957 · First solo balloon flight into stratosphere. The first solo balloon flight into the stratosphere (the upper portion of the atmosphere above 7 miles, or 11.25 kilometers) is made by Joseph W. Kittering Jr. of the United States. In his plastic balloon, *Manhigh 1*, he stays

A Trident submarine under construction.

aloft for 6 hours, 34 minutes, and reaches an altitude of 96,000 feet (29.3 kilometers).

October 4, 1957 · Soviet Union launches *Sputnik I*. The first man-made Earth satellite is launched by the Soviet Union. Named *Sputnik I*, it weighs 184 pounds (83.5 kilograms), contains a battery-powered transmitter, and resembles an aluminum globe. Its easily identifiable "beep" signals are monitored and replayed around the world, giving the Soviet Union a huge propaganda victory over the United States. The United States is forced to recognize that the U.S.S.R. has attained a previously unrealized degree of technological sophistication and possesses launch vehicles with large lifting power. The space age has begun.

June 7, 1959 · First practical air-cushion vehicle. The first practical air-cushion vehicle, *SR.N1* hovercraft, makes a successful trip over water. Designed by English engineer Christopher Cockerell, it is an oval craft with a diameter of 20 feet (6 meters) and weighing 4 tons. It features a flexible skirt that holds the cushion in place as it rides smoothly on a layer of air despite the unevenness of the surface.

September 15, 1959 ▪ First nuclear-powered surface ship. The first nuclear-powered surface ship, the Soviet ice-breaker *Lenin*, makes its maiden voyage. Designed to work in ice up to 6 feet (2 meters) thick, it carries enough fuel to cruise for a year.

May 10, 1960 ▪ First undersea voyage around the world. The first undersea, around-the-world voyage is completed by the U.S. submarine, *Trident*. Following underwater the route taken more than four hundred years earlier by Portuguese explorer Ferdinand Magellan (c. 1480–1521), *Trident* travels 41,519 miles (66,804 kilometers) in eighty-four days.

April 12, 1961 ▪ First human in space. The first human in space and the first to orbit Earth is Soviet cosmonaut Yury Alekseyevich Gagarin (1934–1968). He circles Earth once in his *Vostok I* spacecraft, which flies 187 miles (300 kilometers) above Earth. During the entire flight, the spacecraft is controlled from the ground. On reentry, Gagarin ejects at 22,000 feet (6,700 meters) and parachutes down safely after his 1 hour, 48 minute flight. The Soviets amaze the world and the era of manned space flight begins.

May 5, 1961 ▪ Shepard is first American in space. The first American in space is U.S. astronaut Alan Bartlett Shepard Jr. (1923–) who is launched on a suborbital, ballistic (up and down) trajectory by a Redstone booster rocket. He rides his *Freedom 7* space capsule to a height of 116 miles (186.6 kilometers) and lands 297 miles (477.9 kilometers) downrange in the Atlantic. He is weightless for 5 minutes of his 15 minute, 22 second flight.

February 20, 1962 ▪ First American to orbit Earth. The first American to orbit Earth is John Herschel Glenn Jr. (1921–) in his Mercury capsule, *Friendship 7*. Launched by an Atlas booster, he completes three orbits in space spanning 4 hours, 55 minutes before splashing down safely in the Atlantic Ocean.

June 16, 1963 ▪ First woman in space. The first woman in space is the Soviet Union's Valentina Vladimirovna Tereshkova (1937–), who flies in *Vostok VI*. As a cotton-mill worker and amateur parachutist, she is essentially a passenger in the ground-controlled spacecraft. She has some difficult moments but reenters safely after nearly three full days in orbit.

1964 ▪ Seat belts become standard equipment on Studebaker-Packard cars. Seat belts are first made standard equipment on cars produced by the Studebaker-Packard Corporation. This decision marks a radical break with other major American automakers, but the company goes out of business by year's end.

October 1, 1964 ▪ Japan opens modern high-speed railroad line. A modern high-speed railroad line opens in Japan between Tokyo and Osaka. This is the first of Japan's *Shinkansen* (new railways), which become widely known in the West as "bullet trains." These electric passenger trains will hit top speeds of 132 miles (212 kilometers) per hour.

March 18, 1965 ▪ Leonov is first man to walk in space. The first man to walk in space is Soviet cosmonaut Aleksey Leonov, in *Voskhod II*. During the second orbit, Leonov floats outside the spacecraft, tethered by a cord providing him with oxygen and suit pressurization.

1966 ▪ U.S. Department of Transportation is established. The U.S. Department of Transportation is first established. Its mission is to provide leadership in the identification of transportation problems and solutions, stimulate new technological advances, encourage cooperation among all interested parties, and recommend national policies and programs to accomplish these objectives.

March 18, 1967 ▪ First major oil spill at sea. The first major oil pollution disaster at sea occurs off Land's End, England, as supertanker *Torrey Canyon* runs aground and rips a 650-foot-long (200-meter-long) hole in its hull. It spills about 833,000 barrels of crude oil that soils the coasts of England and France. This is the first of several increasingly disastrous oil spills to occur since the introduction of VLCCs (very large crude carriers) over 100,000 tons.

April 24, 1967 ▪ First person to die during a spaceflight. The first person to die during a spaceflight is Soviet cosmonaut Vladimir M. Komarov (1927–1967). After a successful launch, his spacecraft develops several severe system malfunctions and he attempts an emergency reentry. The Soviets announce that spacecraft tumbling causes his parachute to tangle and fail, resulting in a high-speed, fatal impact.

December 31, 1968 ▪ First supersonic jet transport. First supersonic jet transport, the Tupolev Tu-144, makes its first flight. This Soviet

aircraft soon begins regular service and later becomes the first commercial transport to exceed Mach 2 (twice the speed of sound). **(See also March 2, 1969)**

1969 · Launch of first LASH ship. The first LASH ship, the Japanese-built *Acadia Forest*, is launched. This specialized LASH container ship (*l*ighter *a*board *sh*ip) carries very large floating containers called "lighters." It is equipped with a massive crane that straddles the deck and is used to load and unload lighters. Each lighter has a 400-ton capacity and is stowed in the holds on deck. Loading and discharging is rapid (fifteen minutes per lighter), and no port or dock facilities are necessary, since a group of lighters can be towed onto inland waterways.

February 9, 1969 · Inaugural flight of Boeing 747 jet. The first flight of the Boeing 747 "Jumbo Jet" airliner is made. This wide-bodied, long-range transport is capable of carrying 347 passengers, and is at the time the largest aircraft in commercial airline service in the world.

March 2, 1969 · First flight of Concorde 001 supersonic transport. The first flight of the British Aircraft Corporation/Aerospatiale Concorde 001 supersonic transport is made in Toulouse, France. The product of British-French collaboration, it is assembled in France. In 1976 it becomes the first supersonic commercial transport to operate regularly scheduled passenger service. Both British Airways and Air France offer service to New York.

The liftoff of *Apollo 11,* July 16, 1969. Crew Neil Armstrong, Edwin E. Aldrin, and Michael Collins head for the first successful manned lunar landing.

July 20, 1969 ▪ Man walks on the Moon.

Man first walks on the Moon. The U.S. *Apollo 11* crew of Neil Alden Armstrong (1930–), Edwin Eugene Aldrin Jr. (1930–), and Michael Collins (1930–) achieves the national goal set by President John Fitzgerald Kennedy (1917–1963) on May 25, 1961. Armstrong first steps on the Moon announcing, "That's one small step for a man, one giant leap for mankind." Aldrin joins him minutes later and they both gather lunar samples and conduct and set up experiments during their two hours outside the lunar module. The landing and Moon walk is watched live on television by millions of people worldwide.

November 16, 1970 ▪ Debut of Lockheed L-1011 TriStar wide-body jet.

The first flight of the Lockheed L-1011 TriStar widebody jet airliner is made. This three-engine aircraft can hold as many as 400 passengers and competes with the Boeing 747, McDonnell DC-10, and Europe's Airbus Industrie A300. Wide-body aircraft will soon become the norm for high-density routes where speed is not essential. Passengers sit in long rows separated by two aisles, giving easy access to aircraft exits and facilities.

April 19, 1971 ▪ Soviet Union launches first space station.

The first space station, *Salyut I*, is launched by the Soviet Union into Earth orbit. It is occupied on June 6 of this year by cosmonauts Georgy T. Dobrovolsky (1928–1971) and Vladislav N. Volkov (1935–1971) and becomes the first manned space station. After a successful three-week mission, the cosmonauts undock and attempt to return to Earth. During separation, however, an exhaust valve in their return craft is opened and the cabin depressurizes, killing both men within forty-five seconds. After a routine, remote-controlled landing, the cosmonauts are found dead in their seats. Had they been wearing spacesuits inside the cabin, they would have survived.

1973 · General Motors offers automobile air bag. The automobile air bag is offered by General Motors. This inflatable cushion restraint installed in a car's steering wheel or dashboard inflates in a fraction of a second upon collision and protects the driver or front passengers. The auto industry resists adopting this safety system, and it takes over twenty years to become standard equipment.

September 1, 1975 · Concorde makes four transatlantic crossings in one day. The first aircraft to make two return transatlantic flights (or four transatlantic crossings in one day) is the Aerospatiale/BAC Concorde. This supersonic transport flies from London, England, to Gander, Newfoundland, Canada, twice.

August 12, 1978 · Gas balloon crosses the Atlantic Ocean. The first transatlantic crossing by a gas balloon begins as the *Double Eagle II* establishes new endurance and distance records for gas balloons. Crewed by Americans Ben L. Abruzzo, Maxie L. Anderson, and Larry M. Newman, it flies 3,107 miles (5,000 kilometers) in 137 hours and 5 minutes.

December 19, 1978 · First solar-powered aircraft. The first solar-powered aircraft, *Solar One*, makes a successful but brief hop-flight in England. David Williams and Fred To of England later fly the aircraft for almost three-quarters of a mile on June 13, 1979. Since it uses batteries to store the electricity generated by its 750 solar cells, some argue that it is an electric and not a solar aircraft.

June 12, 1979 · English Channel is crossed by human-powered aircraft. The first human-powered aircraft to cross the English Channel is the *Gossamer Albatross*, designed and built by Paul MacCready of the United States. Flown by bicyclist Bryan Allen whose pedaling keeps it aloft, the ultralight craft crosses from England in 2 hours, 49 minutes. Its wire bracing has high aerodynamic drag (slowing it down), and the tail-first design makes it difficult to fly, especially at higher speeds, but it succeeds.

1980 · New technology sail-assisted commercial ship. The first sail-assisted commercial ship to be built in the past fifty years, Japan's *Shin-Aitoku-Maru*, is launched. The designers of this 1,750-ton tanker use new materials and computer technology to build a sail system that supplements the ship's engines. The entire mast and sail can be rotated mechanically on their own axes from a central control room. The sails are not hoisted or lowered but rather rolled out mechanically from the mast, and the system is able to respond to weather changes and obtain the most favorable angle to the wind.

April 12, 1981 ▪ First winged, reusable spacecraft. The first winged, reusable spacecraft is launched into space as the U.S. space shuttle *Columbia* enters Earth orbit. Flown by American astronauts John W. Young and Robert L. Crippen, the shuttle uses solid-fuel booster rockets that it jettisons after they burn out, marking the first time solid fuel is used in a manned spaceflight. After two days of in-orbit tests, the crew pilots the shuttle to a perfect landing on the lake bed at Edwards Air Force Base, California.

June 18, 1983 ▪ First American woman in space. The first American woman astronaut, Sally Kristen Ride (1951–), is launched into space aboard the space shuttle *Challenger* on mission STS-7. She is accompanied by four male astronauts who, with her, comprise the first five-person crew to be launched into space. During their six-day mission, they deploy three satellites and demonstrate the shuttle's remote manipulator system by retrieving one satellite from orbit. This is the first time a satellite is retrieved by a manned spacecraft.

February 3, 1984 ▪ First untethered space walk. The first untethered space walk is made by American astronaut Bruce McCandless II, during mission 41-B of the *Challenger* space shuttle. During the seven-day mission, McCandless uses the manned maneuvering unit (MMU), a self-contained, propulsive backpack, that enables him to move freely in space without having to be tethered to a spacecraft. The shuttle returns to Cape Canaveral, Florida, marking the first time a spacecraft lands at the place it was launched from.

February 19, 1986 ▪ First permanent space station. Soviet Union launches the core of the first permanent space station called *Mir* or "Peace." It is about 42.5 feet (13 meters) long, 13.5 feet (4 meters) maximum diameter, and weighs about 21 tons. It contains several ports that will accept docking units that can be added on. It can accommodate a crew of twelve.

(See also March 24, 1996)

December 14, 1986 · First around-the-world nonstop unrefueled flight. The first aircraft to fly around the world nonstop and unrefueled is the specially built *Voyager* aircraft. Designed by American Burt Rutan and flown by Dick Rutan (1938–) and Jeana Yeager (1952–), it is constructed of composite materials that include Magnamite graphite and Hexcel honeycomb. It has two British-built, high-efficiency engines, one of which is water-cooled. Its takeoff weight is 9,750 pounds. It covers nearly 24,987 miles (40,212 kilometers) flying westbound from California in 9 days, 3 minutes, 44 seconds. At landing, it has only fourteen gallons of fuel left. This flight more than doubles all unrefueled, nonstop records and demonstrates the possibilities of all-composite structures.

July 2, 1987 · First hot-air balloon to cross the Atlantic. The first hot-air balloon to cross the Atlantic Ocean, the *Atlantic Flyer*, is

A satellite view of the space shuttle *Challenger.* Space shuttles are reusable rockets that take off like rockets, travel like spacecraft, and land like gliders. The first shuttle launched was the *Columbia* in 1981.

launched from Sugarloaf, Maine. Piloted by Richard Branson and Per Lindstrand, the balloon crashes just short of the coast of England after a flight of 31 hours, 41 minutes. **(See also January 15, 1991)**

October 30, 1990 · Eurotunnel links England and France. The first of three of the world's longest undersea tunnels joining England and France is dug, as British and French tunneling crews on opposite sides break through and link up. Eurotunnel will eventually consist of two one-way rail tunnels whose trains will carry both passengers and vehicles. A third, narrower service tunnel will run between and connect them every 1,240 feet (380 meters). The tunneling machines used are 700-foot long (210-meter-long) caterpillars at the working end of which is a 27.6-foot (8.4-meter) digging head. **(See also November 14, 1994)**

January 15, 1991 · First hot-air balloon to cross the Pacific. The first hot-air balloon to cross the Pacific Ocean takes off from Miyakonojo, Japan. Piloted by Richard Branson and Per Lindstrand, it touches down two days later on a frozen lake in the Northwest Territories of Canada.

June 1992 · Full-sized MHD vessel debuts. The first voyage of a full-sized MHD (magnetohydrodynamic propulsion) vessel is made in Japan. The 185-ton research ship *Yamato I* uses a revolutionary MHD drive system that is virtually silent and has no moving parts. The principle behind the ship's propulsion system is one found in all electric motors. When an electrical charge moves through a magnetic field, it is subject to a force (called the Lorentz force) that acts at right angles to the motion of the charge. This new drive system does not use propellers to push the ship through the water but rather employs the Lorentz force (via powerful superconducting electromagnets) to propel seawater out a nozzle at the stern (rear) of the ship, using a form of jet propulsion. This experimental drive system eliminates problems related to propeller systems as well as speed limitations, mechanical vibrations, and even detection by sonar.

February 1, 1993 · Amtrak X-2000 "tilt train" is tested. Amtrak makes the first paying-passenger run of a three-month test of its new high-speed, X-2000 "tilt train." Running between Washington, D.C., and New York, this new train can take curves as much as 40 percent faster than current equipment. It does not have to slow down for a curve since each car tilts into the curve, and passengers feel little or no discomfort. Initial tests show the ride to be extremely quiet and smooth.

November 14, 1994 · Eurotunnel opens. Eurotunnel, the underground "chunnel" connecting France and Britain by rail, opens officially as the Eurostar bullet train makes its first passenger run. Built by the Anglo-French consortium Eurotunnel at a cost of sixteen billion dollars, this undersea bridge is hailed as the greatest engineering feat of the century. The trip between Paris and London takes three hours and is offered twice a day in each direction. Ticket prices are close to those of airfares, and the tunnel is expected to herald a new age in continental travel.

February 3, 1995 · First woman space shuttle pilot. The first woman to pilot a U.S. space shuttle is American astronaut Eileen Collins. She conducts a successful STS-63 shuttle mission.

March 24, 1996 · First American woman boards *Mir*. The first American woman to board the orbiting Russian space station, *Mir*, is astronaut Shannon Lucid. She transfers from a U.S. space shuttle which is docked with *Mir*. Three days later, two Americans, Linda Godwin and Michael Clifford, make the first space walk from the shuttle to *Mir*.

November 19, 1996 · Eurotunnel shuts down because of fire. A severe fire in Eurotunnel, the rail tunnel connecting England and France beneath the English Channel, causes a shutdown but no deaths. A fire starts in a truck being carried on a semi-enclosed, flatbed car at the rear of the train, then spreads rapidly on the speeding train and finally puts the rear electric locomotive out of commission. The train becomes stranded 11 miles (17.7 kilometers) into the tunnel, but the thirty-four people onboard are rescued. The extreme heat does great damage and renders the tube inoperable, forcing single tube operations for some time.

Index

Volume numbers are indicated in boldface type.

Index

Index